D1498357

The Bad Popes

By E. R. Chamberlin
The Bad Popes
The Count of Virtue
Everyday Life in Renaissance Times
Life in Medieval France

The Bad Popes

E. R. Chamberlin

Dorset Press   •   New York

First published 1969

This edition published by Dorset Press,
a division of Marboro Books Corporation,
by arrangement with Harold Ober Associates
1986 Dorset Press

ISBN 0-88029-116-8

Printed in the United States of America

M 10

Contents

I

The Golden City

Rome, A.D. 900   3
The Lord of Rome   10
Donation of Constantine   14

II

The House of Theophylact

Marozia
Senatrix of Rome (926–932)

Rise of the Theophylacts   25
"Pope Joan"   32

Octavian
Pope John XII (955–963)

The Pope-King   40

The Coming of the Emperor   46

Theophylact
Pope Benedict IX (1032–1046)

The Rule of the Magician   62

Sale of the Papacy   67

III

The Lord of Europe

Benedict Gaetani
Pope Boniface VIII (1294–1303)

The Great Refusal   77

Consolidation   87

The High-Souled Sinner   106

Challenge and Response   116

IV

The Wandering Pope

Bartolomeo Prignano
Pope Urban VI (1378–1389)

Avignon, September, 1376   127

Schism: Rome, 1378   136

The Long March   146

V

The Spanish Bull

Rodrigo Borgia
Pope Alexander VI (1492–1503)

Cardinal Rodrigo Borgia	161
The Borgia Family	172
Invasion, 1494	180
Murder of the Duke of Gandia	187
Cesare Borgia	191

VI

The Golden Age

Giovanni de' Medici
Pope Leo X (1513–1521)

The High Renaissance	209
Triumph of the Medici	227
Conspiracy of the Cardinals	233
Luther	239

VII

The Last Day of Italy

Giulio de' Medici
Pope Clement VII (1523–1534)

Giulio de' Medici	253
The Gathering Storm	263
The Sack of Rome	273

Appendix

The Sources   289

Bibliography   291

Notes   297

Index   301

Illustration sections facing pages   *54, 118, 150 and 214*

"*It is now more than a thousand years since these territories and cities have been given to the priests and ever since then the most violent wars have been waged on their account, and yet the priests neither now possess them in peace, nor will ever be able to possess them. It were in truth better before the eyes of God and the world that these pastors should entirely renounce the* dominium temporale: *for since Sylvester's time the consequences of the temporal power have been innumerable wars and the overthrow of peoples and cities. How is it possible that there has never been any good pope to remedy such evils and that so many wars have been waged for these transient possessions. Truly we cannot serve God and Mammon at the same time, cannot stand with one foot in Heaven and the other on Earth.*"

Giovanni de' Mussi, Chronicle of Piacenza, *c. 1350*

I
The Golden City

Rome, A.D. 900

Some time after the Flood, when men began again to move on the face of the earth and grew again in arrogance so that their impiety was confounded at Babel and they were again dispersed, Noah came to Italy and with his sons Jason, Japhet, and Camese built a series of cities upon the seven hills surrounding the Tiber. Jason lived upon the Palatine hill and, aided by Nimrod or Saturn, built the city of Saturnia upon the Capitoline hill. Other kings of glorious name, among them Italus and Aeneas, followed the lead of Noah's children and built other cities in the now sanctified area. Then, on April 17, in the four hundred and thirty-third year after the fall of Troy, Romulus came to surround all these cities with a single wall, making of them one and giving it his name. "And all the nobles of the Earth, together with their wives and children, came to live in this new city of Rome." [1]

Thus, in the tenth century, the Romans viewed the origins of their city, fusing into one picture the strands of Christian and pagan traditions. In it, Virgil and the author of Genesis are accepted as equal authorities, so that Aeneas rubs shoulders with Noah, Saturn with Nimrod, reflecting in literature the fusion of elements which were transforming Rome itself. It would retain its identity as the Eternal City but its ancient substances were taking on new shapes. The vast churches that now dominated it had been built from the materials of venerable temples, and the great monuments of the ancient city that survived were transformed either into fortresses for the ceaselessly warring nobles or into slum tenements for the proletariat.

The peoples of Europe, regarding in wonderment the ancient and imperishable city, wove legends for it that made it a mythological place. They might deplore its tragic fall from greatness, scorn its decadent and violent citizens; but they were touched still by the awe of its mighty past, transforming the reality of its political greatness into magical tales. The Englishman William of Malmesbury tells of how a certain Lucanius, "citizen of this place—youthful, rich and of senatorial rank," in a drunken frolic placed his wedding ring on the finger of a statue of Venus and found himself embraced that night by the goddess herself. "Take me—since you wedded me today." Lucanius is freed by a Christian priest—but the priest himself employs pagan arts to do so. In a subterranean cavern, golden images of the dead sit motionless before an eternal banquet and then are stirred to terrible life when an intruder steals an ornament from the table. And even as reality is twisted into fable, so fable appears as reality, and Malmesbury soberly records the discovery of the body of the giant Pallas, of whom Virgil sang, still incorrupt so that there was visible "the gash which Turnus made in the middle of his breast, measuring four and a half feet." [2]

But, lapped though it was by pagan legend, Rome was pre-eminently the Sacred City of Christendom; and though the thronging pilgrims might marvel at the body of Pallas, they would turn from it with a shudder and cross themselves—the heroes of the old city being the demons of the new—and seek more holy relics. The Romans made much profit by providing these gullible northerners with fragments of corpses—of dubious origins, but sanctified by the fact that they were purchased in Rome. And when the relics had been purchased and the shrines visited and the offerings of copper or gold made at the tomb of Peter, the pilgrims turned to explore the wondrous city, as pilgrims always had and always would. For them there was a species of guidebook, the *Description of the Golden City,* a fantastic mishmash of legend and garbled history compiled by scribes from oral traditions over many generations. Beginning with the foundation of the city by Noah and his sons, it took the pilgrim down to the present, guiding him to the great monuments of the past, explaining in confused and inaccurate detail the complex, interlocking machinery of imperial, papal, and civic government that ruled Rome. It also provided posterity with one of the few descriptions of the city during the dark centuries.

Rome had changed little from the final form established by the emperor Aurelian when he built the great enclosing walls in the third century A.D. They were Rome's final defense. Whatever else was suffered to fall into ruin, the walls were maintained, generation after generation and century after century, encompassing a city that would otherwise have become a shapeless sprawl. In the first decade of the Christian era, during the years of Augustan splendor, there had been a tremendous upsurge in building, culminating in the reign of Nero when vast, gleaming structures swallowed whole streets and areas. After the collapse of the empire the city suffered endless sacks, but it was the Romans themselves who dismantled the classical city and that for the most humdrum of reasons—marble, when burned, yields lime which can be used for plaster.

The scores of limekilns in the city were each fed by irreplaceable fragments of past glory. The great blocks of travertine that formed the core of the walls were broken up to make byres and hovels: Those columns that escaped the limekilns, or were not incorporated into new churches, lay where they fell, protected at least by the accumulated rubbish. But Augustan Rome had been built upon such a colossal scale that, though it was plundered daily for centuries, the center of the city survived as an identifiable entity. A contemporary of Augustus or Nero could still have found his way easily enough around the tenth-century city, recognizing most of the monuments of his day, though he would have been appalled by the filthy condition of the streets themselves. Many were permanently blocked by collapsed buildings; all stank in high summer. The city that had known the splash and play of countless fountains now endured an endless drought, for the great aqueducts were ruined.

Nevertheless, within the circle of the Aurelian walls, the ground plan of the city remained largely unchanged. It was on the other side of the Tiber, on the slopes of the Vatican Hill, that the new age had made its most distinctive mark, creating a virtually separate city that was to control Rome over the coming centuries.

Until 850, the Vatican Hill was outside the walls of Rome. Even Aurelian had not thought it worthwhile to extend his protecting walls to this desolate area. Its plain was a fetid marsh, malarial in summer and—in a land where men naturally gravitated to the summit of hills—its inhospitable upper slopes remained sparsely populated for centuries. Nevertheless, the increasing population in the city made even this dreary region of potential value. Part of it became a cemetery and part of it Nero developed as a great pleasure garden where, in its famous Circus, according to

Christian tradition, the apostle Peter was crucified during that night of insane cruelty in A.D. 64 when the living bodies of Christians were turned into torches, heralding the persecutions under Nero.

The same tradition holds that Peter's body was taken down by disciples and buried in a shallow grave among the tombs near the Circus. By the year 160, a humble but identifiable shrine marked the grave, over which the first basilica of St. Peter's was built in the early fourth century. That basilica—founded, so legend said, by the emperor Constantine himself—was to endure for over a thousand years before it was swept away at last by the impatient surge of the Renaissance.

The fourth-century architects of the basilica were faced with a formidable problem, for the site lay on a slope down which a road ran, flanked by tombs. Work proceeded in haste, and instead of laboriously demolishing the tombs—massive, hut-like structures— the builders merely broke open the roofs, filled the interior with debris and erected the basilica on top. Thus sealed off, the tombs remained untouched for centuries, providing at last a priceless archaeological record when the search for Peter's tomb began in the mid-twentieth century.

The builders began that cannibalizing of material which was to prove far more destructive to Rome than the raids of barbarians. The nearby circus was an obvious source of material but far more beautiful structures were plundered to build St. Peter's. It was an inelegant, brick-built structure of ill-assorted materials hastily put together. The great columns that towered in the gloom of the interior were brought from a number of temples: the columns were not only ill-matched, but the architects had not even bothered to ensure that any given column had its correct base and capital. But though the new building must have seemed incongruous and unworthy of Rome to conservative Romans, it was the outward form of a new way of life. These conservatives still sought to maintain the old religion but its dynamism had been transferred to the new, and with that dynamism went the wealth that had once adorned the temples of the old gods.

In the seventh century the great central door of the basilica was plated with a thousand pounds of massive silver and the shrine of St. Peter itself was similarly adorned. This, the most sacred spot of earth in Christendom, now lay far below among the foundations of the basilica, but the architects had carefully allowed physical, if limited access to it. A shaft led down from the high altar to the tomb itself and the faithful could thrust their heads into the shaft and pray, or let down objects on a line to touch the tomb and thereby receive a rare sanctity. The shrine was a natural object upon which to lavish the increasing wealth of the Church: Less than a century after it had been silver-plated, the silver was torn out, replaced by solid gold sheets. Golden statues, too, ousted the modest silver statues of a poorer age and precious stones added their glitter to what had been a humble shrine of stone.

In vain, St. Jerome protested against the process that was turning the house of God into a treasure chamber. "The marble walls shine, the roofs sparkle with gold, the altars with gems—but the true servants of God are without earthly splendor. Let no one say that the Temple of Solomon was rich with gold—now that the lord has made poverty his own we should think of the Cross and esteem riches as worthless." [3] In this matter, at least, Jerome went unheard. The emperors sought divine favor at Rome's expense, giving permission for more and more of the temples to be demolished in order to adorn St. Peter's. The popes, into whose hands the revenue of Rome increasingly fell, channeled much of it into the basilica. By the beginning of the ninth century, the ugly building contained an enormous treasure in bullion alone, an irresistible attraction to any band of robbers uninhibited by religious scruples.

The basilica remained unprotected for over five hundred years after its foundation. The enemies of Rome were for the most part fellow-Christians, and bitter though the hatred might be between sect and sect, all Christians reverenced the few square feet of earth on the Vatican Hill above which the basilica towered. But over the centuries there grew a new and most dangerous threat from a people unaffected by Christian scruples—imbued, indeed, with active hatred for Christianity and all its works. After the collapse of the short-lived Carolingian empire, the Saracens established themselves in Sicily, spread into southern Italy, and in 846 launched an attack upon Rome itself.

Secure behind the great walls of Aurelian, the inhabitants of the old city watched helplessly while the Vatican suburb was put to the sack. The accumulated treasure in St. Peter's was carried off—the massive silver plate on doors and floors ripped off, the golden statues heaped up, the altars stripped of their precious ornaments. The Saracens appreciated to the full the significance of the basilica, and in an access of fanaticism, broke open the tomb of Peter and scattered the contents. The invaders were driven off after a bitter fight but succeeded in escaping to their ships on the Tiber with most of their loot.

The reigning pope was the energetic Leo IV. He took the lesson to heart, and two years after the sack, he began the enormous task of walling in the entire Vatican area. Work was still in progress when news came that the Saracens were making preparation for an even bigger attack. In a brief demonstration of unity, all Italy combined to repel the threat and the Saracen fleet was destroyed at the mouth of the Tiber before the soldiers could embark.

Again, as in the great days of Rome, Romans beheld slaves working upon their city as Saracen captives were driven by the hundred to labor upon the walls of the Leonine City, as this new walled region came to be called. The emperor helped with liberal gifts of money, Christendom was taxed to provide more, and by the year 852 the work was finished. The walls, over forty feet in height, swept up from the Tiber to the crest of the Vatican Hill and down again to join the river farther downstream.

The key to the Leonine City was the mausoleum of Hadrian. Built originally as a tomb, it stood on the Vatican side of the river and its enormous size and strength ensured that it would be turned into a fortress. By the tenth century, its origins were forgotten, a contemporary chronicler describing it simply as "a castle of marvelous strength and workmanship which stands at the entrance to Rome. A splendid bridge crosses the Tiber opposite its gates and all who enter or leave the city must cross this bridge—if permitted by the guardians of the castle." [4]

The building's name had been forgotten along with its origins, and the Romans knew it now as the Castle of Sant' Angelo, for legend had it that the archangel Michael had once appeared upon its summit. It was immensely strong, consisting virtually of a solid block in which passages and chambers were hewn. A spiral, sloping gallery led up to the great central chamber that had once housed the sarcophagus of Hadrian, and above and around it appeared other chambers, occupied by a permanent garrison. Little now remained of its early beauty. The antique Greek statues that had once adorned its summit had long since been broken up and used as missiles, the hanging gardens destroyed, the marble facings chipped and scarred by countless missiles. Squat, ugly, battered but enduring, it was a fitting representative of Rome itself.

In the sixth century, administrative buildings had begun to appear around St. Peter's, the nucleus of the later enormous Vatican Palace. But for over half the recorded existence of the Roman Church—from the early years of the fourth century until the late fourteenth—the home of the Papacy was not in the Vatican but in the Lateran Palace on the other side of the city. The palace took its name from its onetime owners, the Laterani, a wealthy Roman family whose name was accidentally immortalized solely because they possessed one of the most magnificent private buildings in Rome.

The palace came into the possession of the emperor Constantine, who after his conversion gave it to the bishops of Rome to be their residence in perpetuity. A basilica was erected beside it, smaller than its sister on the Vatican, but destined to be known as Mother of all the Churches. Its secondary name, the Golden Basilica, was testimony to the spiritual and worldly treasures heaped within, including, according to widespread belief, the original Ark of the Covenant, the Tables of the Law, and the most famed relics in Rome—the heads of the apostles Peter and Paul.

The Lateran Palace discharged its honorable, if limited, role as a bishop's residence for some four hundred years. Then, in the late eighth century, the tenuous link that bound the Roman emperor to his titular city was broken, starting the Papacy on its long road of temporal dominion and making the Lateran the center of Roman government.

The Lord of Rome

In A.D. 328, Constantine transferred the capital of the Roman empire to his new city of Constantinople, thereby inevitably altering the center of gravity of the Roman world. Gradually, the imperial throne was occupied exclusively by Greeks, Latin gave place to Greek as the official language, and subtle changes of manners evolved an Oriental civilization that was styled Byzantine from the older name of the city. The link between East and West grew steadily weaker.

Nevertheless, the emperor continued to claim lordship over all Europe and established his representative in Ravenna to enforce his claims. Northern Europe slipped from his grasp but Italy continued to be exploited, brutally, for the benefit of Constantinople. Wave after wave of barbarian invaders swept down the peninsula, establishing scores of petty kingdoms, but the Byzantine garrisons remained passive; their task was simply to enforce the collection of taxes and they performed that efficiently enough.

The ordinary inhabitants of the land, no longer Romans but not yet Italians, accepted the situation, for it made little real difference to them whether they paid taxes to a distant emperor or a present lord. The great chafed under the yoke. It galled the bishop of Rome that he could be summoned to Constantinople like any other official; it galled the new marquesses and dukes that they had to seek legalization of their offices from a distant Greek. But without the support of the amorphous, inarticulate mass of the people, nothing could be done. And the people saw no particular reason to place their bodies at additional hazard; they would revolt only when some gross injustice touched each of them personally and immediately.

The spark was provided by religion, the only subject which, in the total absence of national awareness, bound together all inhabitants of the land.

The Christian emperor in Constantinople had inherited the dual role of priest and king that the pagan emperors in Rome had enjoyed. When the seat of the empire had moved to the East, the bishop of Rome naturally enjoyed rather more freedom than his opposite number, the patriarch of Constantinople, but both, in the eyes of the emperor, were subordinate to him in spiritual as well as temporal matters. Constantinople developed into the true theological center of Christianity, to the accompaniment of endless intrigues and ferocious palace revolutions as religion and politics interacted upon each other.

Nevertheless, there was no major clash between emperor and bishop on a purely religious matter until about 726. The reigning emperor was Leo III, by birth a hillman and by training a soldier, a simple, direct man who brought to the complexities of religious disputations a simple, direct approach. It was disastrous. His Christian subjects had nothing but praise for his edict that commanded the forcible baptism of Jews. But when he issued the first of his iconoclastic edicts, he spelled the doom of his empire in the West. The peoples of Italy were touched, for the first time, on a universally personal matter.

The primitive Christians had attacked image worship as the work of the devil and there had been wholesale destruction of every type of idol when Christianity had at last triumphed. But over the succeeding centuries, the images crept back, appearing under new names but, to the critical eye, with an identical role. It was the Christians of the East who first began to feel that much of the pagan religion that their forefathers had destroyed, at such cost in martyrs' blood, was insensibly being restored. Disturbed by the mockery of the neighboring iconoclastic Muslims, their devotion to images was in addition subjected to a strain of which their Western brethren were free.

In a decade, the infidel Muslims had overcome city after Christian city, each of which had been under the protection of some holy image. In vain, monks made the standard defense of supernatural prophylactics—that it was the lack of faith of the possessor, not the lack of virtue in the image, which rendered it useless. The religious disputation inevitably became political, bringing with it riot and the ever-present threat of civil war. The forthright Leo solved the problem, as he thought, by coming down on the side of the iconoclastics. In 726 he issued his edict commanding the breaking of all images throughout the empire, in the West as well as the East.

In Rome, Gregory II was in the eleventh year of his pontificate, the first Roman-born pope to occupy the Chair of Peter after a long succession of Greek creatures—a fact that was to have profound effect upon Italy. Even as chance had made the unsubtle Leo the spokesman of that substantial part of Christianity which deplored the use of images, chance made of the unsubtle Gregory the authentic and passionate voice of the West which honored them.

Gregory's two letters to Leo, defying the edict and urging him to return to the true path, were a curious medley of legend passing for history, of fact, fiction, and personal opinion all well spiced with hatred for the emperor and his illiterate advisers. It was nonsense to say that Christians had restored the idolatry of antiquity. They did not worship images but honored them as memorials, and in any case, the images of antiquity had been either the images of demons or the products of imagination. The authenticity of the likenesses in Christian images could not be disputed. "Religious men had gathered around Christ in his lifetime—when they beheld him they made a picture of him. They made pictures, too, of James the brother of the Lord, of Stephen, and of all the martyrs. And having done so, they sent them through the world to receive not worship but reverence."

Gregory returned again and again to the theme that he and his followers did not worship, but only reverenced, images. But in referring to a threat of direct attack upon the great statue of St. Peter in Rome, he slipped into a curious and ambiguous phraseology. He himself had no fear of the emperor's rage. "I have but to retire twenty-four miles into the Campania and you might as well follow the winds. But for the statue of St. Peter himself, which all the kingdoms of the West esteem as a god on earth, the whole West would take a terrible revenge." [5] Whether he intended it to be understood that it was the statue, or Peter himself, whom the West held as a god on earth, the statement could have helped little to repudiate the charge that Europe was fast falling into idolatry.

The Italians were indifferent to the theological niceties. The bishop of Rome had spoken for them, clearly and definitively, and they supported him even at the cost of their own blood. It was in defense of their gods of the hearth, the little familiar objects that rendered local and personal the vast impersonality of Christian theology, that they broke the cord that bound them to the East.

Imperial edict was followed by imperial action, and troops who could not be found to defend a province were swiftly available to enforce a theological point. A fierce and bloody war was fought around Ravenna. The Byzantines retreated northward and the scenes of carnage were repeated, so frightful and bloody that for six years thereafter the inhabitants of the Po valley abstained from eating the fish of the river for fear of involuntary cannibalism.

After the violence of open warfare had abated, there remained still a nominal allegiance to the emperor. Gregory himself had no intention of usurping the temporal power but he had charted a path that others could not fail to follow. Just nine months after his death in 731, the effective severance with the East was made when a synod in Rome pronounced excommunicate all those who would attack the images of the saints. It was a discreet enough pronouncement, for the emperor was not mentioned by name. There was doubt, too, as to precisely who was excommunicating whom, but the implications were clear. The emperor and his theologians alike were rejected by Italy and it was inevitable that the bishop of Rome should fill the vacuum of power thus created.

The Donation of Constantine

About a generation after the Papacy had divorced itself from the empire, a certain papal official, Christophorous by name, completed a task of forgery which neatly transferred the temporal crown from the emperor to the pope.

Christophorous based his work upon the legendary life of St. Sylvester, the blameless if mediocre bishop of Rome who ruled over his little flock at the time of Constantine. According to the legend, Constantine was energetically persecuting Christians when he was afflicted with leprosy and, despite the efforts of doctors and magicians, despaired of a cure. Saints Peter and Paul appeared to him in a vision and told him that Sylvester alone could cure him. The old man was brought to the Lateran Palace, where Constantine resided, and there told the emperor that baptism alone would cleanse him of the disease.

Constantine agreed to baptism, and as a result the leprosy immediately vanished. In gratitude, he immediately ordained that Christ should be worshipped throughout the empire and that tithes should be instituted for the building of churches. The Lateran Palace was given to Sylvester and his successors for all time; Constantine himself dug and carried away the first twelve baskets of earth on the Vatican Hill, and so began the basilica of St. Peter.

The legend, though fanciful in its ascription of motives, did not depart widely from known details of fact—the gift of the Lateran Palace, the construction of basilicas, the supreme religious status accorded to Christianity. Christophorous expanded these known elements, skillfully grafting revolutionary theories upon a stock that was both deep-rooted and widespread. He made some blunders that were to arouse the suspicion of scholars centuries afterward: Constantine was made to refer to himself as conqueror of the Huns fifty years before they appeared in Europe; the bishop of Rome was entitled "pope" nearly two hundred years before the title was limited to his office; and Western officials became "satraps of the empire." But Christophorous brought his threads together neatly enough before going on to make his forgeries.

The first forgery was a deletion. The legend had stated unequivocally that the emperor retained in his hands all the apparatus of civil government. The phrase disappeared, the document now implying that all judges as well as bishops were subject to the bishop of Rome. Then, boldly, Christophorous commenced actual manufacture of details. To the "pope" and his successors, Constantine gave the diadem or crown, together with "the purple mantle also and the scarlet tunic and all the imperial trappings. We bestow upon him also the imperial scepter, with all the standards and banners and similar ornaments."

Christophorous was a cleric, anxious to maintain the little privileges and honors of his office and Constantine was therefore made to grant to the clergy a dignity similar to that which the Senate had enjoyed: "to ride on white horses adorned with saddle cloth of purest white, wearing white shoes like senators."

But all this was mere garnishing to the central point—the establishment of the fact that the pope was not merely independent of the emperor, but was actually his superior. Christophorous made it appear that Sylvester had actually been offered the imperial crown, but had declined it as unfitting for the holder of a spiritual office and had accepted, instead, a simple white Phrygian cap, humble forerunner of the great triple tiara. Nevertheless, the fact that he had been offered the imperial crown implied that Constantine afterward possessed it only on the pope's sufferance.

Christophorous went on to make the point abundantly clear by skillfully twisting the true reason for Constantine's decision to establish his capital in the East. "Wherefore, that the pontifical crown may be maintained in dignity, we hand over and relinquish our palaces, the City of Rome, and all the provinces, places, and cities of Italy and the regions of the West to the most blessed pontiff and Universal Pope, Sylvester." Constantine himself would depart forthwith to New Rome, as it was not fitting that an earthly emperor should share the seat of the successor of Peter.[6]

Forged documents were no rarity in these early centuries. It is possible, indeed, that Christophorous had no intention to deceive, that he compiled the *Donation of Constantine* as a wistful exercise in what might have been. His work would probably have gathered dust in some chancery pigeonhole had not an event occurred, soon afterward, that made of it a potent political weapon. He lived to regret it.

The decline of the Byzantine power in Italy had been matched by the rise of the Lombards, the latest and most powerful of the barbarian invaders. Their duchies and "kingdoms" were established throughout Italy, forming the basis of a new society, and as the Byzantine tide ebbed, so they flooded into the cities left temporarily vacant. Eventually, they menaced Rome itself, for though as good Christians they might reverence the pope as spiritual head, they had no intention of recognizing him as a temporal superior. Isolated, threatened at a distance by the Byzantines, actively besieged by the Lombards, the reigning pope Stephen sought a champion. He found him beyond the Alps when Pepin, king of the Franks, offered Frankish aid.

In the winter of 755, Stephen began the long and perilous journey to the Frankish court. It was a measure of his desperation that not only did he, an old man, decide to make the journey in person, but that he undertook the passage of the Alps in the depths of winter. He was received with heartening respect, not merely as a suppliant, not merely as pope, but as the defrauded heir of Constantine, for the papal propagandists had done their work well. The *Donation of Constantine* put out its first root, successfully transplanted from the world of fiction into fact.

In the negotiations that followed, Stephen did not ask just for protection but for land. The territories that the Lombards had taken were to be restored neither to the Byzantine power, which could legally claim them, nor to the republic of Rome, which had created them. They were to be "restored" to St. Peter himself, because four centuries earlier Constantine had granted them to the apostle as represented by Sylvester. It was an astounding claim but one that Pepin accepted without question, motivated perhaps by politics, but also by a genuine piety, a burning desire to champion the prince of the apostles with Frankish swords and so wipe out sacrilege.

Pepin amply kept his promise. In two vigorous campaigns he curbed the Lombards and drew up a treaty which at length and in law made over to the pope those territories outlined in the *Donation*. It was not only the untutored Franks who accepted the *Donation* at its face value: The devious Byzantines, skilled though they were in every aspect of legal intrigue and with much to lose, fell as easy victims. The emperor's representative, far from strongly protesting against the Frank's high-handed action, merely asked him to concede the territories to the Byzantine power that had so long administered them. Pepin refused. It was on St. Peter's account that he had subdued the Lombards, and St. Peter not being present in person to receive the rich gift, he was handing it over to the bishop of Rome. The great iron keys of some twenty cities, including Ravenna and Ancona, Bologna, Ferrara, Iesi, and Gubbio, were brought to Stephen, giving him possession of a great wedge of country along the Adriatic coast, the foreshadowing of the Papal States. The charter recording the gift was placed in a niche in the shaft that led to Peter's tomb, the nearest possible point to the physical remains of the apostle.

Within a decade of Pepin's generous action, Rome learned the full implications of the new splendor of the Papacy. The creation of the Papal States, the so-called patrimony of St. Peter, made the pope a feudal lord, giving a real financial value to his office. The Chair of St. Peter became a prize for the great families of Rome and its neighborhood, creating a more insidious danger for the Papacy than that which Byzantines and Lombards had threatened. There might have been a reluctance to be seated in the chair when all it offered was a spiritual crown and the probability of physical coercion from an only too fleshly emperor. But now that the bishop of Rome held not only the keys of heaven but also the keys of more than a score of cities, each with its revenues, the attraction of the office was considerably magnified.

The first of the papal riots arising from the donations occurred in 767, when, on the death of the reigning pope, one of the numerous local lordlings recognized the opportunity and hastening to Rome, proposed his own brother as successor. The fact that the brother was disqualified because he was a layman was easily overcome, for he was ordained cleric, subdeacon, deacon, and priest— and then consecrated as bishop and pope on the same day. Rival factions immediately arose and two more popes appeared. The first contestant had his eyes dug out and was left for dead. The second was murdered outright and it was only when the third appealed to the hated Lombards for protection that some sort of order was restored. It was perhaps fitting that Christophorous the forger should have perished in one of the brawls, ominous harbingers of the tenth century.

But Pepin's act had done more than give temporal wealth to a spiritual power: It had established the precedent that the German monarch was the natural protector of the Papacy. Fifty years afterward, Pepin's son Charlemagne hastened to Rome at the appeal of Pope Leo III, to put down a rebellion; in return, on Christmas Day, 800, Leo crowned him emperor of the West. Legally, it was a highly dubious act, for there could be but one emperor on earth and he was already reigning in Constantinople. But despite the protests of legalists, the creation of an emperor in Europe was an organic development consequent upon the rift between West and East.

In his own personality Charlemagne combined the contradictory qualities of his time, making his actions a genuine expression of the age. Illiterate, he founded a court of scholars. Unsophisticated, he brought about a legal system that bound together the heterogeneous peoples of his empire. Deeply—indeed, naïvely—religious, he yet limited the activities of the ecclesiastics. His relationship with his protégé the pope was delicate. He formally recognized the gift made by his father, drawing up in turn a charter based on the *Donation of Constantine* through which, in theory, the Papacy claimed "all the regions of Italy and of the West." In practice there was no doubt whatsoever as to the identity of the temporal monarch of Europe.

Nevertheless, in the early application of that stupendous theory which saw the emperor and the pope as the twin vicars of Christ —the one wielding the spiritual sword, the other the temporal, in a holy empire—Charlemagne scrupulously recognized the pope's temporal rights in the territories specifically granted to St. Peter. He even asked formal permission to remove certain mosaics from Ravenna to beautify his own capital of Aachen. The fact that

Charlemagne had not fallen under the spell of Rome helped the business of day-to-day administration. Rome gave him his great title and he therefore intended to influence it—but from a distance. Aachen was the true seat of his empire.

But the new concept of empire could be maintained only by a person of Charlemagne's stature, and even he had a crippling limitation. As soldier he was supreme, but as statesman he was limited still by the tribal concepts of his Germanic forebears. He saw his empire essentially as a personal estate to be passed on to members of his family, and upon his death his son Louis inherited all. Thirty years later, in 843, the empire was divided into three great blocs among Charlemagne's grandsons.

Thereafter, the Carolingian empire was at an end save in name, the fragments now dividing and redividing, now joined arbitrarily so that Lorraine and Italy were one, now dismembered as arbitrarily so that Lombardy could be divorced from Italy, or Provence from the rest of France. Petty kings and marquesses and dukes arose—kings of Italy, kings of Lombardy, kings of Provence briefly ruled, their sole claim being their descent, legitimate or illegitimate, from the great monarch. Each had a claim as good as the rest to the supreme crown of empire and, in pursuing that claim, plunged Italy into uproar. For Charlemagne had added yet another precedent to that established by his father: The sacred symbol could be bestowed only by the high priest of Christendom. The fact was used as a priceless weapon by the Papacy.

In the closing years of the ninth century, the faction battles for the Chair of Peter brought Rome to the edge of social disintegration. In March, 896, the ghastly *Synod horrenda,* which sat in judgment upon a corpse, marked the moment when the city plunged finally into anarchy and delivered, as inescapable result, the Chair of Peter to whosoever was bold enough to ascend it. In that month the triumphant faction, whose leader now ruled briefly as Pope Stephen VII, set in motion a solemn trial of the late Pope Formosus, quondam leader of the rival faction. The act of judgment was no mere formality. The corpse itself was dragged from the tomb where it had rested for eight months and, dressed again in its sacerdotal robes, was brought into the council chamber. There it was propped up in the throne that it had occupied in life while, in a parody of legal form, the "trial" went its blasphemous way.

The corpse was provided with a council, who wisely kept silent while Pope Stephen raved and screamed his insults at it. The pretext for the trial was that Formosus, contrary to canon law, had accepted the bishopric of Rome while he was still bishop of another diocese. But few, if any, in the council chamber, were impressed by the charge. The real crime of Formosus was that he had been a member of the opposite faction and had crowned "emperor" one of the numerous illegitimate descendants of Charlemagne after having performed the same office for the candidate favored by Pope Stephen's party.

But even this crime was illusory, for few people cared which puppet emperor wore the meaningless crown. The corpse of Formosus was being degraded virtually as an act of sympathetic magic, a means whereby his faction could itself be degraded and rendered powerless. There must have been others in the council chamber who shared the horrendous thought of the witness who recorded the scene. Suppose the corpse had replied, as Stephen mockingly urged it to: "Would not all that appalling crowd have fled, screaming with terror? Who, then, would have judged Formosus?" [7]

But there was no divine intervention and the synod obediently condemned the dead and all his acts. Stephen had not yet finished his vengeance. The corpse was stripped and the three fingers of benediction on the right hand were hacked off. It was then dragged through the palace and hurled to the yelling mob in the streets, who in turn dragged it to the Tiber and threw it in. Later, a group of fishermen pulled it out and in compassion gave it a decent burial.

Immediately after the *Synod horrenda* it chanced that an earthquake overthrew the ancient Lateran basilica—an only too apposite omen. Later, too, stories circulated of how the very images in St. Peter's saluted the dead Formosus when at last he was brought back to his place of rest. But it needed no supernatural signs to persuade the Romans that Pope Stephen's party had gone beyond the bounds even of their tolerance. In the early autumn of the same year, Stephen was seized and strangled. Despite the loss of their leader, his party remained active and elected a certain Cardinal Sergius as pope, simultaneously with the election of a candidate by the opposite faction.

But, in a sudden burst of violence, Sergius and most of his followers were chased out of the city. It did not end the battle for the Chair of Peter. Over the next twelve months four more popes scrambled onto the bloodstained throne, maintained themselves precariously for a few weeks—or even days—before being *hurled* themselves into their graves.

Seven popes and an anti-pope had appeared in a little over six years when, with the turn of the century, there came a stay in the rhythm of violence. Cardinal Sergius reappeared after seven years' exile, backed now by the swords of a feudal lord who saw a means thereby of gaining entry into Rome. The reigning pope found his grave, the slaughters in the city reached a climax, and then Cardinal Sergius emerged as Pope Sergius, sole survivor of the claimants and now supreme pontiff.

Throughout this period, contemporary records in Rome were sparse, rude—at times nonexistent. The chronicle of a semiliterate monk in the nearby monastery on Mount Soracte, brief, irregular biographical entries in the official *Book of the Popes,* a handful of epitaphs, some hostile comments by distant enemies—this is the sum of Roman records. In this tenth century the great city that had once spoken for millions was itself dumb, the city that had brought light to the Western world was itself sunken in almost total darkness. The observer gropes, as it were, by the light of a guttering candle which now flares up, now dies away almost to nothingness.

The figure of Sergius looms indistinct in this light. Malignant, unclean, ferocious—these are the epithets commonly applied to him. Regarding him in that uncertain light six centuries later, Cardinal Baronius, first of the great papal historians, could conclude only that such a monster had been unleashed against the church to show the supernatural strength of its foundations; no other structure could have resisted such an onslaught from within. Certainly Sergius had taken an active part in the *Synod horrenda,* and one of his first acts as pope was to provide Stephen with a handsome epitaph and overturn the later judgment that had re-instated Formosus' character. As a result, Sergius became the center of a vicious controversy in which his own character was alternately damned and praised. Out of these confused and conflicting statements only one thing remains clear to posterity: During his seven-year pontificate there began the operation that turned the Papacy into an appanage for the children of the senatrix Marozia, one of whom was his own.

II
The House of Theophylact

Marozia
Senatrix of Rome (926–932)

Octavian
Pope John XII (955–963)

Theophylact
Pope Benedict IX (1032–1046)

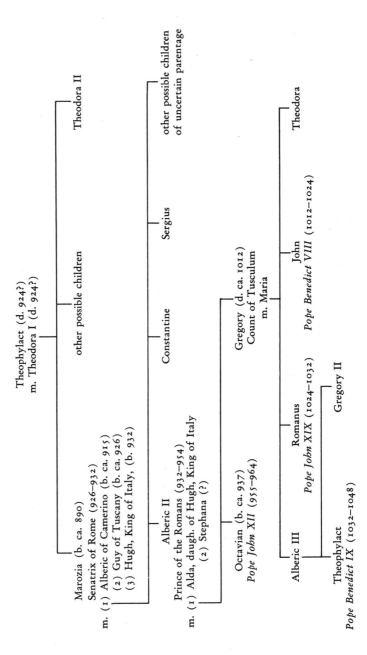

THE HOUSE OF THEOPHYLACT

Conjectured genealogy of the Tusculum branch

Theophylact (d. 924?)
m. Theodora I (d. 924?)

Marozia (b. ca. 890)
Senatrix of Rome (926–932)
m. (1) Alberic of Camerino (b. ca. 915)
   (2) Guy of Tuscany (b. ca. 926)
   (3) Hugh, King of Italy, (b. 932)

other possible children

Theodora II

Alberic II
Prince of the Romans (932–954)
m. (1) Alda, daugh. of Hugh, King of Italy
   (2) Stephana (?)

Constantine

Sergius

other possible children
of uncertain parentage

Octavian (b. ca. 937)
Pope John XII (955–964)

Gregory (d. ca. 1012)
Count of Tusculum
m. Maria

Alberic III

Romanus
Pope John XIX (1024–1032)

Gregory II

John
Pope Benedict VIII (1012–1024)

Theodora

Theophylact
Pope Benedict IX (1032–1048)

Rise of the Theophylacts

Some six hundred years after the Papacy had secured a temporal crown for itself, an unknown genius of propaganda launched into history the bizarre and enduring story of the woman who crept on to the papal throne and ruled under the name of John.

The legend of Pope Joan first appeared in literary form in the thirteenth century when the temporal claims of the Papacy reached their dizziest height. Produced as anti-papal propaganda, the legend's scabrous nature ensured its ensuing popularity so that it passed into folklore. It was told again and again in various forms, reaching its most polished state in the hands of the learned pornographers of the Renaissance. In the main version of the story, Joan was another Heloise, an Anglo-Saxon girl of great beauty and learning who began her career in a monastery disguised as a monk, ultimately went to Rome, and was elected pope. She betrayed her secret only by giving birth to a child during a procession and died shortly afterward through shame and grief.

The story was constructed with a painstaking detail that would have earned the literary approval of the author of the *Donation of Constantine*. The length of Joan's pontificate was given as precisely two years, one month, and four days—from approximately 855 to 858. An ancient statue of a mother and child that had always stood upon the processional route was transformed into a statue of the erring Joan and her innocent betrayer. The fact that papal processions no longer went down that particular street became damning evidence of papal guilt and shame—though other streets were cut out of the processional route from time to time and no sinister motives were imputed. Even the fact that a newly crowned pope seated himself upon a species of marble commode—theoretically allowing a physical examination to be made—was adduced as infallible authentication of the story. After the Reformation, it was believed by Catholics and Protestants alike; and as late as 1600, a bust of *Johannes VIII, femina ex Anglia* was unquestioningly accepted among the row of papal busts that glare out over the heads of worshippers in Siena Cathedral.

Edward Gibbon scotched the story for an English-speaking public, for once appearing as the champion—though a singularly reluctant champion—of the Papacy. Discoursing on the tenth-century faction fights in Rome, he gave the most likely explanation of the origin of the myth.

> The influence of two sister prostitutes, Marozia and Theodora, was founded on their wealth and beauty, their political and amorous intrigues. The most strenuous of their lovers were rewarded with the Roman mitre, and their reign may have suggested to darker ages the fable of a female pope. The bastard son, the grandson, and the great grandson of Marozia—a rare genealogy—were seated in the Chair of St. Peter.[1]

Gibbon erred twice in the passage—once on a matter of fact and once on a matter of charity. There were two Theodoras, and the one Gibbon had in mind was not Marozia's sister but her mother; and they were certainly not prostitutes in the generally accepted sense, for they were the daughter and wife respectively of no less a person than Theophylact, the senator of Rome, civic head of the city. Marozia gained for herself the title of senatrix—the undoubted mistress of Rome, ruling the city between the years 926 and 932 as its lord and so providing a model for the far less colorful "Pope Joan."

Marozia's family came from Tusculum, an Etruscan city on a hilltop near Rome. The beautiful little city had lived in a kind of symbiosis with its great neighbor for centuries. Its ambitious citizens would cross the fifteen miles to Rome, make their names and fortunes there, and return to enrich their native city—if they survived their Roman foray.

Some time about the year 890, Marozia's father Theophylact made the journey from Tusculum that so many of his forebears had undertaken, and established himself in Rome. Theophylact, the titular head of the family, is a wan and shadowy figure, his bare identity and office alone surviving through the medium of a few legal records. He bore the resounding titles of duke and senator and was one of the judges appointed by the emperor. But the present power and future notoriety of his house were derived less from his judicial powers than from the more potent if more dubious elements supplied by his wife and daughter. So, at least, the bitterly partisan chroniclers imply; but the man must have had courage and skill in plenty to survive and in part to control the murderous situation that he found in Rome.

During the violent battles that followed the *Synod horrenda,* Theophylact had achieved the double success of supporting Sergius' party even while it was in exile, and yet of surviving to welcome it when it returned. How and why such an obviously competent man lost ground to his wife and daughter, the chronicles did not see fit to inquire. The fact, presumably, was sufficient, for the "monarchy of Theodora" was undoubted fact: From the year 900 onward it is her name, not her husband's, that predominates in the sparse annals of the city.

The Theophylact women emerge suddenly, in three dimension, from the dark background, bathed in the same lurid light as shone on Sergius. But unlike Sergius, they had their own chronicler, a bitterly hostile one who destroyed what good name they might have possessed in exchange for the immortality he granted them. His name was Liudprand, bishop of Cremona, a Lombard by birth and therefore a bitter enemy of all that Rome and the Romans stood for. Marozia and her mother are introduced into his history in a passage of concentrated venom which established their reputation for centuries to come. Cardinal Baronius, struggling in the sixteenth century with the task of writing the first papal history, had no choice but to follow Liudprand and coined the vivid term "pornocracy" for that period of the Papacy which the two women dominated.

"A certain shameless strumpet called Theodora at one time was sole monarch of Rome and—shame though it is to write it— exercised power like a man. She had two daughters, Marozia and Theodora, who were not only her equals but could surpass her in the exercises that Venus loves." [2] Liudprand, like Gibbon after him, certainly traduced the younger Theodora, a blameless young woman who seems to have passed her life in conventional good works. But other sources, scanty though they are, give only too good grounds for Liudprand's attack upon her mother and sister. *The Book of the Popes,* in an entry neutral if only by its brevity, recorded the one solid piece of information relating to Marozia's early years. Shortly after puberty she had a child by Pope Sergius—a boy—who in time ascended the papal throne.

Liudprand probably did not trouble to analyze the springs of Theodora's power because, from his viewpoint, they were self-evident. The true master of Rome was Pope Sergius and Theodora owed her influence to the fact that her daughter Marozia was Sergius' mistress. An element of sheer self-preservation alone would have encouraged Sergius to maintain his alliance with the family that had contributed to his success. But alliances in Rome were fragile structures, apt to be overturned or shattered by even minor shifts in self-interest. Far more enduring would have been the living link between the Theophylacts and Sergius provided by the young body of Marozia, then in the first flower of that beauty which later proved her most valuable weapon.

In whatever manner Theodora exploited her position, by the time of Pope Sergius' death in 911 she had moved from indirect to direct control. Rome might, reasonably, have expected another murderous prelude to the next election. Instead, two of Theodora's nominees ascended the throne with the minimum of fuss, reigned for a little over a year each, and quietly descended into the grave. Only then did she turn her attention to the boldest, most cynical act of all her career: the transferring of a lover from the bishopric of Ravenna to the bishopric of Rome.

The contemplated move was in total defiance of that same canon law which had been pretext for the "trial" of Formosus. In executing it, Theodora showed the extent of her control over both Rome and the Papacy. Liudprand of Cremona is again the major—and at times the only—witness to the events that led to the consolidation of the family's grasp upon the tiara. His account is garbled, spiced with his habitual salacity, filled with detectable errors, but it is the only one that tells a coherent story, filling in the gaps left by other chroniclers.

According to him, Theodora fell in love with a certain John, an ambitious young cleric in Ravenna who frequently came to Rome on official business. Under Theodora's protection, the young man progressed steadily in his career and was at last made bishop, a post that ended his frequent trips to Rome. "Thereupon Theodora, like a harlot fearing that she would have few opportunities of bedding with her sweetheart, forced him to abandon his bishopric and take for himself—O, monstrous crime!—the Papacy of Rome." [3] In 914 Bishop John of Ravenna became Pope John X.

Shortly afterward Theodora provided Marozia with her first husband. The girl was still in her late teens, and now that Sergius' death had placed her again on the market, she was used to tie another powerful man to the house of Theophylact. He too was a newcomer to Rome, a soldier of fortune who bore the name of Alberic. His name was German but he came to Rome with an Italian title—marquis of Camerino. The title was undoubtedly gained by the simple means of violence—indication, at least, of his proficiency as a soldier, for titles meant land, which now could be gained only by the sword.

Alberic probably came to Rome at the invitation of Theophylact. A professional soldier with a band of veterans behind him could tip the balance in a faction fight and Alberic swiftly made himself indispensable to his host. As a reward, he received Marozia as wife and moved into the domestic apartments of the family palace on the Aventine hill. There, in due course, Marozia's second child was born, christened with his father's name of Alberic.

The three men whom chance had brought together at a critical moment in Rome's history were each supremely competent in his own field. Despite his dubious entry into Rome as Theodora's protégé, Pope John proved to be a statesman of the first rank; he became, too, a firm ally and friend of Theophylact's, a piquant situation that the Romans must have enjoyed. Theophylact himself, though overshadowed by his wife, continued to play an important part in the governance of the city; he was still, after all, a judge appointed by the emperor. And Alberic the soldier had already proved his ability by climbing unaided into the upper levels of power in Rome.

The fields in which the three men operated overlapped, but they succeeded in establishing a species of triumvirate in which each supplemented the deficiencies of the others, yet refrained from interfering in their legitimate spheres. Casually evolved, it was as short-lived as were all such experiments, but it was effective while it lasted. There was desperate need for men of such caliber in Rome at that time, for its very existence was threatened by a new wave of Saracens.

The city had poured out its energies for nearly a century in internal battles, ignoring the changing conditions in the world outside. It had not only abdicated from world responsibility but was now incapable of defending even the narrow limits of its home territories. In the north of Italy, the despised Lombards held waves of invading Huns in check, but there was no such barrier in the south against the Saracens. They had moved steadily up the peninsula and by the year 924 they were established less than thirty miles from Rome. The abnormal became the norm; the sight of Saracens in the heart of Italy was an everyday occurrence, Italian merchants paying toll to African tribesmen in Italy as a matter of course.

The establishment of a temporary equilibrium between the factions in Rome released energies for a rare Roman military action against the external enemies of Rome. All Italy united before the threat of total Saracen dominance, looking once again—and for the last time—toward the imperishable city on the Tiber, which effortlessly reassumed its ancient role of leader. Even the Byzantines forgot their endless grievances and united with their fellow Christians against the Muslim. Briefly, the darkness lifted from Rome as poets and chroniclers, stirred by the event, recorded the last triumphant foray of the Roman army, providing a brilliant light by which posterity could mark the march of the triumvirate. Pope, nobleman, and soldier, combining and fusing for the moment all that was great in Rome, led an immense army down upon the Saracens, destroyed them utterly, thus removing the menace that had hovered over Italy for two generations. They returned to Rome in triumph.

And after that, the darkness again descends upon Rome; when a glimmer of light appears a few years later, Alberic has disappeared, and with him, Theophylact and Theodora. The total absence of records allows almost any interpretation of the end of Alberic and the first generation of the house of Theophylact. One of the many vague rumors persisted and was picked up by later chroniclers. It seemed that Alberic reached too high and was destroyed. He aimed for total domination, was driven out of the city, and ended as he began, a robber baron in a hill fort, besieged and then killed by the people who had once called him hero and savior.

There is nothing inherently improbable in the story. A man who had gained high rank by the sword was only too likely to be tempted by the chronic anarchy and seek to rule by the sword, particularly if he were married to such a woman as Marozia. The fate of Marozia's parents is utterly unknown. They may have been caught up in Alberic's disgrace; they may have been destroyed by him, or by their daughter on her upward path. By whatever means it was brought about, the Roman stage was clear for Marozia by the year 926.

"Pope Joan"

The key to the tumultuous events in Rome during the mid-tenth century lies wholly in the personality of Marozia. She was a lay person, yet she controlled the supreme sacerdotal office of Europe. She was a woman, yet she dominated a purely masculine society, twisting the complex constitution of the city to serve her own ends.

She was not unique. Her mother had demonstrated the heights to which a woman could rise, and throughout Italy and even beyond the Alps there prevailed a curious dominance of women who pursued and maintained political power through sexual means. The tendency was exaggerated by the prurience of celibate chroniclers, but it was a very real element in a supposedly masculine world. In a society that looked upon a second marriage as a species of adultery, these women succeeded in marrying two, three, or even four times, the deaths of the successive husbands bringing them added riches. Women were never again to enjoy such power until the coming of the Renaissance.

Marozia was not unique, but she was indubitably the most flamboyant. Lacking official status, she was thus deprived of even the arid praise of official apologists who might have given some corrective to the otherwise universal bias of the chroniclers. Benedict, the monkish chronicler of nearby Mount Soracte, had watched over the affairs of Rome for years, and he of all people could have essayed some assessment of this remarkable woman, who seems to exist in a vacuum. But he contented himself with the bald statement that she, like her mother, was senatrix—lord of the city. He gave some idea of his opinion on the situation in his brief remark—"The Roman power was subjugated to women—even as we read in the prophet 'the effeminate shall dominate Jerusalem' " [4]—but that was all. He was a monk, and the idea of a woman exercising power in the sacred city was sacrilege enough, without going into details as to whether that power was exercised for good or ill.

The fact that he gave no hint as to the means by which Marozia gathered the civil power of Rome into her hands was understandable. The threads of power were tangled beyond hope of unraveling and she profited by the confusion. But ultimately, her power derived from her ability to maintain the loyalty, or feed the ambition, of her fellow citizens. She could not command the enormous wealth, drawn from an empire, that had allowed the earlier masters of Rome to keep the mob in subjection with the anodyne of pleasure. The only military power was that provided by reluctant militia, or maintained by private wealth. Her two sons were children still. Her sister, though loyal as were all Theophylacts to each other, preferred to follow the more conventional path open to a patrician woman and occupy herself with domestic affairs and the more harmless religious practices. Marozia exercised power not only illegally but alone.

Outside the pages of Liudprand of Cremona, there exist only vague indications of her nature: sensual, but capable of employing her beauty coldly as a political weapon; fierce, debauched, revengeful—but also highly competent, highly intelligent. Liudprand fills in some of the details but ignores the rest. His motives for painting Marozia in the darkest possible colors are obvious: She was a Roman and she was the grandmother of that pope who gave endless trouble to Liudprand's beloved master the emperor Otto. Indeed, she was the ancestress of a line of popes who defied the emperors of the West.

Already predisposed to salacity, Liudprand chose to attack Marozia at the most vulnerable point of a woman in high office— her chastity. It was totally irrelevant, and as an attack, defeated its own end, for it threw a smokescreen over the rest of her activities, bad and possibly good alike. In the universal corruption that marked Roman society, Marozia's morals would have passed unnoticed. What was conspicuous was her ability to mold people to her will, and this Liudprand ignored, except to imply that it was done purely through the bedchamber. And, even if this were so, the most besotted Roman politician must have occasionally regarded his shrinking future with dismay.

Marozia's parents had gone no further than to create alliances between the family and the Papacy. Their daughter boldly pushed the principle to its furthest possible extent—the Papacy and the family were to be one. She appeared totally indifferent to the universal pretensions of the office, seeing it simply as the necessary badge of success for a Roman family, a means whereby the rich revenues of St. Peter could be channeled directly into Theophylact coffers. She already had a candidate, her eldest son John, fathered by Pope Sergius and now in his early teens. The role her second son, Alberic, was to play was less certain. Later, evidence provided by Alberic himself showed that he was forced into the background, humiliated, though he was the legitimate son of the one-time hero of Rome. John was to be Marozia's major piece upon the board, presumably because the coronation of a pope's son as pope could promote the hereditary principle.

But whichever of her two children she openly favored, the position of the reigning pope John was one of considerable danger. He was a vigorous and brave man, but bereft of Theodora's protection he was now isolated in a city controlled by an enemy. For Marozia loathed her mother's paramour. Her hatred may have arisen from that dark sexual spring which colored the motives of her unhappy, violent family; or she may have seen in the tough and canny pope an obstacle to her own ambitions. For whatever cause, she had early decided upon his destruction.

The tigress of Rome, with two cubs to provide for, must have presented an unnerving spectacle to a man who had had personal experience of the power of a Roman matron, and Pope John looked outside Rome for an ally. There was one to hand—Hugh of Provence, yet another man who boasted that Charlemagne's blood ran, though illegitimately, in his veins. Hugh agreed to help the pope if the pope would anoint him king of Italy. John went to Ravenna to discuss the details.

But he had moved far too slowly. While the lengthy negotiations were under way, Marozia offered herself to, and was accepted by, Hugh's half-brother Guy, a feudal lord of Tuscany who brought to the marriage his own dowry in the form of soldiers. With her new husband's aid she completed her grasp on Rome by occupying the Castle of Sant' Angelo, key to the city. Secure both militarily and politically, she calmly awaited the return of the pope.

John returned and managed to survive another two years, defended by a devoted but dwindling bodyguard. In the summer of

928 it was overwhelmed in a sudden fierce riot, John was seized and hurled into one of the dungeons of Sant' Angelo. There, a year later, he died either by suffocation or starvation, the first of the popes to be created by a woman, and now destroyed by her daughter.

Three years later, Marozia achieved the first of her long-range ambitions when her son by Sergius ascended the throne. Two shadowy figures had kept the throne warm for him until he was of an age that would not offend even the easy tolerance of the Romans, but even then he was not much more than twenty years of age when he became supreme pontiff. Shortly afterward, Marozia dispensed with her husband. She had overcome the last shreds of resistance with his aid, and like the luckless mate of a mantis that has performed its sole function, he was expendable.

Marozia too looked out beyond Rome to the same Hugh of Provence who had been anointed king of Italy by the luckless pope John. With such a man beside her, she could aim for the highest goal in the land—the imperial crown itself—for in her son's hands lay the power that could turn a king into an emperor. Hugh of Provence hastened to Rome at her call.

Liudprand knew the man well, for he had been a page at Hugh's court and rather liked him. Now he was appalled, likening Hugh to an ox which went to sacrifice at a woman's summons, assuming that he did so for the basest reasons. Certainly Hugh was the most accomplished satyr of his day, his royal court resembling a brothel at which Italians marveled. But though Marozia was doubtless a powerful attraction for such a man, even stronger was the attraction of the dowry she could bring him. He was already married, but that problem was easily overcome. There was another problem in that, Marozia having been married to his half-brother, the projected union would be, technically, incestuous. Unhesitatingly Hugh defamed his mother's memory, branding his half-brother bastard, and when another brother furiously protested, had his eyes dug out and imprisoned him.

In the spring of 932 Hugh arrived in Rome for his marriage to its mistress. There was a certain murkiness about the wedding atmosphere. Behind the groom were the specters of a wife who had conveniently died, a defamed mother, a brother blinded and in a dungeon. The hands of the bride who awaited him were only too probably stained with the blood of his half-brother, and were certainly stained with the blood of a pope. But her son was performing the ceremony and he, supreme judge of morals in Europe, saw no just impediments to the marriage.

The wedding took place not in a church but in the Castle of Sant' Angelo, and there the shadowy though legal power of the king of Italy was strengthened by the illegal, but very real, power of the mistress of Rome. It seemed, on that day, that there was nothing they could not do, that now nothing stood between them and the imperial purple. The pliant twenty-year-old pope had only to perform another ceremony and Hugh and Marozia would be emperor and empress of the West—Marozia of all people could have transformed that hollow title into a meaningful one. But at that moment of penultimate triumph, a forgotten figure stepped out of the shadows and knocked the cup from their hands.

The figure was Alberic, son of Marozia's first husband, half-brother to the pope. He was then perhaps eighteen, and throughout his young life his mother had kept him deliberately in the background. He possessed perhaps too much of the vigor of his father to make a sufficiently pliable pope, and neither could he claim that genetic link with the Chair of Peter that his half-brother possessed.

Marozia's second marriage had thrust Alberic even further into obscurity, depriving him still more of his rightful position as heir of the hero of Rome. Though her second husband Guy had disappeared, there now appeared the ruthless Hugh. Apart from feelings of affronted pride, Alberic knew well that he stood in immediate and terrible danger, for there could not be room for two such men as himself and Hugh in the city. His new stepfather, arrogantly confident, made no secret of the fact that he intended to blind his young rival—the universal method of rendering an enemy helpless—and Marozia raised no objections. It was only a question of finding a pretext for the disposal of a young Roman patrician in a manner that would not rouse even his abject fellows.

The pretext came sooner than Hugh expected, but it was not he who profited from it. During one of the numerous drunken feasts in Sant' Angelo that followed the wedding, Alberic "was pouring out water, at his mother's bidding, for his stepfather Hugh to wash his hands"—probably a deliberate humiliation that Marozia had imposed upon her son to emphasize his subordinate role. The young man clumsily spilled the water and Hugh struck him across the face.

Alberic ran out of the castle, shouting to the Romans to rise, to defend their honor and their lives.

The majesty of Rome has sunk to such depths that now she obeys the orders of harlots. Could there be anything viler than that the city of Rome should be brought to ruin by the impurities of one woman and that those who were once our slaves should now be our masters? If he should hit me, his stepson, when he had only recently come as our guest, what do you suppose he will do when he has taken root in the city? [5]

The Romans responded. It was as though Marozia had exerted a Circe-like spell upon them for nearly six years, reducing the most ferocious mob in history to an apathetic mass of slaves. Whatever the spell, it broke at that moment, shattered by Hugh's too-hasty desire to taste the fruits of tyranny. They could see, as clearly as Alberic, the portent of the blow. The mob rose and, howling, advanced on Sant' Angelo.

Hugh's army was encamped outside the city walls, for his bride had deemed it unwise to introduce a mass of foreign soldiery among her volatile subjects, and the castle was garrisoned only by citizen militia. The squat building was impregnable, however, and had Hugh put up even a token resistance his army could have entered and carried him off, together with Marozia and the passive pope who could still have bestowed the crown upon them.

But Hugh did not even try. As soon as he knew that the Romans had revolted he had no thought but to save his skin, abandoning the castle, his wife, his hopes of future greatness. He let himself down by a rope at a point where the castle touched the city walls, escaped to his army and immediately marched away from the perilous city. The garrison now had no incentive to hold Sant'

Angelo against their fellow citizens; the mob swarmed in, captured Marozia, and handed her over to Alberic.

Marozia disappeared from history at that moment, as though she had never been. Alberic took the only course open to him. She was his mother, but she was also the wife of his deadliest enemy, and was quite capable of murdering her son to gain the glory of which she had been robbed. Yet Alberic, as his later actions showed, shrank from such a crime as matricide. Marozia was therefore conducted down to the lowest depths of the very castle that had seen her brief reign as queen. There she was immured and remained—a woman still young and beautiful, enduring a living death but one that did not stain her son's hands with a terrible murder. And while she raged her life away, in the sunlit streets of the city above her a nonviolent revolution brought her son to a power the like of which Rome had not witnessed for centuries.

Alberic ruled Rome as its supreme prince for twenty years, purging it of the gross decadence that had made the city an object of contempt for all Europe. It speaks much for his ability that he, a youth scarcely out of his teens, grasped the reins of power with a sure and certain hand. It speaks even more for his personality that under him the Romans—notoriously the most venal, the most undisciplined people in Europe—resisted both the attacks and bribes of Hugh of Provence, who returned to take tardy vengeance on his stepson.

Alberic's rule restored self-respect to the wild, mixed group of people who still bore the sacred name of Romans. Rome benefited, but the Papacy benefited more, for Alberic's first act was to deprive his half-brother of the temporal power. He invested it in himself as prince of Rome, again divorcing the spiritual from the temporal power after the disastrous fusion made two centuries earlier. Again, the office of pope had little attraction for the avaricious and the effect upon the characters of the popes was immediate, dramatic and, so long as Alberic ruled, enduring.

Even the sourest of churchmen, the most dedicated of Alberic's critics, were forced to concede that the supreme office of Western

Christianity was discharged with high honor during the two decades that it was untrammeled by temporal power. Under Alberic, the popes enjoyed the fullest freedom in their priestly and papal roles. Edicts continued to go out to distant bishops, who in turn sought the guidance of their spiritual superior. The vast and complex machinery of the Roman Church continued to move around its ancient center, unaffected by the fact that the bishop of Rome was no longer the lord of Rome. Not for another nine hundred years was the Papacy to be free again of the burden of temporality, and this brief respite granted it was perhaps Alberic's highest achievement. Ironically, it was Alberic himself who destroyed this respite when he fused the spiritual and temporal offices for the sake of his depraved young son Octavian.

The Pope-King

Octavian, son of the prince of Rome, was born about the year 937, for his mother had been the passive instrument of a peace concluded between Alberic and Hugh of Provence the previous year. She was Hugh's daughter and Hugh may have intended to use her as a stalking horse and so at last gain entry into Rome. But shortly afterward he deemed it prudent to retire from Italy altogether, his debauches and tyranny having at last undermined what little power he possessed as king. In one last round of robberies he collected a fortune, then retired to Provence and there comfortably lived out the rest of his life. A new "king" of Italy was elected, but he ignored both Rome and Alberic. The latter, resigning himself to the fact that his wife was the heiress merely of a retired bandit, devoted himself thereafter to the restoration of Rome.

The name Alberic chose for his first legitimate child was demonstration of his pride in Rome's past and belief in its future. The Romans themselves had forgotten, or were contemptuous of, their heritage, turning to the Greek court at Constantinople for their models of social behavior. Alberic's own grandparents, Theophylact and Theodora, had borne Greek names although they were Romans. For Alberic, the name "Octavian" had a double significance. It was the personal name of that Augustus Caesar who was the epitome of the majesty of Rome; but it was also the name of a long-dead Etruscan prince of Tusculum who had led the Etruscans in their last battles against Rome over a millennium before. Perhaps Alberic intended only a symbolic link with the city of his maternal ancestors, but descendants of his family were in time to claim a blood link with the great Etruscan, calling themselves counts of Tusculum, transforming the murky origins of their family into a dizzy ancestry.

The childhood of the young Octavian is wrapped in almost total obscurity. His father probably raised him as soldier, rather than future priest, for while he later displayed some military proficiency, it was obvious that his book learning had been scant. In his maturity, as a young pope called to preside over the councils of learned men, he was derided for his elementary ignorance of Latin. It did not seem to trouble him, nor act as a handicap. The house of Theophylact bred politicians and soldiers rather than scholars, and in the abysmal state of learning in Rome, it would have required an unusual youth to achieve even that level which was accepted as the norm for people of his class elsewhere. And in this matter, at least, Octavian was by no means unusual.

But whatever species of training the boy enjoyed, it was cut short almost as soon as it had begun, for he could not have been more than sixteen years old when, in the autumn of 954, his father died. Alberic himself was scarcely forty when the lethal fever that lurked in the Roman Campagna seized him. Characteristically, he was in the middle of a military preparation when his last illness came upon him, but it was not the campaign that caused him urgently to summon the Roman nobles to St. Peter's.

It seemed that Alberic knew he was about to be cut down while his long-term plans for himself, for Rome, and for his son were still in a state of flux. With the sweat of death upon him, he therefore had himself carried to the most sacred spot in Christendom, the altar above the tomb of St. Peter, and there called upon the nobles to swear upon the bones of the apostle that they would elect his son prince upon his death, and pope upon the death of the reigning pontiff. The nobles loved him and so swore—and ensured the destruction of all that he had created.

Despite his breadth of vision, his quality of daring imagination, Alberic was still essentially a child of his time, unable to view events save through the spectrum of family loyalty. He had purged the Theophylacts, made it a great house, and according to the moral climate of his day, would have been lacking in piety had he not ensured its continuance.

It is possible that, had time been granted him, he would have bred Octavian up in his own image as prince, initiating the youth in the control of the subtle balance of forces that enabled the offices of prince and pope to be distinct but harmonious. But time was not granted him, and in his last hours the statesman gave ground to the family-conscious nobleman who saw only that the fortunes of his house, now in the hands of an inexperienced youth, must be shored up by the power and wealth of the Papacy.

He died, and Octavian took his place as prince. A year later the reigning pope also died and the Romans, obedient to Alberic's last command, elected his sixteen-year-old son as pope. Thus, both offices were again combined in one person, causing a critical mass that must in time explode.

On his coronation, young Octavian took the style of John XII, establishing the enduring custom of a papal name. It was an expression of his dual role, for he employed the name Octavian in his capacity of prince and the name John in that of pope.

The young man possessed qualities which, had they been allowed to develop under his father's guidance, could have made him a worthy successor—as prince. He had a certain attractive insolence, an ability to talk his way out of tight situations, and considerable personal courage. He was eager to copy his great father, but only if it could be done without too much effort. He had neither the desire nor intention to spend his days and nights in laborious groundwork fit only for clerks. Impulsive, he lacked the ability to maintain that steady and comprehensive control of men and actions necessary to both his offices. In the first months of his reign he led a hastily planned, badly organized military expedition against a rebel lord in the Papal States who had risen, with ominous swiftness, on news of Alberic's death. The expedition was a fiasco. A resolute show of arms sent the papal army scampering for shelter, the young Holy Father leading the rout. The military life was plainly not for him, and he returned to Rome and embarked upon a course of living that startled even the not particularly impressionable Romans.

The return of temporal power to the Papacy had again thrown the tiara to the mob. The factions, dormant for twenty years, rose again, and murder, arson, and rape returned to the streets as casual incidents of everyday life. John encouraged faction as enthusiastically as his father had suppressed it—a rowdy young noble striving to overtop the rowdiest of his companions, and succeeding. He was the son of the heroic Alberic, but he was also the grandson of Marozia and Hugh of Provence, the two most accomplished debauchees that Italy had seen in many years. It was their malign strain that swiftly dominated his nature, already under the corrupting influence of absolute power, and smothered whatever might have been noble.

The city that his father had cherished John saw as a treasury to be plundered, he himself protected by the swords of a faction for whom he could do no wrong so long as he maintained it in power. Rome lacked that middle class which, in her daughter cities of Italy, brought about even the limited democracy of the later centuries. There were no merchants to create wealth and so act as buffer between nobles and people; for Rome's chief income came through the coffers of St. Peter, her chief industry the production of priests and the exploiting of pilgrims. The sullen, inarticulate mass of the people was a wholly unpredictable element that could destroy but never mold, save when led by most rare geniuses. The power of the city lay wholly in the hands of great families, ensconced with private armies in indestructible castles. John was able to draw upon the revenues of the Papal States to maintain his own armed gangs. They proved useless against outside enemies but were adequate enough to terrorize Romans.

In his relationship with the Church, John seems to have been urged toward a course of deliberate sacrilege that went far beyond the casual enjoyment of sensual pleasures. It was as though the dark element in his nature goaded him on to test the utmost extents of his power, a Christian Caligula whose crimes were rendered peculiarly horrific by the office he held. Later, the charge was specifically made against him that he turned the Lateran into a brothel; that he and his gang violated female pilgrims in the very basilica of St. Peter; that the offerings of the humble laid upon the altar were snatched up as casual booty.

He was inordinately fond of gambling, at which he invoked the names of those discredited gods now universally regarded as demons. His sexual hunger was insatiable—a minor crime in Roman eyes. What was far worse was that the casual occupants of his bed were rewarded not with casual gifts of gold but of land. One of his mistresses was able to establish herself as a feudal lord "for he was so blindly in love with her that he made her governor of cities—and even gave to her the golden crosses and cups of St. Peter himself." [6]

Fornication was one thing, but alienation of lands was another, striking at the rights of that class upon whom he depended for support. It was a characteristically rash and arrogant gesture, but for the moment John was immune. The opposition to him was fragmented, without a leader of even his shabby caliber: For what it was worth, he was the sole, constant center of Rome.

So he pursued his course for three headlong years until there rose an enemy outside Rome, the new king of Italy, with whom his enemies within the walls might make common cause. This new king was, if anything, worse than the old. His name was Berengar, a duke of one of the old Lombard duchies, who had fought his way to power by the usual means of murder and treachery, and maintained himself in power with the usual band of semibandits, who would support him just so long as they gained profit in return. The reign began in murder and continued with a violence, a depthless cupidity, that outreached even the reign of Hugh of Provence. Of Berengar's wife, Liudprand remarked caustically that it was only her daughter's character which robbed her of the title of the worst woman alive. Her avarice was insatiable: The ladies of her court learned to appear before her innocent of jewels, for that which she coveted she instantly demanded.

For some time after his coronation Berengar plundered the north of Italy, then, inevitably, began to move south, attracted, as all were attracted, to Rome. The army behind him more closely resembled a brigand horde than the army of a king, but its members were tough fighters, intent upon the loot all believed to be in the city. John's pleasurable career was brought to a sudden halt. Behind him were citizens on the brink of riot, before him a ruthless enemy who was also a skilled soldier. The mantle of prince fell from him, displaying only a frightened young man whose one thought was to save his life, and if possible, his pleasures too.

He was now prince in name only; but he was still pope, and as supreme head of the Christian Church he could appeal to the deepest and noblest instincts of all her children. In the year 960 John summoned to his aid the emperor Otto of Saxony.

The Coming of the Emperor

Over 150 years had passed since Charlemagne had been crowned emperor of the West by Pope Leo III. During that century and a half, the crown of the empire had become the debased pretext for faction war, a hollow title for which even such as Marozia and Hugh could aim. Yet still there lingered the memory of the high compact made on that distant Christmas Day when the warring nations of Europe had been again united under a single head. The unity had not outlasted Charlemagne's lifetime, but thereafter men were to look back upon the Carolingian Empire as a lost Golden Age. The knowledge remained that the bishop of Rome could create a supreme lord of Europe who would bring back law and, with it, peace.

Therefore, when a truly great king, Otto of Saxony, arose in Germany, it was as though he stepped upon a stage that had been waiting for its protagonist for over a hundred years. He found Germany divided into five great dukedoms, each racially distinct: He welded them into one and placed himself at its head.

Otto could not claim descent from Charlemagne for he was not even of the same race, being a Saxon. But, like his great predecessor, personal might overcame the arguments of lawyers, and to emphasize his goal—the reestablishment of the Carolingian Empire—he reenacted Charlemagne's coronation. He received the German crown in the beautiful circular church that Charlemagne had built in Aachen and was given, successively, the Frankish monarch's great sword, scepter, and the priceless Sacred Lance—the very spear that had pierced Christ on the cross. The court he established was modeled upon Charlemagne's, and though it could not compare in intellectual qualities, yet it rose above its time as the powerful young king attracted the most diverse peoples from distant corners of Europe. Among them was the Lombard bishop of Cremona, Liudprand, whose vivid histories, only sure guide to the whole dark century, enshrined the memory of Otto as the prince of all virtues.

But it was not his intellectual and imperial pretensions that made Otto great in the eyes of peoples far beyond his German forests. Imperial pretenders were commonplace and intellectual pursuits were best left to clerks. What he had done was to smash the terrifying Hun threat that had loomed over Europe for a generation and more.

In the eyes of Europeans, the Huns had appeared like goblins from some diabolical mythology as, a million strong, they had swept in from the East. The little men with their deeply sunken eyes and partially shaved heads were totally alien from anything that Europe had known. They habitually fed upon raw flesh, giving rise to the belief that they devoured the corpses of the slain. Incredibly hardy, superb horsemen, they terrified even those who had experienced the bloodlust of the Norsemen, the refined cruelty of Greeks and Saracens.

Germany was in the front line of this new wave of migrants, and in combating it, the Germans found a national hero and a national identity. Otto's father had organized the eastward defenses of the country and brought the Huns to a halt in a tremendous battle. Stunned, they paused for a generation, and then, shortly after Otto had established himself, they poured across the frontiers in a horde so numerous that they could boast their horses would drink the rivers dry and pound the cities to dust with their hooves.

Otto met them outside Augsburg on the tenth of August, 955. The dead on the German side alone climbed into the tens of thousands, but the Hun dead were uncountable. It was the end of the menace. Western Europe had shown that it could protect its reborn civilization and the Huns ebbed back to the East.

With the prestige of Augsburg added to his demonstrated skill as statesman, Otto towered in Europe without equal, his influence stretching from England to Spain, even the Danes acknowledging him as virtual overlord. But still there was the memory of that Christmas Day compact to haunt him, as it would haunt so many Germans to their nation's cost. He was clothed in Charlemagne's mantle; he ruled as de facto lord over much of Charlemagne's empire; after Augsburg his troops had spontaneously hailed him as "Imperator"—but still he had not been anointed by the successor of the priest who had anointed Charlemagne. And until he received the sacred oil he was a pretender, a barbarian king who happened to have the military might to dominate Europe. So at least he thought, and with him, most Europeans.

When, therefore, John summoned him to Rome to champion the apostle and to receive the crown of empire as reward, Otto came in haste. Berengar, a bully but no coward, marched from Rome to meet him in battle but the outcome was never in doubt, the veterans of Augsburg more than a match for the bandits of Italy. After exacting promises of good behavior from him, Otto set Berengar at liberty—foolishly, his advisers thought—and continued on to Rome, coming in sight of the great Aurelian walls in the first weeks of the new year of 961.

The coronation of a German pretender in Rome a century earlier had led directly to the macabre trial of Formosus with all its long train of violence. Now the Romans were called again to witness the glorification of a barbarian, this time conjured up by the son of the man who had restored their self-respect.

In spite of Otto's pretensions to culture, in the eyes of the Romans his army was barely preferable in appearance to the Huns it had destroyed. "Terrible of aspect" were these Germans, huge, bearded, shaggy men from the northern forests, wolves scarcely leashed in by their king, as contemptuous of the effete Romans as the Romans despised them for barbarians. The Romans had long since forgotten the art of open warfare but they were bred to that tradition of street fighting where a mob, familiar with every alley, could put an army to flight. But, though there were incidents, there was no concerted gesture of defiance. The bulk of Otto's army remained, as both custom and prudence demanded, outside the city walls whose great bulk acted as an insulator.

On the morning of February 2, Otto entered the city in formal procession, accompanied by a very strong bodyguard. The crowds were sullen but passive and the Germans marched without hindrance to the base of the marble steps which led up to the great open court before St. Peter's. There the bodyguard fell away, but Otto had already taken his swordbearer Ansfried to one side and warned him to be prepared for anything, even within the sacred precincts of the basilica. "When I kneel today at the grave of the

Apostle, stand behind me with the sword. I know only too well what my ancestors have experienced from these faithless Romans." [7]

Ansfried accompanied his lord up the steps to where young John, gorgeously robed, awaited them; the procession, now augmented by priests, moved across the courtyard and entered the vast dim basilica. But again there was no incident and above the shrine of Peter —a shrine stripped of its treasures, the shaft to it still blocked with rubbish—Otto knelt and received that crown whose weight eventually crushed the crown of the German kingdom. On February 2, 961, the Holy Roman Empire came into being, tying Italy and Germany in a bitter marriage that would continue for another nine hundred years.

John XII, the dissolute young noble who initiated the process with all its incalculable results, was merely following established precedents. Other popes had crowned other pretenders to this or that crown for purposes little more worthy than his own. Otto's coronation oath must have been extremely encouraging to him.

> I shall exalt the Church and thee, its overseer, according to my powers. Never shalt thou be injured in life or limb with my sanction and knowledge. I will never hold a court, or make laws, within thy jurisdiction. Whatsoever of St. Peter's property comes into my hands I will restore to thee. To whomsoever I shall bequeath the kingdom of Italy, he will swear to be thy helper in defense of the ecclesiastical state. [8]

On the surface, it was a highly profitable transaction for John. In return for what he believed to be an empty honor, a resounding but meaningless title, he was to receive the direct military protection of the most powerful monarch in Europe. The lucrative cities that Berengar had captured would be returned to him to enjoy as he wished, and he would continue in sole power in Rome. Otto's promise was in keeping with the unsophisticated German mentality, which John's ancestors had always manipulated easily.

But there was one major flaw in John's reasoning. The Otto who had knelt at his feet in St. Peter's was, in many ways, the uncomplicated tribal chief that he seemed; but he was also a statesman of the first rank. He had gained a great state by force of arms, but he maintained his power by diplomacy as well as force. Gradually, he had gathered around him the foremost legal and political minds in Europe, men who could gauge the remotest effect of the simplest act, who knew precisely the weakness and the strength of the forces that supported John.

John's court, by contrast, was composed either of rowdy young men like himself or sycophants who told him only what was agreeable, and who were prepared to change sides at the slightest pressure. Indifferent to everything but his own immediate desires, lacking competent advisers, John acted with the arrogance born of supreme ignorance. Initially, his attitude gave him an advantage over Otto. The cautious German, threading his way through the intricacies of international politics, was again and again to display his bewilderment at the sudden and heedless actions of the young Roman. Even when he was convinced that the apparent stupidity did not, after all, mask some devious Latin plot, he showed himself reluctant to take that firm action which he took in every other field, looking, it seemed, for the plot behind the plot.

Throughout, his personal relationship with John was engagingly avuncular. Otto was then past his fiftieth year—an age that was patriarchal in a society where disease or violence took off most men by their fortieth year—and John was still in his early twenties. In public, they were emperor and pope. In private, Otto's sure knowledge of his own power, and the disparity between their ages, encouraged him to treat John as the adolescent he was, displaying a sincere, if clumsy, intent to guide and help the hotheaded young patrician who also happened to be high priest. Immediately after the coronation ceremony he took John aside and treated him to a homily on the vices of his past, urging him to reform his ways. John made easy repentance; the age of saints, it would appear, was about to dawn again in Rome.

Otto left the city after a stay of only two weeks. Rome, with its sullen citizens on the edge of rebellion, could have had little attraction for him. Additionally, there was the need to encompass the destruction of Berengar, who predictably had broken his oath and with his son Adalbert had gone back to the old ways as though Otto had never existed. And as soon as Otto had left the city, John offered the imperial crown to Berengar, the very man whose menaces had earlier caused him to cry to Otto for help.

The twisted motives of John XII are probably beyond hope of reconstruction. The lunatic gesture may have arisen from the most trivial form of pique, a means of hitting back at Otto for his heavy-handed lectures. He may perhaps have wished to show that he could summon a king, make him an emperor, and unmake him if he so pleased. He may perhaps have seen—though he did not usually look ahead—that the Roman faction which had supported him as the son of Alberic would infallibly reject him as the protégé of Otto. From whatever cause, he deliberately set about his own destruction.

Berengar failed him, for Berengar was fighting for his life against Otto. Nevertheless, Berengar's son Adalbert was still at large, having made common cause with a Saracen enclave in Provence. John, persisting in his lunacy, wrote to him, offering to transfer the imperial crown to him if Adalbert would only come and free Rome from the yoke of virtue imposed by a German. It might entail introducing Saracens into Italy again, but it was a small price to pay. Adalbert, with good reason, hesitated to cross swords with the formidable emperor, and while he hesitated, John began negotiations with the Huns in the north and the Byzantines in the East.

In all of John's bizarre career, nothing better displayed his lack of balance than these successive appeals. He had absolutely nothing to gain from them, except perhaps a return of that chaos in which people of his like flourished. Saracens and Huns could bring only murder into the land. The Byzantine emperor wanted only the return of a breakaway province, when the bishop of Rome would be stripped of his pretensions and made again a subordinate court official.

John himself had had firsthand experience of the tyranny and faithlessness of both Berengar and his son. Even with his limited knowledge of affairs he must have known that neither could begin to equal Otto, and in appealing to them he had placed himself in grave danger from the emperor. No matter how lenient, how avuncular Otto might be, he could not fail to react violently against an attempt to stir up rebellion.

Otto's first response was, predictably, bewildered. Only a few months before, he had delivered the young man from Berengar's violence and had guaranteed him not only protection but sovereign authority within his own sphere. And now this. There was little that Otto could do at the moment. He was several days' march from Rome, and committed to a military action against a tough enemy who had established himself in a secure fortress. Otto therefore sent not an army but an embassy to Rome to find out exactly what was happening.

The envoys returned a few days later with a fantastic story of John's activities in Rome. Violence had again returned to the city as John's partisans ensured their leader's supremacy with the sword, while their leader himself returned to his life of debauchery. The pilgrim traffic had dried up entirely and the Romans, ever more vulnerable in their pockets than their consciences, were talking of overthrowing their prince and summoning the emperor themselves.

But they had as yet taken no direct action, and Otto, reluctant to offend them by deposing their prince—reluctant too, perhaps, to believe that his exhortations had been ignored—clung to his hope that reform could be worked in John.

> He is only a boy and will soon alter if good men set him an example. Berengar must first be dislodged—then let us address some words of admonition to the lord Pope. His sense of shame will soon bring about a change for the better and if he is forced into good ways he will, perchance, be ashamed to return to his old habits.[9]

Otto's hope that a Theophylact could be affected by a sense of shame speaks rather more for his own sense of honor and lack of imagination than for his knowledge of Roman morals. Hearing of the emperor's reaction, it must have seemed to John that there was nothing he could not do. He had negotiated with the terrible Huns, held out a hand to a rebel vassal of the emperor, contacted the emperor's rival in Constantinople; and Otto, instead of descending upon Rome in outraged majesty, had contented himself with more vague exhortations. Blind to the gulf that was opening before him, John continued on his path, though he was prepared to supply moral protestations if Otto wanted them.

The envoys he thought prudent to send to Otto opened their embassy with a glib apology. It was true that the pope had indulged in youthful indiscretions, but now he was reformed and would henceforth live in a manner pleasing to the emperor. That accomplished, they proceeded to a remarkable attack upon Otto, impugning his honor directly: He had failed to render back to St. Peter those territories which he had promised to restore; he had given shelter to two high officials who were disloyal to the pope.

Otto still remained calm. To the first part of the accusation he made the reasonable retort that he could hardly restore the disputed territories to St. Peter until he had wrested them from Berengar. As for the two treacherous officials, "We have neither seen them nor welcomed them—we understand that they were taken prisoner at Capua." With them were two other men, known to be personal friends of John, who had been sent to stir up the Huns against Germany. "We would not have believed that the lord Pope could have acted thus, whoever told us. But his letter—sealed with his seal and bearing his signature—compels us to think that it is true." [10] But still Otto wanted final, indisputable proof of John's treachery before acting. Accordingly, he sent a last envoy to Rome, choosing his most skilled Italian adviser, Liudprand, bishop of Cremona.

The entire text of the *Deeds of Otto,* one of Liudprand's three major works, relates exclusively to the events in Rome that arose from his mission. It is from Liudprand's other books that posterity gains most of its knowledge of the careers of John, his father Alberic, his grandmother Marozia. The broad outlines are accurate enough, substantiated by other, lesser, writers; but the details are colored with the enduring hatred that Liudprand held for the entire stem of Marozia.

He was a highly skillful writer, his books springing out of the barren field of tenth-century Italian historiography like luxuriant oases, but their very attractiveness presents a trap for the unwary. Generations of later writers praised their vividness while deploring their obscenity, and certainly there runs throughout such a bitter contempt for feminine chastity as to result in distortion of fact. But the obscenity itself is harmless enough, smacking of the tavern rather than the court. It is the deliberate distortions that undermine

Liudprand's otherwise priceless value as guide through the maze of the tenth century. He gives every appearance of honesty, going out of his way to state which of his material he can personally vouch for, and which is only hearsay. But the objectivity is dubious, for he does not hesitate to blacken an enemy's character so thoroughly that it is impossible to ascertain the truth without recourse to other sources. His admiration for Otto is the most attractive part of his character, but in building up his hero, he unfortunately found it necessary to overstate the depravity of his hero's Italian enemies. Otto's character needed no such artificial strengthening.

In characteristic generosity, Otto had received Liudprand as a penniless refugee scholar into his court: He found that he had acquired a highly competent Italian adviser who proved of incalculable value to him. Liudprand knew personally most of the major figures in both Italy and Constantinople, and was able to guide his German master through the perilous shoals of Italian faction politics.

Liudprand was forty years old at the time of Otto's descent into Italy. He had been born in Pavia, and according to his own lively account, because of the beauty of his voice he became a singing page at the court of Hugh of Provence, where doubtless he acquired his opinion of feminine virtue. After Hugh prudently decided to retire from Italy, Liudprand entered Berengar's service, on whose behalf he made the first of his trips to Constantinople. Berengar tricked him. Searching through his luggage for the customary rich presents for the Byzantine emperor, Liudprand found only a fulsome letter, and so was forced to make the gift out of his own shallow pocket. The shabby trick enraged him, and when the opportunity came, he deserted Berengar, joining the stream of Italian refugees who found shelter at Otto's court in Saxony. Later, he had the profound satisfaction of recording the destruction of Berengar at the hands of his hero Otto.

Throughout Otto's campaign Liudprand was by his side, analyzing the endless Italian problems that presented themselves daily, hourly, for the German's attention and action. It was natural that Otto should choose him to go on the last embassy to Rome, to attempt to bring John back to a rational course.

St. Peter's, interior. Fresco, 17th century.
Church of S. Martino ai Monti, Rome.

Panorama of Rome. Tempera, late 16th century. Ducal Palace, Mantua.

Above : — Crown of
Charlemagne.
Schatzkammer, Vienna.

Facing page: — Head of
Emperor Constantine. Marble,
4th century A.D. The
Metropolitan Museum of Art,
Bequest of Mary Clark
Thompson, 1926.

Right : — Tiara of Julius

Boniface VIII. Arnolfo di Lapo. The Vatican, Rome.

Liudprand arrived in Rome to find that John had not the slightest intention of honoring his promise of reform. That was unsurprising. What was startling was his pretended belief that Otto himself was breaking his oath, that he was not returning the Papal States as he had promised. His belief was obviously a pretext, and the thinnest of pretexts, for repudiating Otto: All Italy knew that the emperor and Berengar were still fighting for those states. Nevertheless, Liudprand went through the motions of protest, obeying the emperor's instructions even though he was skeptical of their value. If John still doubted the emperor's word, he said, he was empowered to choose a champion to defend the emperor's honor, or to swear an oath that it was not yet possible to return the States. John declined to accept either the oath or appoint a champion, and contemptuously dismissed Liudprand.

Liudprand left Rome, but before he arrived back at the imperial camp, Otto learned that Adalbert had at last overcome his hesitation and had entered the city to receive the crown from John. And even Otto could not ignore the presence of a pretender in Rome itself.

It was now July, and the fierce heat of an Italian summer incapacitated the emperor's northern soldiers. Until the end of August the army remained in the relative coolness of the Umbrian Hills; then, with the beginning of the cooler weather of autumn, Otto began the march on Rome.

It was a swift and easy campaign. John was still surrounded by the ruffian element who had everything to lose by the reestablishment of order, but the bulk of the Romans turned upon him, pinning both him and Adalbert within the Leonine City. The young pope went through the motions of defiance, appearing in armor to lead a halfhearted attack, but his nerve failed when Otto was reported nearing the city. Hastily plundering St. Peter's of what portable treasure remained, he fled to Tivoli with Adalbert. Otto entered on his heels, and three days later, summoned a synod of the Roman Church to consider the whole situation.

The synod was under the direct control of Otto throughout. As a result, both he and Liudprand were aware that it had to be conducted with the most scrupulous honesty. Indeed, Otto was later accused by papal apologists of deposing John illegally. The murder of one pope by another, the deposition of others by obscurely appointed ecclesiastical councils, wholesale sacrilege—this was as nothing beside the temerity of a layman deposing a priest.

It was to avoid the obvious charges of bias that Liudprand, opening the proceedings in the emperor's name, warned the synod that hearsay evidence could not be accepted, that all charges must be specific and substantiated. Liudprand was not only Otto's chief adviser but also his sole apologist in Rome; and for his record of the trial he departed from his usual racy, casual style. Every member of the synod was identified by name and rank. Archbishops, bishops, cardinals, even the single representative of the common people, "the commoner Peter, also called Imperiola," each had his speech attributed to him. Any one of these people, directly associated with the verdict, could afterward have given Liudprand the lie had he departed from a strict record of the proceedings. None did so.

Otto prefaced his address to the synod with an expression of regret that John had not thought fit to attend. Such a remark from any other man could have been uttered only in irony. Otto intended it sincerely, for Otto, possessor of all the knightly virtues, quite lacked a vestige of humor. He then went on to outline the course the trial should take—for trial it undoubtedly was. Charges were to be preferred by individuals, one by one, and the synod would then consider what course to adopt.

Thereupon the cardinal priest Peter got up and testified that he had seen the Pope celebrate Mass without himself communicating. John, Bishop of Narni and John, cardinal deacon, then declared that they had seen the Pope ordain a deacon in a stable. . . . Benedict, cardinal deacon, with his fellow deacons and priests, said they knew the Pope had been paid for ordaining bishops. . . . On the question of sacrilege, they said, inquiries were hardly necessary as it was a matter of eyesight, not of hearsay. As regards the Pope's adultery, they had no visual information but they knew for certain that he had copulated with Rainier's widow, with Stephana, his father's concubine, with the widow Anna and with his own niece. He had gone hunting publicly, blinded his spiritual father Benedict, caused the death of cardinal sub-deacon John by castrating him . . . drunk wine for the love of the devil. . . .[11]

The catalog was brought to a close and Otto again emphasized that he expected the witnesses to be prepared to substantiate their charges. The accusers confirmed their statements on oath and the synod passed on to consider the next action. It was decided that John should be summoned to defend himself.

It was left to Otto to give substance to the summons, Liudprand casting it into his flowery Latin. It was a dignified letter. Otto remarked again that he was surprised at John's absence. The pope had been accused of actions "that would have been the shame even of play-actors," and it was imperative that he should immediately come to Rome to clear himself of the charges. He anticipated John's natural reluctance to put himself among enemies, by giving him his imperial word that "no action is contemplated contrary to holy canons."

It must have given John little comfort to learn that he was to be judged only by the holy canons. He had not actively preached heresy; that apart, it would have been a matter of some difficulty to find a canon that he had not outraged. His reply was a model of brevity, if not of grammar, and again added a stupid insult by pointedly ignoring the presence of the emperor in Rome. His letter was addressed simply: "To all the Bishops—We hear that you wish to make another Pope. If you do I excommunicate you by almighty God and you have no power to ordain no one or celebrate Mass." [12]

On November 22, another embassy set out on the short journey from Rome to Tivoli, bearing the synod's answer to John. Some pedantic merriment was made at the expense of the pope's grammar—"more fitting for a stupid boy than a bishop—we always thought that two negatives make an affirmative." The pedantry was probably Liudprand's, but the threat that followed was undoubtedly Otto's. Unless John presented himself in Rome, he, not the bishops, would be excommunicated.

John was not at Tivoli when the envoys arrived. A later chronicler implies that his absence was due to fear, and that, while the envoys waited, he was hiding like a beast in the nearby woods. Certainly, any sensible man would have had reason to fear. His ally Adalbert had promptly deserted him when he saw the strength of the opposition and the high ecclesiastics of Europe were unanimously in support of the emperor.

But John was anything but sensible and Liudprand's account of his absence is far more characteristic. The pope, having hurled his casual thunderbolt, had contemptuously dismissed the whole affair and gone off hunting. In his own mind he was invulnerable, and the threats of a ponderous German could have no effect upon him, supreme pontiff and prince of Rome. Someone, somewhere, would come to his aid. Meanwhile, there were the pleasures of Tivoli to be enjoyed.

Otto made no further threats or pleas. The Romans invariably mistook patience for weakness and his leniency was already beginning to undermine his prestige with them. On December 1, John was formally deposed by the synod and a nominee of the emperor's emerged as Leo VIII.

The new pope was Roman-born but, created by the will of the emperor, his existence was an affront to all Romans. There was no lawful reason why the election of the universal pope should be at the will and desire of only the Romans. Indeed, the fact that they had the right to elect the bishop of Rome had extinguished the right of all other Christian communities to elect their pope. In effect, Otto was acting on behalf of all such disfranchised Christians when, overriding the desires of the Roman mob, the Roman families, he nominated a pope.

So the imperial lawyers argued with some justice, but in Rome the argument was merely an exasperation. The Romans saw only that their prince, elected by themselves, had been overthrown by a foreigner, a barbarian. John had little of the magnetism of his great father and if the election of his successor had been left to the Romans, they would have forgotten John quickly enough. But when Otto deposed the pope he also deposed the prince, and in defending the one the Romans were also forced to defend the other.

A month after Leo was elected, they rose in revolt. This, the first of countless bloody rebellions against imperial rule, was put down easily enough. The citizens were far from united and the imperial army was still camped outside the walls. Otto could afford to treat the insurrection leniently.

But he could not remain in Rome forever; neither could he afford to leave a garrison. His army was composed of feudal levies, serving their lord for a fixed objective and a limited period. It had been dwindling steadily during the protracted campaign, and he now had barely sufficient force to give the *coup de grâce* to Berengar and Adalbert. When at length he marched out of Rome, only a token contingent was left behind as bodyguard for Leo.

As soon as the emperor had gone, John returned. The council that he summoned in February, 964, was composed of very frightened men, for most had voted for his deposition in November. But though John's desire for vengeance was limitless, circumstances forced him to place a curb upon it. Over one hundred high ecclesiastics had attended the November synod: Fewer than thirty attended his own council, spectacular evidence of his collapsing power. The Romans might riot in protest at their prince's deposition, but the bishops of Europe, whose superior he was, had taken all that they could stomach.

During his eight years' rule, John had not so much debased his office as rendered it void of all significance outside Rome. Even in Rome itself, a growing imperial party reflected the growing discontent with the system that placed the supreme spiritual office exclusively in the hands of a few great families. Outside, the authority of Rome as center of the Church was compromised almost beyond redemption by the grotesque debaucheries of those Roman popes of whom John was prime example. "Where is it written that the innumerable company of the priests of God, scattered over the earth and adorned by learning and merit, should be subject to monsters devoid of all knowledge, human and divine, and a disgrace to the world?" [13] the bishops of France later demanded in a council that threatened to separate the Gallic from the Roman Church. Simpler men might learn to distinguish between man and office and, dazzled by the splendor of the claims, accept spiritual gifts from foul hands.

The powerful bishops of Europe, in regarding the rich prize clutched firmly in the hands of Romans, were firmly on the side of the emperor.

But though distant bishops could issue defiances bravely enough, those within actual reach of John thought it better to compromise. The motives of even those few who attended his council were highly dubious. Two of them were later to emerge as popes approved by the emperor, evidence of the Roman ability to hunt with the hounds and run with the hare. Most were Romans, uneasily aware that their livelihood was at stake and that this screaming pope had displayed an uncanny instinct for survival. He might yet again triumph and they, exiled, would be reduced to camp followers of the emperor.

They were not wholly helpless, for their existence gave a legal gloss to his actions. The judgments were his, but the actions effected emanated as the actions of a group, the church in council. John confined his rage to those who had been foolish enough to make specific accusations against him. One had his tongue torn out, his nose and fingers cut off; another was scourged; the hand of a third was hacked off. Loyalty being thereby reinforced with terror, John set about overturning the decrees of the synod. Leo VIII, who had fled to Otto as soon as John returned, was excommunicated and Rome returned to its domestic wars as though Otto were on another planet.

The emperor heard, but could do nothing. He had destroyed Berengar but his campaign against Berengar's son Adalbert was approaching a crucial point: To abandon it now would be to lose all the advantages gained over the past year. Leo VIII trailed after him, a standing reproach to his pretensions, until at last Otto had gained the upper hand over Adalbert and was free to deal with John and Rome.

But it was not by the hand of the Holy Roman Emperor that Christendom was freed of its burden. The imperial army was still marching to Rome when news came that John had died, violently, but not in battle or by a political assassin. The champion of Christendom was an outraged cuckold who had caught his Holy Father in the act and cudgeled him so severely that he died three days afterward. Or so the gossip ran in Rome, to be picked up by Liudprand

and elaborated into a moral tale in which the injured husband was transformed into the devil himself, come to fetch home his most faithful servant.

There were no tears for John, the young man who had broken under the colossal weight of his double crown. But his death brought no peace to Rome, to the church, or to the emperor. The Roman hydra that had lain dormant since the beginning of the century, first drugged by Theodora and Marozia, then chained by Alberic, had at last been released by John and again it raved and tore at its enemies, its friends, itself.

The papal crown was the symbol of Roman sovereignty, and to gain control of that symbol, emperor and city were prepared to destroy each other and themselves. Otto descended from Germany and subjected the city to a terrible vengeance—but it rose again. Again he smashed it down, but again it rose, and again. The great emperor died and his son Otto II continued to pour out the wealth and power of Germany, seeking the double goal of a purified Papacy and a Roman crown. And when Otto II died, his son Otto III inherited the task.

With the approach of the millennium—that year 1000 which men had thought would bring Christ in judgment—a curious lull came over Rome. It seemed that the youthful Otto III was about to achieve the miracle of Charlemagne, welding together the Papacy and the empire into an indestructible whole whose two elements gave mutual support. But even while the idealistic Otto and his scarcely more realistic pope Sylvester went about their great work, the descendants of Marozia, transformed into legal counts of Tusculum, prepared their own, more lasting, modification of papal power.

The Rule of the Magician

The pattern of power in the district that encircled Rome and stretched to the Adriatic had changed radically. "Patrimony of St. Peter" was now a vain, virtually a sacrilegious, title, for successive popes had alienated the territories through fear or cupidity, and the patrimony was a mosaic of petty principalities. Each hilltop bore its fortified town, the seat of one of the new barons who defied what centralized power remained, periodically issuing out to plunder the once mighty city, contribute to the uproar attending the "election" of popes, and return with their booty.

Tusculum formed one of these baronial centers. The city was ancient, but little remained to serve as physical link with its heroic past when as an Etruscan power it had led the opposition to the growing might of the city on the Tiber. Rome had absorbed it and turned it into a pleasure city. But even the memorials of its life during the golden afternoon of the classic empire, when Tusculum had served as a retreat for the wealthy, were fast disappearing. The ruins of Cicero's enormous villa served as a useful quarry of ready-hewn stone. The market gardens that had once kept Rome ablaze with flowers had long since been trampled over. Goats tended by semi-barbaric herdsmen wandered over the spot where Lucullus had given his fantastic banquets.

But in the iron age that had again come to Italy, men turned again to Tusculum, attracted by its strategic situation though they remained indifferent to the beauty that had made it famous. The theater, the villas, the temples provided stones for military fortifications, and even the crudest husbandry could wring food from the rich, easily defended fields. Secure behind its new walls built of ancient stones, Tusculum woke from its long sleep to begin again a cycle of conquest under the descendants of Marozia.

The house of Theophylact had maintained its identity and much of its power throughout the chaos of the second half of the tenth century. The rule of women had long since passed into history, and at the head of the family in the last years of the dark century stood

Count Gregory of Tusculum, son or grandson of the great Alberic. Gregory's title of count was legally gained, for he had obtained it from the only person who could bestow it—the emperor Otto III, grandson of Otto I. With the matter-of-fact treachery that passed for politics in Rome, Gregory had abandoned the Roman allies of his family and made himself the faithful servant of the temporarily ascendant emperor. Then, having obtained what he wanted, in turn he abandoned the emperor to the wolves of Rome and set up as an independent lord in Tusculum, waiting for the opportunity to drag the Papacy once more into the possession of his house.

It had not been too difficult to deceive the youthful Otto, a dreaming adolescent of eighteen, with the fantastic notion of resurrecting the glories of ancient Rome. A greater obstacle to Tusculan ambitions was the scholar-pope Sylvester II, whom Otto had placed upon the chair in the last year of the old millennium. Sylvester had been young Otto's tutor but he was no mere tool of the emperor. A scholar by inclination, as a young man he had been thrown by chance into some of the bitterest political battles in Europe. The experience could have throttled one side or the other of his character, forcing the statesman to develop at the expense of the scholar, or inhibiting the scholar from playing an active role. It did neither, instead fusing the two strands of his nature into a formidable personality. He awed even the unimpressionable Romans, who believed him to be a magician, on intimate terms with the devil.

Sylvester's major weakness was his belief in Otto's mission, and were it not for the unconscious evidence provided by his letters, he could perhaps be suspected of remarkable depths of cynicism. A statesman of his experience must have found it difficult to take the boy's plans seriously, for they implied nothing less than the recreation of the court of imperial Rome, down to the last palace and the last page. But Sylvester's letters show that he possessed a certain boyishness, an attractive if dangerous impulsiveness toward new ideas. Otto's plans might be extreme but they were in the right direction. In addition, the pope was French by birth and had had very little experience of the unstable Romans whose cooperation was a prime requisite for the establishment of the new Roman

Empire. Like Otto, he saw only the violence and disorder, and was ignorant of the deep-running pride of race that made the Romans prefer chaos to order imposed from without.

"*Romam caput mundi,*" the opening phrase of Otto's decree, was the key to all his plans. Rome was the capital of the world and on its ancient foundations the new imperial court would be erected, not symbolically but actually. A great new palace arose on the Aventine hill and round the person of the young emperor was created a complex ceremonial. Here Otto departed from his model, for it was not the austere Latins that he copied, but the great Byzantine court that had dazzled the world with its splendor for seven hundred years. His German courtiers reluctantly learned Greek or, if that proved beyond them, attempted to write their solid German names in its outlandish characters. Eunuchs, the characteristic Oriental courtiers, ousted the unglamorous German tribesman with his real but unsophisticated virtues. It was a curious, bastard culture that Otto created: half-remembered rites and myths from Latin antiquity combined with Byzantine customs and modern needs in an exotic flowering which could not outlast its creator.

The Roman barons were swift enough to take advantage of any new office that might be created, and were perfectly prepared to acquiesce in the outward form of empire. Count Gregory of Tusculum, still apparently the friend and ally of the emperor, received the grand title of prefect of the fleet. The fleet was not yet actually in being but that troubled Gregory not at all. The prefect had very useful powers over the mouth of the Tiber, powers that could be used to channel yet more revenue into Tusculum. But if Otto believed that he could bind such a man as Count Gregory by the grant of resurrected ancient titles, he was rapidly disillusioned. A slight shift in the balance of power in the city found Gregory aligned again with his fellow Romans, leading an attack upon his late benefactor. For three days and nights the emperor of the world, the youth who styled himself Italicus, Saxonicus, in the ancient manner, was pent up in his grand palace on the Aventine. He appealed to them in a tragic, curiously moving speech. "Are you my Romans for whom I have forsaken country and relatives? Are you those for whom I have shed the blood of my Saxons and Germans

—yea—even of my own?" [14] The speech touched some spring in the Roman character and there was a brief reconciliation. But Gregory of Tusculum, sensing that this was the moment when Otto's power toppled irrecoverably, led a renewed attack. The dwindling supporters of Otto and Sylvester urgently advised them to leave the city while there was yet time. On February 16, 1001, the emperor and his pope stole out of Rome together.

The remaining eleven months of Otto's life were a tragic anticlimax to all that had gone before. He had no troops, for his love of Italy had cost him the loyalty of the Germans, and he and Sylvester drifted indecisively here and there in Italy, with Otto now planning a triumphant restoration, now contemplating an ascetic life withdrawn from the world. So, in a twilight of endeavor— neither defeated nor victorious, neither rejected nor accepted—the Wonder of the World passed his last months. He died on January 23, 1002, within sight of the city that had ignored him. He was not quite twenty-two years old.

Sylvester returned to Rome after Otto's death. He had now nothing to hope for and very little to fear. The Romans left him alone, for though he was an old man, his mental powers were undiminished, and those who would not have hesitated to murder a pope were reluctant to tangle with a magician. He survived his brilliant, erratic pupil by barely sixteen months, dying in May, 1003. His epitaph, written by one who endured the result of his death, summed up the sorrow that afflicted all thoughtful men at the ending of a splendid dream. "The world, on the brink of triumph, its peace now departed, grew contorted in grief and the reeling Church forgot her rest." [15]

The writer of the epitaph achieved a degree of accuracy unusual in his craft. The curious calm that had prevailed in Rome during Sylvester's pontificate was shattered, as the supreme prize was again available for the strongest and the reeling church fell into the waiting arms of Gregory of Tusculum. Two obscure popes were successively elected after Sylvester's death, but they were the creatures of only temporarily dominant factions. When Gregory at last moved in strength, his grasp upon the Papacy was immovable. Backed by the swords of his hillmen, financed by his own wealth, he obtained the election of one of his three sons. When that son died, the tiara passed without a hiatus to his brother. And when the brother died, the debased but still lucrative office touched bottom. In the autumn of 1032 Count Gregory's fourteen-year-old grandson Theophylact was "elected" and ascended the Chair of St. Peter as Benedict IX.

Sale of the Papacy

"The Romans have found a singular means to palliate their insolent traffic in the election of popes," the French monk Raoul Glaber observed. "When they have made choice of a pontiff which it pleases them to raise to the Holy Seat, they strip him of his own name and give him the name of some great pope so that his want of merit will be obscured by the glory of his title." [16]

Octavian, the son of Alberic, had established a useful precedent when he changed his name to John XII. The pious or distant observer of Roman events saw only a stately procession of great names, conveniently masking ignoble identities, ascending the chair. Under the noble name of Benedict, there now appeared a youth who rendered his office not so much shameful as ludicrous. Octavian-John had behaved like a Roman prince with some of the virtues as well as all of the vices; he at least had not lacked courage and was equally prepared to fight Roman mobs or German emperors. Theophylact-Benedict added cowardice to cruelty, introducing an element of knockabout comedy into the consistent tragedy.

The annals of Rome were still barbarously sparse and Benedict did not possess even such a hostile biographer as Liudprand had been for John XII. Rome was again in total chaos, and the only occasions on which the young pope fully appears from out of his dark background are when he is fighting for his life and office against a sudden attack. The first attack came just six months after he had been installed in the Lateran, when the dwindling opposition faction set a plot in motion to remove him from the throne. They were faced with a formidable problem, for Benedict was all but invulnerable, hedged in by the swords of his Tusculan followers in the Lateran Palace, now indistinguishable from a castle. But even Benedict was obliged to keep up the outward appearance of his office and to celebrate mass in the sacred—and unfortified—basilica of St. Peter. He would be murdered there.

Choosing a feast day, the plotters entered the basilica, unnoticed among the great crowds. They could not carry swords, a too obvious declaration of intent, but each had a length of rope. It was intended that a disturbance would be made, and those nearest the Holy Father would seize him and strangle him before the guards could intervene, trusting to get away during the resultant confusion.

But, "about the sixth hour of the day there occurred an eclipse of the sun which lasted until the eighth hour. All faces were as pale as death, and everything that could be seen was suffused with the colors of yellow and saffron." [17] The timely phenomenon saved Benedict, for as the unearthly light stole through the basilica, the assassins lost their nerve and with it the exact timing needed to bring off the murder. Benedict was warned by the initial disturbance and fled the basilica, not stopping until he was well away from Rome. It was the first of many flights.

The abortive plot of the eclipse involved relatively few Romans, for it had simply been the attempt of one faction to eliminate the head of another. Three years later, however, Benedict was all but engulfed in a major rising. Benedict had been a purely passive instrument of his family's policy, and while his extreme youth had rendered the formality of his "election" a solemn mockery, it had also protected his office from the more sensual degradations. As he achieved maturity he gave ample evidence that he was upholding the traditions of the Theophylacts.

Later, legends told how he had been in league with infernal powers: Magic books were found in his palace and countrymen swore that they had seen the youthful pope in earnest consultation with demons in remote places at night. Similar legends had been told of Sylvester, but they had grown from the ignorance of men observing a skilled chemist and astronomer at work. The rumors attending Benedict were probably based on jealousy. His infernal powers were used for limited ends—the gaining of women. Or so the Romans believed, and dropped their differences to rid themselves of a lunatic youth.

Benedict again escaped the city, but this time, instead of hovering irresolutely outside waiting for the upheaval to simmer down, he had a goal. A great monarch, Conrad, had again risen in Germany, and falling victim to the lure of Italy and the consistent German desire to gain an imperial crown, had begun to march southward.

A formidable alliance in Lombardy, led by Milan and its archbishop, blocked his path and Conrad settled down to destroy it.
Benedict hastened to join the imperial camp, attended by a handful
of followers.

There could be few more preposterous pictures than that presented by the eighteen-year-old pope on his journey northward,
solemnly presiding over councils of mature and learned men, granting privileges, pronouncing judgments. Every man who sued for
his favors, or endured his childish arrogance, was well aware of the
background of this new Holy Father. Every man knew that the
vast and venerable machinery of the Roman Church moved, if
haltingly, under the control of a robber baron in the Alban Hills.

Yet still the office was the hub of the Western world. A few years
before, Canute, the tough but pious king of a newly established
England, had come to Rome during the pontificate of Benedict's
uncle. There he wrote an ecstatic letter to his subjects that summed
up the reverence Europeans felt for the mother city of Europe.

> I have lately been to Rome to pray for the forgiveness of my sins,
> for the safety of my dominions, and the people under my govern-
> ment . . . worshipping and adoring according to my desire. I have
> been the more diligent in this, for I have learned from the wise
> that St. Peter has received from God great power in binding and loos-
> ing, and that he carries the Keys of the Kingdom of Heaven.

St. Peter and the reigning bishop of Rome were one, and the eye
of faith was blind to the incidental discrepancies. No lay monarch,
no matter how powerful or virtuous, could hope to attract to himself the deep instinctive reverence that men felt for the successor
of St. Peter, no matter how unworthy—a successor who was also
the inheritor of the ancient capital of the world. From this all else
flowed. "A great assembly of nobles was present," Canute went on.
"I spoke with the Emperor himself and the Sovereign Pope and the
nobles who were there, concerning the wants of my people, English
as well as Danes. . . ." [18] Despite its decrepitude, Rome was still the
meeting place of Europe; despite his manifest unworthiness, Benedict IX was still the unique living successor of St. Peter.

The German emperor recognized this with the rest and bowed

to the pope while he mocked the youth. The Germanic hope for a new City of God in which a holy pope would be protected by an honorable emperor was dormant, not extinct, but the time had not yet come for its arousing. The counts of Tusculum had identified themselves, when it suited them, with the cause of the emperor, and Conrad could overlook the peccadilloes of the pope so long as he could rely on Tusculan support. In return for Conrad's promise of immediate help, Benedict obediently excommunicated the archbishop of Milan and returned to Rome under the protection of German swords.

He enjoyed another two years of relatively undisturbed rule, two years in which it seemed that John XII was again in the chair, with rape and murder again a commonplace, the remaining wealth of the Papacy again squandered in brothel and banquet room and the upkeep of private armies. The Germans withdrew, the factions clashed, Benedict fled—but only as far as Tusculum where he cowered under the protection of his uncle the count. During his absence from Rome, another baron-prelate appeared as pope: John, bishop of the Sabine Hills, who had the temerity to take the great name of Sylvester. He ruled for three uneasy months, and in his turn fled to his own tribesmen in the Sabine Hills when Benedict returned at the head of a Tusculan band.

Benedict could have claimed, in defense of his curious conduct, that his high office had been none of his choosing for it had been thrust upon him by his family. Certainly, he had paid dearly enough for his unsophisticated pleasures, his bouts of riotous living enjoyed under almost permanent threat of death. In his absence in Tusculum he had come to a decision: He would rid himself of the dangerous honor. In Rome it was generally believed that the decision was forced upon him; he wished to marry but the girl's father, although inured to the spectacle of papal depravity, balked at the idea. Benedict could have his daughter only if he resigned the Papacy.

Benedict was prepared to do so, but he was not prepared to contemplate the loss of income that would result from abdication. Those of his predecessors who had been hurled from the chair were usually able to show a profit by plundering St. Peter's before they fled from Rome. But the treasury of St. Peter had long since been scraped clean. If Benedict wanted money, he would have to anticipate the revenues of the church—he would have to sell the Papacy itself. He found a buyer in the person of his godfather, Giovanni Gratiano, archpriest of the venerable church of St. John at the Latin Gate, and closed with him for the price of 1,500 pounds of gold.

Benedict's career was the target for virulent attacks from both friends and enemies of the Papacy. But Gratiano's act indicated more clearly than the bitterest accusations the depths to which his godson had dragged the Papacy. Gratiano was learned, a good Christian, and an honest man; some thought him simple to the point of idiocy. The money he paid over came from his own pocket—he had, in fact, amassed it for the honorable purpose of repairing the more dilapidated of Rome's great churches. But he had nerved himself to commit the ultimate sacrilege and subject the Chair of Peter to its greatest humiliation in the honest belief that he was saving it from worse.

So, at least, the more thoughtful of his contemporaries believed. He was not acting alone, nor without competent advisers: Two of his most loyal supporters, the monk Hildebrand and the hermit Peter Damian, later played leading roles in European affairs. Both men belonged to the growing movement of protest and reformation that had been engendered by the corruption of the hierarchy, though they took different paths to arrive at the same goal. Hildebrand took the conventional monastic path, and ultimately, as pope himself, grappled with the enormous task of reforming the entire European clergy, not merely that of Rome. Damian harked back to an older form of protest and became a hermit, scarifying the degraded clergy "in the world" from an anchorite's inviolable cell.

Hildebrand was an unknown young man at the time and his support of Giovanni Gratiano was of comparatively little value. But Peter Damian already had a European reputation for both sanctity and satire, and courageously he backed Gratiano, although in a congratulatory letter to him he made use of a curious argument to approve the unparalleled act of simony. "May Simon, the false coiner, no longer strike his base money in the court. The greed of those who aspire to the Bishopric [of Rome] must be repressed, the tables of the money-changers overturned." [19]

Giovanni Gratiano entered upon his pontificate in May, 1045, taking the name of Gregory VI. Faithfully, Benedict promised to leave him in full enjoyment of the office, and took himself off to the Alban Hills. There was some doubt as to his exact status: A pope could perhaps abdicate—but could he sell? Did the actual crime of simony on such a scale cancel out his authority at the moment when it was committed, and so, paradoxically, confirm him in his office? There were no precedents to guide, but in any case the new pope Gregory had little time to debate the niceties of spiritual authority.

Rome and the Papal States were in the convulsions of ultimate anarchy, the Papacy powerless to restore order in the very area where it claimed all power. There was not even money enough to pay for the day-to-day running of the court.

> Pope Gregory found the power of the Roman pontificate so reduced by the negligence of his predecessors that, with the exception of a few neighboring towns and the offerings of the faithful, he had scarcely anything on which to subsist. The cities and possessions of the Church, at a distance from Rome, were forcibly seized by plunderers. The public roads and highways throughout all Italy were thronged with so many robbers that no pilgrims could pass in safety unless strongly guarded.[20]

There was no safety even when they reached Rome. Pilgrims had grown accustomed to being swindled by the rapacious citizens, but now they were physically robbed, despoiled of the gifts intended for the altar of the apostle. The factions, divided and subdivided in their allegiance, were indistinguishable from robber bands. Under the continual pressure of violence, Gregory himself was forced to become little more than a captain of militia, paying out of his own pocket for soldiers with whom to police the distracted city. He earned thereby the hatred of everybody, for his mercenaries robbed all, impartially.

Gregory's task would have been difficult even had he possessed the absolute power for which he had paid. Such was rendered impossible by the return of his two rivals. Benedict, perhaps disappointed in his love affair, or finding that the office of even a paper pope was more lucrative than that of a hilltop bandit, resumed his pontificate. The so-called Sylvester III returned too, and maintained his court in Rome, supported by the arms of his tribesmen. Twenty months after Giovanni Gratiano had purchased the Papacy, three popes ruled in Rome, each powerless to eject the others, each claiming the unique possession of the keys of heaven.

And the Romans revolted, not violently as was their immemorial habit, but coldly, soberly. A group of citizens and priests went off to find the emperor and yielded to him, totally and freely, the ancient city which their ancestors had so jealously preserved to themselves for generations. They asked in return only that he should cleanse the sty that was Rome, as his ancestors had attempted to do so often—but on this occasion, emperor and Romans would be working toward a common end.

The emperor came, and on December 20, 1046, presided over a synod that considered the fate of the three popes. Only two of them were present, for Benedict had cannily retired to Tusculum as soon as the emperor had entered Italy. The preposterous Sylvester III presented no problem to the synod: He had never been pope and was condemned out of hand and imprisoned. Gregory's case was far different. He had acted for the best and, as a man, would honorably have filled his office. But the Romans, both lay and clergy, wanted a clean sweep. He fought hard, but at last admitted sadly that evil could not be used to drive out evil and voluntarily abdicated, going into exile in Germany with his loyal chaplain Hildebrand.

That left only Benedict. Three days later he was canonically deposed, an act that tacitly admitted he had been pope throughout Gregory's pontificate, and a new pope of the emperor's nomination was elected.

It was one thing to depose Benedict, but quite another to ensure his deposition. He had the example of his illustrious ancestor John as guide and as soon as the imperial forces had been withdrawn from Italy, he marched back to Rome, depending on the ancient Roman hatred of a "foreign" pope to give him support. There was sufficient anti-imperial sentiment to enable him to maintain a precarious rule in Rome for some eight months. But when, in July, 1048, the emperor Henry III himself marched into the city, Benedict's few partisans abandoned him totally and he fled for the last time, passing out of history and into legend. No man knew for certain when he died, or where. Peter Damian recorded a story that Benedict had been seen after his death in the form of a monster, half bear, half ass, doomed to prowl the surface of the earth until the last judgment. Another, more charitable, rumor claimed that he repented and entered a monastery, and in the end died a humble Christian.

Benedict's death finally broke the grasp that the house of Theophylact had exerted upon the Papacy for nearly a century and a half. His brother, the ruling count of Tusculum, made one last effort to place another Tusculan upon the throne—and actually succeeded in doing so for a matter of months. But times had changed—radically—and under the monk Hildebrand, Italians and Germans united to crush the last impudent attempt. Benedict's bizarre career had worked paradoxically to the benefit of the Papacy: Extreme corruption had brought about extreme reaction, creating an atmosphere in which the power of the Holy Roman Emperor could be directed toward reform, instead of expending itself in sterile struggle with the Romans. Under the protection of the imperial sword, the Papacy refashioned itself and reformed its enduring parts. The right of election was taken from the Romans and invested in the nascent college of cardinals, creating thereby a closed cycle of power.

And when, at length, the Papacy stood upright on its own, it saw that the power that had protected it while it struggled out of its chrysalis was its sole rival in Europe. It set about to destroy the rival and succeeded. At Canossa, in 1077, the monk Hildebrand, now Pope Gregory VII, literally brought the emperor to his knees; and though Gregory personally paid for that act of humiliation, his successors profited from it. By the end of the twelfth century, the emperor had become a shadow and the pope stepped forward to claim dominium over all the world.

III
The Lord of Europe

Benedict Gaetani
Pope Boniface VIII (1294–1303)

The Great Refusal

On July 5, 1294, nine weary, stubborn men met yet again in conclave as they had been meeting over the past eighteen months. There had been twelve of them when the reigning pope had died in 1292, but even this tiny Sacred College had suffered further depletions during the long debate. The old dean of the college had died, another cardinal now lay grievously sick, and on this July morning a third was mourning his brother's death.

The conclave was taking place not in Rome but in Perugia, for Rome was in the grip of plague. When the disease had struck, most of the cardinals had hastened away, seeking the coolness and health of the mountain cities. But the Roman cardinals, well aware that their power was rooted in the city, had remained, accepting the heat and stench of a plague-stricken Roman summer for the sake of political advantage. There arose a threat of schism as those who remained in Rome claimed that they formed the true conclave; the prime purpose of the conclave was sidetracked as this secondary issue was thrashed out. The Roman cardinals gave way at length and, in October, 1293, joined their colleagues in Perugia, the grim-walled city on its high slope.

They met desultorily throughout the winter of that year. In spring came the king of Naples, dubious ally of the Church, to urge, with scarcely concealed threats, the necessity to bring this scandalous delay to a close. The cardinals were breaking the strict law designed twenty years before to prevent just such a delay. The election of 1271, preceded by three years of intrigue and uproar, had been brought about only when the citizens had torn off the roof of the palace in which the conclave was meeting and so forced a decision. At every election hereafter, it was decreed, the cardinals were to be walled up, their food reduced day by day until they came to a decision. But cardinals ever pleaded comfort before duty, King Charles stormed: They had suspended this "terrible law" as they called it and, in consequence, wandered and argued still.

The king's reproaches were met by a violent outburst from

Benedict Gaetani, the most outspoken member of the college. The election of the new pope lay in their hands alone, he reminded the king: If they sat until all eternity, no man had the right to put pressure upon them. No matter that all Christendom waited, the cardinals would make their choice as and when they saw fit. Charles departed in anger and the conclave continued, week after week throughout the spring and early summer until there seemed no reason why it should ever end.

Eleven men, it would seem, should be able to come to an agreement easily enough. But the conclave was divided between two great Roman families, the Colonna and the Orsini, perpetuating within the college the faction struggle that made murderous the streets of Rome. The last pope had been an Orsini, and the Orsini could not bear to contemplate the loss of that great power. But neither could the Colonna contemplate its revival; and so the members of the two great houses faced each other in conclave through the weary months, their powers too equal for one to destroy the other.

The neutrals hung uneasily around the fringe. Some, like Benedict Gaetani, were biding their time, others were reluctant to incur the automatic hostility of one family by supporting the other. In vain, the dean of the college, the aged and ailing Latino Malabranca, had urged upon his colleagues the need to forget family interests. Only a fool, he said, would wish to take up the heavy weight of the tiara. "The times were evil." The Saracens had retaken Acre and Tripoli; the kings of France and England were plunged in a war that threatened the unity of Christendom. Sicily, the church's own domain, was threatened by the barbaric Spaniards. Malabranca was ignored. The nations of Europe might consider the Chair of Peter to be raised above nations but the cardinals saw it for what it was—the supreme prize for a Roman family.

In the heavy heat of a July day the cardinals sat on. Soon, as they had done so often, they would break up yet again to go to their palaces, there to bathe the sweat from themselves, to eat and rest and recoup energy for the next encounter. All arguments that could be used had been used, all threats that could be made had been made and countered. No one man among them could count on sufficient support necessary for a two-thirds majority, and so it seemed they must meet again—and again throughout the sultry heat of summer, throughout another autumn, throughout the raw mists of a Perugian winter. They had that morning attended the funeral of Napoleon Orsini's brother and an unusual solemnity pervaded the conclave, the shadow of death touching even these sophisticated men. Certainly, the endless talk of politics had petered out. It was then that Latino Malabranca, speaking to no one in particular, mentioned that he had received a most urgent letter from a holy hermit, foretelling divine vengeance upon them all if a pope were not soon elected.

The cardinals felt no particular urge to follow up the matter: Holy prophets with messages of damnation had been common enough over the past year. Benedict Gaetani looked up with a smile and said sarcastically, "I suppose this is one of your Peter of Morone's visions." [1]

Everyone knew that Malabranca was a disciple of Peter of Morone, the holy man who hung his cowl upon a sunbeam, whose hours of devotions were marked by the tolling of a supernatural bell. Irritated by the sarcasm, Malabranca admitted that the letter was indeed from Peter, and the conversation swung, still idly, toward a discussion of this famous hermit of Monte Morone.

Peter of Morone more closely resembled the fanatical anchorites of the early centuries of the church than a modern Christian. Nevertheless, lover of solitude though he was, he had found time to establish an order, dedicated to the Holy Ghost, which had spread with remarkable rapidity. Its members called themselves the Spirituals, and though it had received official blessing, the more conservative members of the hierarchy viewed with considerable suspicion its near fanatical devotion to poverty and simplicity. Peter himself had gained an undesired fame and spent much of his time dodging hordes of pilgrims by moving from one remote mountain of the Abruzzi to another. He was now established in a cell high up on Monte Morone and from there had addressed his letter to Malabranca.

The casual conversation became more animated as the cardinals retailed the legends of Peter, some perhaps with concealed scorn, others with genuine conviction. Then Malabranca said loudly, "In the Name of the Father, the Son, and the Holy Ghost, I elect brother Peter of Morone." [2]

It seemed a fantastic idea, an almost miraculous demonstration of the doctrine that, ultimately, it was the Holy Ghost who guided the decision of the conclave. In the past, that guidance had been manifested in perplexing ways, but here it seemed was a pure and unequivocal choice—a holy man already dedicated to the Holy Ghost, elected spontaneously. Five cardinals immediately assented. Their motives, unlike Malabranca's, might be very mixed, although the Colonna claimed that they had been moved to elect Peter solely "by the fame of his sanctity." Nevertheless, even mixed motives would break the deadlock without giving advantage to either of the embattled families, and the Orsini followed the Colonna.

So did Benedict Gaetani. It had been his mocking question that had indirectly led to the decision—one that he certainly had neither expected nor desired. Throughout the eighteen months this cold and arrogant man had kept his own counsel, contributing to the deadlock, for he had declined to cast his vote for either of the main parties. He was related, though distantly, to both families and it was not unreasonable to hope that the conclave, finding it impossible to choose either Orsini or Colonna, must turn to him. And now it seemed that the conclave had been struck by a collective madness.

But he voted with the rest. Peter of Morone was an old man, well into his eighties, and in the nature of things, his pontificate would be brief. Benedict Gaetani was in his early sixties, in good health though troubled by the gout and the stone. There would be time enough.

After most normal elections, informing the new pope was a minor matter of routine, for if he were not actually in the room at the moment of election, he would be waiting anxiously not many doors away. But the man whom the Holy Ghost had chosen was even now in his mountain cave, over one hundred fifty miles away. Protocol demanded that the cardinals themselves should wait upon him with the news and gain his formal consent. But the moment of impulsiveness was already past. It would be beneath the dignity of the princes of the church to make the wearisome journey to the desolate mountain range where Peter had his cell. The task was delegated to three lesser men, one of whom, James Stefaneschi, made a record of the remarkable affair.

It took the papal party five days to make the tedious journey, and it arrived to find that others were ahead of it. Charles, king of Naples, had not thought it beneath his royal dignity to wait in person upon the newly elected pope. He was moved less by piety than by politics, for Peter of Morone was a subject of his kingdom —suddenly a very important subject.

The papal and royal parties, mutually suspicious, began the steep ascent of the mountain to Peter's cell. They were still scrambling up the stony track, sweating in their incongruous finery, when a late arrival from Perugia joined them. Cardinal Peter Colonna had obviously had second thoughts about maintaining dignity at a distance: Rich benefits could be reaped from such an unsophisticated pope as this during the first bewildering hours of his reign and Colonna intended to be there at the reaping. So Stefaneschi noted, disapprovingly, then dismissed the officious cardinal from his mind in order to record the fantastic scene that met his eyes at the end of the journey.

Peter of Morone had chosen a cave over a thousand feet up on the desolate mountain. It was set upon a narrow plateau, with a sheer drop upon one side, and there the party was forced to crowd. News of the approaching cortege had filled Peter not so much with dismay as outright terror. He had intended to fly yet again to one of his remoter refuges, but his disciples, with a keener awareness of the fruits involved, had dissuaded him. When Stefaneschi saw him, he was peering out through the bars of his cell, his eyelids swollen and darkened by tears, his face emaciated. He barely seemed to understand what was being said to him; then he threw himself upon the ground, prayed, arose, and with infinite reluctance, accepted.

It was a scene that could have been a subject for one of the fashionable allegories. A crowned king of the earth with his sons and his court, a prince of the church and other high prelates, prostrating themselves on the stony ground before a simple holy

man, vying with each other to kiss the hairy buskins that protected his legs, acclaiming him universal pontiff. By the time they
had edged themselves off the plateau and organized a rough procession, the lower slopes of Morone were covered with pilgrims,
come in their hundreds to see this new miracle. Chanting their
triumphant hymns, laymen and ecclesiastics descended to the valley
—and there their brief amity was shattered.

The papal party had expected to turn northward to Rome as
soon as the old man was capable of traveling. But King Charles of
Naples did not intend to lose his prize as easily as this. The new
pope was to remain in his kingdom, preferably in Naples itself
where he could be manipulated according to Neapolitan needs.
The ecclesiastics objected—strongly—but there was nothing they
could do about it for Peter himself declined to go north. In this
matter alone was he firm. All his life had been spent in the south
and nothing could induce him to brave the unknown dangers of
the north.

The pope refusing to go to the cardinals, reluctantly the cardinals came, one by one, to the pope. The last to come was Benedict
Gaetani, very much aware that he was entering the territory of
the same king whom he had abused so violently in Perugia. But
King Charles, having gained a major point, was happy enough to
overlook a minor quarrel in order to secure the friendship of a man
of Gaetani's stature, and the two men were amicably reconciled.

The coronation took place in Aquila on August 29, when Peter
of Morone took the name of Celestine. Two hundred thousand
people were reported to have crowded into the little town, peasants
and citizens from miles around flocking in to see the apotheosis of
the south. Pope Celestine V was a fellow countryman and, backed
by the power of the king of Naples, should do much to bring back
the power and glory of the south, so long oppressed by the arrogant north. So the thousands thought, and apparently had their
hopes justified when, in October, Celestine announced that he was
setting his seat in Naples. Gaetani again was the spokesman for
Rome—a violent spokesman—for he was almost beside himself
with rage at the news. "Go with your saint," he yelled, "for I'll
not come with you—nor let the Holy Ghost deceive me further

about him!"[3] The blasphemy did not go either unnoticed or unrecorded.

Gaetani went nevertheless, as did the rest of the court, and in Naples the situation passed rapidly from comedy, through farce, to tragedy. Celestine made his headquarters in the great Castello Nuovo, the five-towered fortress that even today dominates the harbor. His first act was to order the construction of a wooden cell in one of the great chambers of the castle and there he hid himself, as Stefaneschi put it, like the pheasant that thinks itself invisible and safe when it hides its head. The poor old man was utterly at a loss, utterly out of his depth in the sophisticated society into which he had so suddenly been thrown. The cardinals frightened him: They were worldly, experienced men while he, all his life, had fled from the crowds. He could not even talk to them in the accepted language of the court; condescendingly, they abandoned their polished Latin to converse with this rustic pope in the vernacular, which was all that he could understand. His immediate advisers and confidants were the monks he had known in his lowly days. With them alone was the unhappy pope at ease.

He ignored all work of the vast organization of which he was now head save the furtherance of privileges for his own monastic communities. The ancient Order of the Benedictines—particularly the powerful abbey of Monte Cassino—was despoiled in favor of the semifanatical Spirituals, sowing deep seeds of later hatreds. Place-hunters swarmed at the court. Celestine had no conception of the value of the rich gifts he could now dispense, and was bewildered by the hunger for benefices, granting them casually at request. Blank bulls made their appearance, peddled by the unscrupulous officers of the chancery to purchasers who filled them in as desired. The elaborate banquets and entertainments that had become a commonplace of court life disappeared, not by edict but quite casually. Celestine, the lifelong ascetic, was not so much offended by the display of luxury as puzzled by it. He is pictured as wandering from room to room of the castle, pining for the open air of Monte Morone, munching a dry loaf, declaring that it was the only savory food.

The election of a simple good man, who was taken from his

cave to mount the most splendid throne in Europe, had first astonished and then delighted Christians. It seemed as though they were witnessing the working out of those recent prophecies which foretold a new dispensation, when the meek would rule the mighty. Such a pope as Celestine might perhaps have found a place in the earlier centuries of the church, before the machinery of government dwarfed the men who had built it. In the thirteenth century he was an anachronism, as out of place as a first-century martyr would have been in the ruins of the Colosseum.

In a little over a month, Celestine reduced the bureaucracy to chaos with his casual gifts and retractions, creating an inextricable tangle that his successor could only cut, not resolve. Aware of his inadequacy, he sought to find a way out of his difficulties by creating a species of regency composed of three cardinals. Luckily, the Sacred College persuaded him to abandon the dangerous experiment, which would have given the church four simultaneous heads; but rapidly the situation approached the intolerable as Celestine cowered away from his insupportable burden.

His life was made no easier by the knowledge that somehow he was betraying those he loved, those Spirituals who had hailed his coronation as the dawn of a new age ruled by love. Their spokesman was Jacopone da Todi, one-time sinner and poet, now part saint, part fanatic, modeling his life upon that of St. Francis—but taking Francis' asceticism to extremes. From his distant cell, Jacopone gave perspicuous warnings to his old master now wandering lost among worldly cynics. "Beware of place-hunters, of men with skilled but twisted tongues. Beware, above all, of the wrath of God which will assuredly descend upon him should he neglect this priceless opportunity to reform the world." [4]

Celestine was in an impossible position. On one side were the men to whom he had given a new order and a new hope, exhorting him to begin the reign of love. On another were the tough and cynical papal bureaucrats who were either employing him for their own ends or were attempting to force his whole way of life into an alien mold. And exerting a third pressure was King Charles of Naples who expected solid returns for his protection. Obediently, Celestine flooded the Sacred College with nominees of Charles's, creating one of them cardinal quite casually—"after dinner," as another indignant cardinal reported. Seven of these new cardinals were French, for Charles, himself a descendant of the house of Anjou, was ever anxious to maintain his links with France. The Sacred College, in whose hands lay the exclusive right of electing a pope, was composed solely of Frenchmen and Italians, first clear hint of the schism that lay ahead.

At exactly what point, or on whose advice, Celestine turned his mind toward the thought of abdication, no man could afterward say. Later, the Colonna put it about that Benedict Gaetani had begun the insidious process of self-doubt by introducing a hidden speaking tube into Celestine's cell, and in the silence of night, he simulated a supernatural voice warning him to abdicate or face the flames of hell. Dante, for one, believed some such story, for after Gaetani had won his way to the throne, Dante accused him of having "gained the Fair Lady by fraud."

It was natural that Celestine would turn to a lawyer of Gaetani's status to seek advice on such an action as abdication. The precedents were both obscure and unsavory, involving as they did that sale of the Papacy one hundred and fifty years earlier. Latino Malabranca, Celestine's original sponsor and the only man from whom he could have hoped to receive competent and disinterested advice, was dead. Gaetani was at least neutral among the factions of the college—if only because he was pursuing strictly his own ends.

Whoever first approached the other, from the moment that Celestine made his decision it was Gaetani who piloted it through the dangerous legal and political shoals. The news leaked out and there was immediate uproar. Celestine's own monks, aware that their master's abdication would not only put an end to the long-awaited rule of love but would also strip them of their privileges, stirred up the Neapolitan. For his own reasons, King Charles too put pressure on the old man to change his mind. Under Gaetani's guidance, Celestine pretended to reconsider, while the legal machinery ground on. On December 13, just fifteen weeks after his coronation, Celestine summoned his cardinals for what was to be the last consistory. Gaetani was probably the only one among them who knew what was about to happen.

Pale, trembling, but for once resolute, the old man read a prepared deed of renunciation that he and Gaetani had drawn up. In the astonished silence that followed, he slowly descended the steps from the throne, and with his own hands stripped himself of the gorgeous robes that symbolized for him not power, but imprisonment. He left the chamber, then returned a few moments later, clad in his own familiar coarse garments.

So ended the great experiment in love. The majority of the cardinals accepted the decision with relief, even if none were so unwise as Gaetani as to accuse the Holy Ghost of deceit. Outside the college, reaction ranged from the sympathetic to the cruel. "On St. Lucy's Day Pope Celestine resigned the papacy—and he did well," [5] was perhaps the kindest comment. It was left to Dante to pin a badge of shame on a broken man that was to pass as history's verdict. He put Celestine not in hell but in its dismal approaches, wandering with those who had been neither friends nor enemies of God, for they had lacked the courage or passion to ally themselves with good or evil. Dante recognized some, among them "the shade of him who made through cowardice the great refusal." [6]

Ten days after Celestine's abdication, the conclave met and, within twenty-four hours, elected Benedict Gaetani. He took the name of Boniface VIII.

Consolidation

The new pope was in his early sixties, and his election seemed a logical conclusion to an energetic and competent career. Behind him lay some forty years' experience at the very heart of papal politics, experience gained not only in the claustrophobic atmosphere of Rome but in the rough and tumble of legations in foreign lands. As a young man of thirty he had gone to England in the legate's entourage at the time when the land was convulsed in the struggles centered around Simon de Montfort. Years afterward, Boniface recalled how he, with the rest of the papal party, had been besieged in the Tower of London by Montfort's allies, and how the young Prince Edward had rescued them. Young Edward became Edward I, and that timely rescue probably played no small part in the mutual admiration that later sprang up between the two rather similar men.

After the defeat of Montfort, Gaetani returned to Rome and the center of things, disappearing from sight but moving steadily upward, for when his name appears again, in 1281, it is in a document that empowered him to hold the numerous benefices in England, France, and Italy that he had gained in the interim. There was nothing unusual in this plurality of benefice; unusual, perhaps, was the tenacity with which they were held, the dedication with which others were added. Here now could be seen, superadded to the figure of the discreet lawyer, the man of property, goaded by hunger for land and the gold with which to purchase it—"gold wrung from the groans and tears of the poor."

Gaetani's successful career was doubtless due to his fortunate connections: His mother was the niece of a pope and he was distantly related to other families who had gained the papal throne. But, though family influence aided him, personal vigor maintained him on his path to power. He displayed that clearly enough nine years after his visit to England. On this occasion he was in France, legate in his own right, come to chastise the all-powerful University of Paris, which dared to interfere in papal business.

"You Paris masters at your desk seem to think that the world should be ruled by your reasonings. I tell you this is not so—it is to us that the world is entrusted, not to you." [7]

In a characteristic outburst of violence, he went on to warn them that Rome could, and would, destroy the University if it continued to prove recalcitrant. Paris saw, in addition to the lawyer and the landlord, the third aspect of Gaetani's character: the arrogant cleric, sure of himself and of the vast organization in whose power his confidence was rooted.

This was the man who had sat impatiently throughout the long conclave; who had then watched incredulously as a holy hermit brought the machine of government to a halt; and who, when opportunity presented itself, seized it, confident that his high ends justified any means whatsoever. Unlike the Roman cardinals, locked still in their sterile battle with each other, he had taken the precaution of ingratiating himself with Charles of Naples, whose creatures now swamped the college. Their support, together with that of the remaining neutrals, probably accounted for the speed of election.

The crown secured, Boniface had not the slightest intention of remaining in Naples. Quite apart from the attraction of Rome was the danger to his person represented by the Neapolitans themselves. They had taken the resignation of Celestine very hard indeed. Lawyers might argue the hairbreadth morality of the abdication, and come to the conclusion that it was legal: To the people, it was a betrayal of hope. At the center of the disturbances remained Celestine's band of monks, in search of vengeance now that they had failed in their first task, goading the Neapolitans to attack the usurper. Boniface got out of the dangerous city as soon as he possibly could. He was elected on Christmas Eve, and by the end of the month he was on his way out of Naples—so swift a departure, indeed, that the bulk of the papal luggage was left behind. Celestine was ordered to accompany the party back to Rome. The ex-pope was utterly dismayed. The whole reason for his renunciation had been to enable him to go back to the life he knew and loved. Rome meant nothing to him—it was a vast, hostile city even farther than Naples from his beloved and familiar hills. En route, he and a small band of disciples managed to escape from the straggling caravan and he made for his old cell on Monte Morone.

Boniface knew nothing of the escape until he arrived in Rome. It came as a shock. His entry into Rome on January 17 had been greeted by genuine popular delight, the Romans welcoming back their pope after an absence of more than two years. But Boniface also heard of another popular demonstration, in Naples, where news of his supposed death had been greeted by jubilant crowds in the streets. Already rumors were circulating that he had brought pressure to bear upon Celestine, that he was a usurper. Now he learned that Celestine was at large, free to attract a rebellious following if he chose. He immediately gave orders that the old man was to be arrested and brought back to Rome, by force if need be. Celestine was warned and, with remarkable courage and agility for a man of his age, left Monte Morone in the depths of winter and began wandering in the remoter mountains, keeping just ahead of the papal officials seeking him. A monk who had remained in the cell to break the news to Boniface's enraged and fearful soldiers paid for his devotion with his life.

It was an ominous opening to a new pontificate, but after his initial reaction Boniface was not unduly troubled. It could only be a question of time before somebody betrayed Celestine, and meanwhile there was his own coronation to be celebrated with all the pomp that was dear to him. Celestine had ridden to his coronation mounted upon an ass—to some, an almost blasphemous symbolism. He, Boniface, would ride like the Roman emperor he resembled, displaying himself for the adoration of the tumultuous Romans.

The ceremony of papal coronation fell naturally into two parts: the consecration and coronation at St. Peter's, followed by a procession to the Lateran Palace where the new pope took formal possession of the ancient seat of civic government. On January 23, Boniface was duly consecrated at the altar of St. Peter's and then, clad in the stiff and splendid garments of supreme pontiff, moved in procession to the square in front of the basilica. There he seated himself upon a throne before the great doors. It was a bitterly cold day but considerations of mere physical comfort could not deter Boniface from the supreme part of the ritual, the crowning of the pope before the gaze of thousands.

The archdeacon removed the bishop's miter from his head and in its place settled the great conical tiara, outward expression of the claim to universal earthly power. A little over two centuries earlier, the "crown" of the pope had still been the simple white cap that was all that the legendary St. Sylvester had accepted from Constantine. Even the Tusculan popes had been content with the symbol that made them temporal lord only of Rome and the Papal States. But, imperceptibly, it had grown with the growing status of the Papacy, and was now a crown as splendid as that of any emperor, a pretension made explicit by the formula uttered at the moment of coronation: "Take the tiara, and know that thou art the father of princes and kings, the ruler of the world, the vicar on earth of our Saviour Jesus Christ, whose honor and glory shall endure through all eternity." [8] It was a formula that Boniface had every intention of turning into fact.

Rising, Boniface descended the steps of the piazza to the road below and there mounted a great white horse. Again, tradition accorded him a high honor, for his horse was led by the kings of Hungary and Naples, trudging humbly in the slush below him. Constantine was supposed to have acted as groom to St. Sylvester, so that now the highest-ranking monarchs present in Rome deemed it an honor to take the lowliest task in the procession.

Passing on through the crumbling arches of the great emperors of the past, the procession flowed past a solitary tower and halted when Boniface himself came abreast of it. At its foot stood a deputation of the Jews of Rome, come to make their peace with the new ruler of Rome and accept his ritual spurning. The rabbi offered the law of Moses to Boniface, who took it, then returned it with the words, "We acknowledge the law but we reject Judaism, for the law has already been fulfilled through Christ."

The procession moved on again through the enthusiastic crowds. The Romans loved it all. They had decorated their houses that lay on the processional route. The brilliant gonfalons, glowing in the thin sunlight, brought color into the wintry streets, foretaste of the color and glory being brought back to Rome. This was to be the last homecoming of a pope to the Lateran, for Boniface was the last to take up residence in the ancient and sacred palace. A little over a generation afterward, it was a gutted ruin, a millennium's history shattered in casual violence.

But in January, 1294, the Lateran Palace was still the heart of the temporal Papacy. Outside the palace, a curious ceremony took place, an inverted reflection of the one that had taken place outside the Vatican. There, Boniface had been seated upon the Chair of St. Peter; here, he sat down upon an ancient red marble chair, with a pierced seat that bore a strong resemblance to a commode. Originally, the chair had stood in one of the great public baths of the city, but its humble origins had long been forgotten now that it was, like so much else from the great past, swept into papal ceremony and refurbished. It was probable that its antiquity and beautiful color had led to its being adopted as the throne on which the new pope took formal possession of the Lateran. But its curious shape gave rise to the pious belief that the pope sat upon it in a gesture of self-abasement from which he was raised up by his cardinals. A few years before Boniface's coronation, less pious but even more vivid imaginations had begun to spin the story that the purpose of the throne was to allow a physical examination of the new pope, and thus avoid a repetition of another "Pope Joan." The rumors so thrived that two centuries later there existed a complete pseudoceremony of examination, faithfully recorded by the more credulous chroniclers and historians, to give substantiation to the story of Joan.

Seated upon the chair, Boniface received a girdle from which hung seven keys and seven seals. Then rising, he thrust his hands into a bag.containing a mixture of gold and silver coins and three times cast a handful into the crowd, chanting, "God and silver are not mine, but what I have I give." He then entered the palace itself, where a similar ceremony was repeated. Again he seated himself on a pierced marble seat, receiving on this occasion the keys of the Lateran Palace and of the basilica. More largesse was scattered, the palace officials advanced to kiss his foot, and the prelates came to ask and receive the customary gifts from a newly crowned pope.

And after the public ceremonies came the only slightly less public banquet, where powerful nobles of the city brought dishes to the pope and a king acted as his cupbearer. Lateran banquets had always been magnificent occasions; but that celebrating the coronation of Boniface VIII probably surpassed all those the palace had ever witnessed before, a fitting enough climax to its life. Stefaneschi was there and recorded it in wonder, marveling at the profusion of costly wines and delicate foods, the priceless drinking vessels of gold and precious stones, the jeweled platters, the brilliant tapestries upon the ancient walls. Rome, plundered again and again, had yet been able to prepare, from its inexhaustible treasury, a fitting welcome for its magnate.

But despite the outward signs of his stability, Boniface did not forget Celestine, the doddering ancient who could yet topple him from his solid throne—or who could be used to topple him. King Charles of Naples had joined in the hunt for Celestine, but the old man had eluded both papal and royal forces, aided by those who loved him and hated his successor. Ironically, it was their very love that betrayed him.

Wisely, Celestine had recognized that Italy was too small for both himself and Boniface and, arriving at the Adriatic coast, he took ship for Greece. It was perhaps a measure of his desperation that in the closing months of his life he should abandon not merely the few square miles of mountain that he loved but Italy itself. Nevertheless, he did not escape. A storm arose, his ship was thrown back, and landing among too enthusiastic followers he was recognized by royal troops as his well-wishers proclaimed him true pope. Charles, who had first encouraged him, now used him; it must have seemed a profitable transaction to exchange a half-wild holy man for the gratitude of the splendid Boniface.

Celestine was brought before both Charles and Boniface for judgment to be passed. Travel-stained, deathly weary, stung still by pangs of conscience, it was perhaps then that the old man made his prophecy at whose seeming exactness generations were to marvel.

"You have entered like a fox," he told the impassive Boniface. "You will reign like a lion—and you will die like a dog." [9]

Boniface went through the motions of consulting his cardinals, but Celestine's fate had already been decided: He could not be allowed to wander at will, a focal point for the rebellious. His last home was to be in the isolated fortress of Fumone, used in the past for the more important prisoners of state. The imprisonment was in fact an unwitting kindness, and when Celestine saw the tiny cell prepared for him, he rejoiced; it resembled closely enough his preferred type of home. But the two brothers who elected to share his imprisonment broke down under the rigorous conditions, and rumor inevitably spread of deliberate ill-treatment. His disciples made much of that humble cell and of how he lay dying upon naked boards, while "he to whom he had left the Papacy reposed like a god on a couch adorned with purple and gold." [10]

Certainly, Celestine did not long survive imprisonment, dying some ten months afterward to the expected accompaniment of rumors of murder. His bones were piously cherished, among them, the skull with a hole in it, together with the nail that was supposed to have been driven into it. It is wholly unlikely that Boniface would have employed such a crude means to destroy a man whom unaided nature would soon remove from the world. But the manufacture and cherishing of such a macabre story was evidence enough of the hatred which Pope Boniface VIII had inspired within a few months of his coronation.

The Papacy had been virtually without a ruler for well over two years and Boniface threw himself wholeheartedly into the task of reimposing order. According to Boniface's account, Celestine had expressly asked him to repair the damage made by unthinking gifts. Whether the statement was true or not, Boniface's first act was to condemn all that Celestine had done, canceling with a stroke of the pen the wholesale appointments that Celestine had distributed with a free hand. It was a task well suited to a man of Boniface's legal mind and powerful will, but it also gained him innumerable enemies. To those enemies who had genuinely regretted the lost possibilities of a new order, were added those who were now deprived, tactlessly if justly, of illegal benefits.

In the larger field of European affairs, Boniface moved with a sure and firm step, acting with skill and justice during the opening stages of the conflict between Edward I of England and Philip the Fair of France. Neither he nor the contestants could know that this conflict was itself merely the curtain raiser to the protracted struggle that later generations termed the Hundred Years' War. In 1298 it seemed a simple enough matter of arbitrating about Flanders and the English possessions on French soil. True, the embattled kings called upon him to arbitrate as lawyer, not as pope, specifically referring to him as "Benedict Gaetani," not as "Boniface VIII." True again, the Flemings complained among themselves that it was impossible to get justice in Rome without paying for it. "The court of Rome is insatiable, its appetite bottomless—one must always bring many gifts." [11] But though Boniface played the role of arbiter of Europe for all it was worth, he gave good advice, gaining considerable prestige—but gaining, too, a fatal taste for power in temporal affairs.

In domestic affairs, Boniface plunged straight into the shabbiest of papal crimes, simony and nepotism. To gain the gold to buy the land with which to establish the Gaetani family—this was the leitmotif of his policy, its narrow, unworthy parochialism undermining all else that might have been great and enduring. In Boniface's opinion, a pope could not, by definition, commit simony, for he was the church and the church was he and all that it possessed was at his ordering. Rome was a vast mouth gulping the gold of Europe, and though much of it went out again to finance legitimate missions, more of it remained in Rome. Even this loss could be defended on the grounds that the earthly sinews of the church required earthly nourishment. When, however, the earthly power and wealth of the Church were diverted for the aggrandizement of a single family, Boniface exceeded his demands on even the cynical tolerance of the times.

Nepotism was a comparative newcomer to the range of papal sins, its appearance coinciding with the final degradation of the empire. The papacy was the only goal in Italy for such ambitious men as Boniface, who under other circumstances would have aimed for an ordinary crown. But by the time such a man had battled his way through decades of intrigue, it was to find that he had gained a species of Dead Sea fruit. Celestine's tragedy had underlined the fact that a spiritual pope was an anomaly—the power to be exercised was the same type as that exercised by any other monarch. Its range was greater, but the papal monarch suffered one enormous handicap: He could not transmit the gathered power to his children. The vivid sense of family that characterizes Italians throughout their history made this limitation a real penalty, placing the occupant of the throne under great temptation. In the tenth century, and again in the sixteenth, the office became all but hereditary. It was the cardinals who checked the process, if for no better reason than that each had the right, and hoped, to become pope.

Deprived of the natural means of transmitting power, regarding his relatives as his only sure allies, Boniface began the process of family aggrandizement that reached its logical conclusions under the popes of the Renaissance. His very real love of family was, of itself, one of his most attractive virtues. On the news of the death of his brother and his nephew, he burst into bitter—and indiscreet—lamentations, cursing the God who had brought these things on him. But the Gaetani were a fertile stock and there were other nephews upon whom he could lavish his love and pride—at the expense of the church.

Legally, his position was unassailable. The lands he was buying for his family lay in the States of the Church and he could argue that by securing such loyal vassals, tied to him by both blood and gratitude, he was protecting the interests of the church. But his observers and victims saw only a hitherto modest family suddenly sprawling over the hills and valleys of the Campagna. Even if this generation of beneficiaries remained loyal to the church, what of the next? No one was more tenacious of land than an Italian noble.

Steadily, Boniface went on acquiring rich cities and their adjacent territories, until a clear-cut chain of Gaetani cities could be seen extending over the hills from Rome southward to Caserta and the distant sea. The equivalent of two years' revenue of the Holy See was poured out for their purchase—a quarter of the entire revenue that came in during his reign. Long-established families were dispossessed in the process, some fairly, their pride assuaged with gold, others shouldered aside to join the ranks of Boniface's enemies. And of all those who watched in smoldering discontent, the most dangerous was the family of the Colonna.

The Colonna were old and the Colonna were powerful. They claimed their descent from the counts of Tusculum, and through them, to the near mythical Marozia. The Romans had arisen at last and destroyed their impudent rival Tusculum, and thereafter the Colonna had ruled their widespread territories from the hilltop city of Palestrina. Over the years, their predominant enemy had been the Orsini. Now they saw an upstart family, the Gaetani, backed by the power of the Keys, encroaching upon their lands. Direct conflict between Colonna and pope was unavoidable.

In the early days, the two Colonna cardinals, James and his nephew Peter, had maintained friendly if not exactly warm relationships with their colleague Benedict Gaetani, looking upon him as a possible ally. Even when that colleague became transformed into a master, they had supported him, if only on the lukewarm principle that a Gaetani pope was better than an Orsini. But very soon afterward the relationship began to deteriorate. Not only were the Colonna forced to witness the glorification of the Gaetani at their expense, but they now saw their old enemies the Orsini creeping back into power. Boniface too had seen that a clash between himself and the Colonna was inevitable—and so made allies of Colonna enemies. The Sacred College was proving merely another arena where the great Roman nobles would fight out their differences.

In their search for an attack on Boniface, the Colonna found a weak point in his armor and a powerful support for themselves. The legality of his election might be acceptable to canon lawyers, but for the common people who lamented the loss of a kingdom of heaven on earth, the arguments in favor of Boniface were arid and meaningless. All they saw was that Pope Celestine, the chosen of the Holy Ghost, had been shouldered aside by Pope Boniface, the lawyer usurping the place of the saint.

Most opponents were content merely to murmur, but here and there strange cults arose, bizarre outgrowths of the deep-rooted hope that Boniface had cut down. The strangest of these developed in Milan, where a pious but otherwise undistinguished lady called Guglielmina had died and left a large sum of money to a Cistercian monastery. The monks had honored her with a chapel, convenient miracles occurred around her tomb, and rapidly an extensive cult developed. Guglielmina was now the incarnation of the Holy Ghost and would come again, throw down the usurper Boniface, and place a young Milanese girl, Maifreda, in his place. An inquisition was ordered, the wretched Maifreda with her devotees was duly burned, and the Guglielmites withered. But others rose to take their place. Consistent at the center of opposition were those monastic fanatics who took their name from Celestine himself, abandoning their earlier nickname of "Spirituals" for that of "Celestinians." They lent themselves readily to any form of attack upon the usurping Boniface and the Colonna made firm allies of them.

Boniface learned to hate, above all men, the Celestinian leader Jacopone da Todi, erstwhile adviser of Celestine himself. As a young man, Jacopone had been a wholehearted rake—until he had been plunged into a sudden, private hell by the death of his beautiful young wife. He nearly went out of his mind, the experience so totally altering his character that when at length he had fought through the dark valley, he became a Franciscan monk, embracing virtue as wholeheartedly as he had embraced vice.

But in spite of his spiritual change, he still possessed his considerable talent for poetry. He employed it now, not for the creation of gay lilting verses full of springtime and love, but for hymns of a remarkable grandeur, the surge of the poet within him transforming the stiff Latin into sonorous, living music. He had abandoned love poetry, but his restless, many-sided nature still needed a more frivolous outlet than that provided by hymnology; this by-product of his poetic activities took the form of lively political satires.

Convinced that Boniface stood for all that was worldly within the Church, for all that was ultimately corrupting, Jacopone took him as prime target for his stinging darts. For other Celestinians, Boniface loomed like Lucifer, "an angel from the abyss, supported by malicious spirits." Jacopone, divining the man behind the imposing pope, directed his unerring aim at that man's shabbier vices —the avarice, the simony, above all, the unfailing nepotism. Jacopone and the Colonna, working for different ends, proved a formidable combination when hostilities came into the open.

The final breach between Boniface and the Colonna occurred on the afternoon of Thursday, May 3, 1297—a significant date for Boniface, for the tiny, almost invisible, crack that then appeared in the foundation of his monolithic power was to spread until the whole was riven. Late on that afternoon a caravan of mules heavily laden with gold was passing not far from Rome when Stephen Colonna swept down upon it and carried off the gold. The money was intended for the purchase of yet more territories for the Gaetani, and Stephen's act could not have touched Boniface on a more tender spot.

The storm broke swiftly. At nine the following morning, a raging Boniface ordered the two Colonna cardinals to present themselves at the Lateran on that very day. They delayed their appearance until Monday. There was not the slightest doubt that Stephen, a hotheaded young man, had put both himself and the entire family in the wrong, and family pressure was immediately exerted upon him. Obediently, he agreed to restore the gold and it was with the knowledge that reparation was being made that the cardinals faced Boniface.

They learned very quickly indeed that simple reparation was not sufficient—by no means sufficient. Boniface demanded the person of Stephen himself, the sacrilegious young man who had dared lay hands upon sacred Gaetani gold. He demanded more. The Colonna were to accept papal garrisons in their chief cities, Boniface speciously pointing out that the Colonna themselves were eternally disputing among themselves the ownership of these cities. He would grant the cardinals until the following Friday to think it over.

James and Peter returned to their city and summoned an urgent family conference. There was, in fact, little to debate, for it needed no great exercise of the imagination to foresee that "papal garrisons" meant "Gaetani garrisons" or—worse still—"Orsini garrisons." Plainly, Boniface meant to exploit the situation and lever out the Colonna, with the aid of the Orsini if need be. Doubtless, later, there would be a dogfight between Gaetani and Orsini over the division of spoils but it would not, by then, be of much interest to the ruined Colonna.

The only real point to be discussed was how the Colonna were to reply to the immediate threat. Jacopone da Todi, with five powerful French prelates, was present at the family conference, and between them, the allies decided that their attack was to be a legal one. Over the next two days they hammered out their policy and by the early morning of Thursday, May 10, they had drawn up a manifesto in which the legitimacy of Boniface's election was impugned and appeal made for a general council to settle the doubts and rumors. Several copies were made, and shortly after sunrise, trusted messengers rode off to Rome with them.

Rome stirred early with the approach of summer and the Colonna heralds were observed as they galloped through the fresh streets of morning, each to a prearranged spot. Curious, but carefully neutral, faces watched as copies of the manifesto were nailed up on church doors throughout the city. One bold spirit even penetrated into St. Peter's itself and left his copy on the high altar. Their task done, the heralds galloped out again, passing through the great city gates without opposition.

The impudent manifestos were still fluttering in the morning breeze when Boniface met in full consistory with his loyal cardinals. He, and they, and all Rome now knew of the direct challenge to his authority. The Colonnas had no allies in the Sacred College. It was dominated by Romans, each of whom saw the overthrow of the Colonna as the destruction of a rival, and Boniface had his will. By the evening of the same day he had published a bull with one of those resounding titles in which he delighted.

"In excelso throno" rehearsed the injuries he had received from the Colonna, excommunicated and deposed the two cardinals and as an afterthought demanded their appearance before him within ten days. The Colonna replied on the following day with a detailed attack. Boniface now was accused not merely of fraud but of parricide, of having been the direct cause of Celestine's death. Yet again, a bull thundered in reply. Excommunication was extended to include every member of the cardinals' branch of the Colonna family "even unto the fourth generation," its oldest and youngest members declared heretical, outside the law, the legitimate prey of those who could overcome them.

There was now no retreat for the Colonna and they stepped up the war of words. Advised by their French allies, they addressed their appeal to all Christendom—in particular to France, exploiting the grumbling element of conflict that lay, still hidden, between Boniface and King Philip of France. Specifically, they addressed themselves to the University of Paris, that powerhouse of the Roman Church, which in despite of Rome formed European opinion on theological matters. The story of the abdication was told yet again, with embellishments, and an accurate enough summary given of Boniface's character and the court molded by him —of its venality, of his own ceaseless hunger for gold, of his tyranny in consistory. To oppose him on the most trivial matter was to run a knife into him, they said. He was not content to reign without opposition over priests "but boasts that he presides over kings and kingdoms in all affairs, deeming himself a god on earth." The cardinals themselves had been deposed as though they had been the meanest of officials: "not summoned, not warned, not convicted, not confessed, not accused, not denounced, not indicted." [12]

But if the Colonna hoped for immediate aid from France, they were disappointed. Philip the Fair did not want an open break at this stage, and Boniface's field was, for the moment, clear. On August 17, 1297, open war was declared against the Colonna and the machinery of the Church began to grind against her children.

Excommunication as a spiritual weapon was one that was now thoroughly blunted. Among the great mass of inarticulate Christians, and even here and there among the sophisticated, the threat of being expelled from the mystical Body of Christ was both real and terrible. But excommunication had been used too often for debased political reasons to retain its religious terrors in the higher levels of society. Nevertheless, though its spiritual potency was diminished, its legal powers remained. An excommunicated man was thrust out of society, placed outside the law: Acts which would be illegal against any other person in the community were deemed not merely lawful but actively virtuous when directed against him. Thus, on September 14, Boniface specifically absolved from sin those who had sacked the Colonna property in Rome—the thieves were no longer thieves but avengers of Christ. The mob was probably indifferent to the fine theological distinction but it was nice to know that the stolen property now lawfully belonged to those who had got away with it.

Three months later Boniface brought about the final debasement of the spiritual weapon with the proclamation of a crusade against the Colonna. From his point of view it was a very useful device that enabled him to lay his hands, legally, on money collected throughout Europe for the old-fashioned crusades against the infidel in the Holy Land. The great military Order of the Knights Templar could be asked for military aid, humble Christians in distant lands could be persuaded that cash contributions would purchase remission of sins.

Comparatively few joined in this curious new holy war. The Orsini were delighted to be numbered among the enemy of the Colonna and some Italian cities sent token contingents in exchange for civic privileges. But Italy, and Europe as a whole, saw this crusade for what it was: a vicious contest between Roman barons, one of whom happened to possess the power to employ the weapons of the Church in a private war. The Romans themselves, hardened to civil turmoil though they were, protested at this fratricidal war which was tearing open the vitals of the state. It was an unusually deadly struggle, even by Roman standards, for the papal troops enjoyed that dispensation which freed crusaders from even the rough and ready contemporary rules of war. In the light of the ruling that "God would know his own," the crusader could plunge his sword where he wished, depending upon divine intervention to turn the blade aside should the destined victim be a true believer.

It was not merely the rebellious Colonna who suffered, but all connected to them by even the remotest of feudal ties. The peasants on their lands, the women and children in all the villages which happened to be within the boundaries of their lands—all these now could be killed or sold into slavery, their pathetic goods becoming the property of the "crusaders." The ancient olive groves, each tree a vital possession of some family and tended through generations, went up in flames. Crops too green for harvesting were destroyed. Suicidally, Romans were destroying the sustenance of Rome. The senator of Rome, the civic head of the city, went between Colonna and pope in a desperate attempt to make peace. It was futile. Boniface received him "with paternal care," but he had no intention of losing this chance to crush, finally, the family that stood between the Gaetani and glory; and the Colonna, too, knew that this was the final test of arms.

Throughout the winter and spring the ferocious warfare continued, until by the late summer of 1298 it had all but achieved its object: With one exception all the Colonna cities had fallen to the "crusaders." Each city, as it capitulated, was handed to one or another of the pope's allies, the rich reward for their brief support. The exception was Palestrina itself. Here the family had gathered at the last, entrusting their defense to the strange, grim John Colonna, the veteran soldier who bore the significant nickname of Sciarra—Quarreler. Secure behind their city's giant walls, amply provisioned, their defense ably handled by Sciarra, the family should have been able to hold out indefinitely. Besieging commanders had long since learned that treachery was the only possible method of defeating the inhabitants of a walled city who were determined to resist.

Treachery duly came—not from within but from without—in the form of perjury on the part of Boniface. Or so, at least, the bitter accusations afterward maintained. Giovanni Villani, the neutral Florentine, gave his cautious opinion in favor of the Colonna. According to his account, Boniface offered to pardon them, "promising to restore them to their high state of dignity if they would yield the city. But this was not done—instead, he destroyed the city of Palestrina. And this false and fraudulent treaty the Pope made at the counsel of the Count of Montefeltro, at that time a friar, who gave to him the evil words 'promise much—fulfill little.' " [13]

Dante picked up the story from a common source and elaborated on it, telling how Guido of Montefeltro, the "wolf turned friar"—the ex-bandit who had become a Franciscan—had been approached by Boniface, who wanted to know how to get the Colonna out of Palestrina. Guido the soldier knew that there was only one solution, but Guido the repentant monk was reluctant to give it. Then, at Boniface's direct order and promise of absolution beforehand, he counseled:

> Father, since thou washest me
> Of that sin into which I now must fall,
> The promise long with the fulfillment short
> Will make thee triumph in thy lofty seat.[14]

Lunga promessa con l'attender corto—it was not particularly original advice and it seems unlikely that Boniface could not have thought of it himself. But however the promise was conceived and framed, it worked, and the Colonna surrendered in the belief that their possessions would be restored to them.

Boniface had an enduring delight in making grand public appearances. At almost every crisis he would appear, clad in full pontificals and surrounded by obsequious officials, to seat himself upon a throne—preferably in the open air before some great church or city gate. On this occasion he was at Rieti, and like some Roman general, had set his throne outside the city gate, there to receive his vanquished enemies. To him, at length, the Colonna came: cardinals James and Peter, Sciarra, Stephen, bearing halters around their necks. They threw themselves upon the ground, kissed his feet, craved his pardon. In this, his hour of triumph, Boniface appeared magnanimous enough. The two cardinals were not reinstated in office, but did retain their freedom. Stephen, the immediate cause of the whole trouble, was to go on an expiatory pilgrimage and the whole matter of the dispute was to be discussed at a later stage. On Jacopone da Todi alone fell the immediate weight of Boniface's vengeance: He was thrown into prison to rot for the rest of his life. In the event, he was fortunate, for Boniface's own death secured his release.

The implication that the dispute was to be discussed when tempers were cooler gave the Colonna hope. But it also gave Boniface a breathing space to accomplish an act that made a mockery of his magnanimous gestures. Palestrina was destroyed.

It was an act without precedent in papal history. Palestrina was one of the seven pillars of the Roman Church, for it had been the seat of a bishop from the remotest days. Its monuments dated back to the days of imperial Rome, protected by the Colonna, whose family seat was the great palace supposed to have been built by Julius Caesar himself. The family had gathered within the walls those treasures of the past which their contemporaries despised or ignored, making of the city a priceless museum. Boniface did not intend the usual token destruction—the demolition of a section of wall or of a tower or two—but the total eradication of one of the ancient cities of Italy. The cathedral alone was spared.

It was a hard task, the centuries-old mortar defying the destroyers, but it was done. And when all had been accomplished, when the inhabitants had been driven out and the once proud city was a desolate acreage of rubble, the terrible Roman symbol of plow and salt was reenacted. In the edict that encompassed the destruction of Palestrina, Boniface made his emulation of a Roman general explicit: Even as Carthage had been plowed and the furrows sown with salt, so, he said, was Palestrina to be plowed and rendered eternally barren. The symbolism was appallingly accurate, for Palestrina never recovered. Still following his Roman model, Boniface ordered that a new city should be built on the lower slopes of the hill. *Civitatis papalis*, he called it, but it was a poor enough community. Indeed, its life was less than eighteen months, for in the spring of 1300, in a sudden access of rage, he ordered that even this poor relic was to be destroyed; and the inhabitants once again went off as exiles, this time for good.

Boniface, to the casual eye, had triumphed utterly, but he paid dearly for that vindictive pleasure. In destroying Palestrina, he destroyed any hope of reconciliation with the Colonna, and they shared the Italian taste for vengeance to the full. "Vengeance," the proverb ran, "is a dish best tasted cold"—and they were adept at such dishes. In his comfortable burgher's house in Florence, Giovanni Villani recorded the end of the first act of the distant tragedy with a troubled mind.

The Colonna, finding that they had been deceived, their noble fortress of Palestrina destroyed, rebelled again against the Pope and the Church before the end of the year. And the Pope excommunicated them again with terrible processes, and for fear of being captured or killed through the Pope's persecution, they left the land of Rome. And some went to Sicily and some to France, traveling from place to place wherever they were not known. And thus they remained in exile while the Pope lived.[15]

Among those wandering Colonna was Sciarra. He was captured by pirates, but Philip of France paid his ransom and brought him to France. There was much hard and dangerous work ahead for Sciarra, the fruits of which brought him a vengeance that left even the Italians appalled.

The High-Souled Sinner

Boniface VIII, the last of the papal monarchs on the heroic scale, is the first of the popes to stand clear of his background, the first who can be viewed in the round, through the medium of art as well as letters. Loving magnificence, he drew to his court the first of those artists who were working in the predawn light of the Renaissance, and in return they left his image clear for posterity. Throwing himself into one of the decisive struggles of Europe, battling with its dominant monarch, he became an object for the wondering gaze of all Europeans; and in England and Ireland, in France, Germany, and Spain, chroniclers recorded his activities. In his native land during his reign, the art of true history was reborn, in Florence, and it is his figure that looms in the opening pages of the great Florentine prose writers. And in that vast gallery of saints and sinners, the *Divine Comedy,* he throws a shadow larger than Lucifer's, for he appears in each of the three books.

Outside the pages of poets and historians, his activities were detailed minutely by an army of lawyers. He spoke for himself through his resounding bulls, for loving the law above all other intellectual activities, it was through it that he best expressed himself. Ironically, it was the law that crucified his memory, the king of France pursuing him even beyond the grave with a posthumous trial in which every foul action, attested or merely rumored, of the man's violent life was dredged up to create a portrait of scarcely human depravity. Between them, the poets and the lawyers, the historians and the artists, built up a figure that towered like a colossus and made an epoch of a reign that lasted barely eight years.

Until the coming of the Renaissance, there are few popes whose physical features are so authentically preserved as those of Boniface. Appropriately, it is through the medium of sculpture that posterity best knows him, for Roman in this as in all else, he preferred that art above all others. Indeed, his love for it later provided basis for the charge that "he ordered silver images to be set up in churches in order to induce men to idolatry." The stupidity of the charge was equaled only by its malice, but certainly an unprecedented number of statues of a living pope appeared during his reign.

Many were erected at his direct order, but many were paid for by communities who hoped to profit through flattery. His best-known portrait, the seated figure by Arnolfo di Cambio, was erected in Florence, not in Rome. Boniface was not a particularly outstanding art patron, the law was his preferred subject and art but a by-product, a luxury. Nevertheless, there was a sensitivity about the man which enabled him to discern the new forms then emerging, to pay honor to artists at a time when most men looked upon them merely as a form of craftsman. Vasari's story of how Giotto demonstrated his skill by drawing a perfect circle freehand throws as much credit upon Boniface's ability to interpret, as on Giotto's to execute, the subtle gesture.

Giotto came to Rome, but most of his work there, like so much else inspired by Boniface, did not survive. Only fragments remain of the frescoes and mosaics he executed for St. Peter's, but one of those fragments shows a living Boniface. It is a poignant survival, for Giotto painted him in the act of proclaiming that first Jubilee of 1300 which marked at once the apotheosis of his power and the beginning of his downfall.

Boniface VIII was an imposing figure, over six feet tall and proportionately massive, though the hands were curiously delicate and sensitive. He was capable of wearing even that fantastic crown, the towering Oriental tiara of the popes, as though it were part of his normal costume and not an irrelevant weight threatening to topple the wearer. Giotto had no need to flatter, to exaggerate the stature of his subject, in order to allow him to dominate the little group that surrounds him.

Arnolfo's statue reflected the arrogance of the man, but Giotto's painting shows something of introspection and melancholy. Neither artist necessarily contradicted the other. Boniface indubitably possessed the violent, aggressive will to force through a titanic scheme, nothing less than the creation of a world power with one head, but behind the will there had to be a spirit capable of visualizing such a scheme. In the end, neither will nor spirit failed, for

Boniface was defeated not by a man but by the tide of history itself.

Chroniclers throughout Europe referred to Boniface, but it was in Florence that the final judgment was made, the definitive portrait etched. Boniface himself recognized the intellectual status of the Florentines, then gathering themselves for that astonishing burst of activity that culminated in the Renaissance. "You Florentines are the fifth element," he cried out when a group of Florentine ambassadors, each representing a different European or Italian state, ranged themselves before him.

Giovanni Villani gave the first reasoned assessment of the man's character.

> He was very wise in learning and natural wit, and a man very cautious and experienced and of great knowledge and memory. Very haughty he was, and proud and cruel toward his enemies and he was of great heart and much feared by all the people . . . a man of large schemes and lordly who sought for much honor.[16]

Dino Compagni, the young nobleman who recorded the tumultuous events in Florence precipitated by Boniface, echoed Villani. "He was of great boldness and of high understanding, and he guided the Church as he wished and thrust down those who did not consent. He reigned most cruelly, and fomented warfare, undoing many people." [17]

Villani and Compagni were citizens of a merchant city, accustomed to weighing men in the precise scales of commerce where errors of judgment cost money. Villani, particularly, was very much a Florentine in this matter, cautious, sober, disliking the extravagant. In the summaries of these two men occur the key words which appear again and again in the writing of lesser men—haughty, proud, violent, courageous, lordly. Many crimes were laid, with justice, at Boniface's door, but none could deny him the larger qualities.

To the judgment of the prose writers was added the more terrible judgment of the poet Dante Alighieri. Dante hated Boniface with a double hatred, personal and ideological, for Boniface had usurped the sacred role of the emperor and created the conditions in Florence that led to Dante's lifelong exile.

The restlessness of the Florentines was a byword throughout all Italy, accustomed though Italians were to the endless revolutions in the city-states. But Florentine restlessness was purposive, the city moving, though erratically, toward a concept of true political liberty. The year before Boniface had won his crown, the Florentines had passed a remarkable law asserting that all citizens were equal in rights. The Florentines were ever more capable of launching heady political theories than putting even simple ones into practice, but though the new law was ignored as often as it was honored, it acted as a leaven, giving hope to the inarticulate masses. It was an astounding experiment, and dangerously, the Roman people sought to copy it. Boniface smashed the infant republicanism in Rome but was vividly aware of the danger of contagion spreading again from the neighboring Florentine state. Where might such an experiment end?

He hungered, too, after Tuscany: To add this jewel of Italy to his own Papal States, to extend the temporal power of the tiara throughout central Italy—this would be a glory that would enshrine his name forever. He began to work cautiously, conspiring with those discontented Florentine nobles who saw the rise of the people as the end of the state. The intrigues were discovered, his agents fined, and he reacted with his customary violence, threatening excommunication and interdict.

"Is not the Pontiff supreme Lord over all? Do not emperors and kings of the Romans yield submission to us, yet are they not superior to Florence?" He demanded absolute and humble obedience; otherwise he would "inflict the utmost injury on their citizens and merchants, cause their property to be pillaged and confiscated in all parts of the world, release all their debtors from duty of payment." [18]

It was the precise method he had employed with the Colonna. But Florence was not a Roman barony ultimately dependent upon the good will of the Roman pope, but a tough-minded republic that had fought off even bigger enemies than Boniface. Riots and tumult followed in the city between Boniface's allies and the republicans. He hurled a papal army against the city, led by a general bearing the ironical title of Pacifier. The city sent embassies to him, one of them including the magistrate Dante Alighieri. All failed. In a final convulsion, the noble party triumphed over the popular, whose leaders, including Dante, were thrust into exile.

To do Boniface justice, he merely exploited the Florentine genius for discord among themselves. Compagni's account is an unedifying story of talebearers hastening from Florence to Boniface, each hoping to get his story in first and discredit the other side. Apart from the danger of having a republic on the borders of the Papal States, Boniface believed, or was led to believe, that the popular party was in alliance with the Colonna. And that hated name would have caused him to destroy Rome itself, were it necessary.

But whether Boniface was a direct or indirect cause of the tumult that retarded the birth of democracy in Florence, he earned Dante's undying hatred. Later, Dante rationalized that hatred when he developed his theme that mankind could only know happiness under an emperor appointed by God, that the temporal power of the popes was an offense to heaven which condemned all mankind to chaos. In the *Divine Comedy* he drags Boniface through hell, through purgatory, through paradise itself, there to be arraigned before St. Peter, condemned by the apostle himself in an appalling indictment:

> He who usurps my place upon the Earth,
> My place, my place, my place,
> Has made of my cemetery a sewer
> Of blood and stench whereby the Evil One,
> Who fell from here, below there is appeased.[19]

It may be a measure of Boniface's misfortune that while his defense is in the hands of little men—colorless officials grinding out stereotyped posthumous praises—his condemnation is in the language of Dante and Villani. But the rolling periods of these high masters of Italian, though they might distill the essence of the pope, missed something of the man; and it is from the pen of other little men, agents of enemies though they were, that posterity gains the more intimate pictures.

Boniface had a gift for pungent, pithy speech, a liking for witty, frequently punning epigrams which he tossed out regardless of their propriety, indifferent to the fact that busy little men might be recording them. Sexual immorality? Why—there is no more to going to bed with women and boys than in rubbing one hand against the other. Immortality? A man has as much hope of survival after death as that roast fowl on the dining table there—a remark made on a fast day at that, the shocked witness recorded. It was difficult to assess his true beliefs, but his obiter dicta seemed all of a piece: the clever remarks of a learned man who was indifferent to, or even skeptical of, the inner mysteries of the religion he professed. The god that the world saw him worship was the god of power.

The cardinals, who came into intimate daily contact with him, learned to hate him with a personal bitterness that surpassed even Dante's. Inordinately proud men themselves, his pride and arrogance overtopped theirs, crushing them, reducing them to the status of court officials, contemptuously ignored unless their signatures were required on documents. Much of the trouble with the Colonna had sprung from his refusal—his inability—to recognize any will, any objectives but his own.

"The Cardinals all desire his death and are weary of his devilries," Gerald of Albalato, residential envoy from the king of Aragon, reported to his master. Gerald was a toadying little man, eagerly picking up gossip from the "big dogs of the Curia" and relaying it to his master who, like so many others, was waiting for Boniface to make a false step. But Gerald's very spinelessness made him a safe recipient for the spleen of which the cardinals disburdened themselves. "Cardinal Landulf says that it is better to die than to live with such a man. He is all tongue and eyes but as the rest of him is rotten, he won't last much longer. We have the very Devil to deal with." [20]

"All tongue and eyes"—a vivid phrase, summing up the impotent hatred of a subordinate writhing under the lashing of a master of invective, raked by the coldly contemptuous glance of a confident superior. But Landulf's brutal remark that Boniface was rotten gave some explanation for the pope's outbursts of uncontrollable rage. He was a sick man, his old complaints of the gout and the stone exacerbated by the endless problems of high office.

A man of his temperament was unlikely to prove an easy patient and his doctors were endless, each arriving with soothing promises, each departing with burning ears and quaking heart. A quack could very easily be proved to be a heretic, particularly if the patient who suffered his administrations of theriac and crushed diamonds and dried mandrake was the supreme pontiff.

Yet ironically, it was a condemned heretic who preserved Boniface's health, and probably his life. The man was Arnold of Villanova, a Spanish doctor, theologian, and prophet who had already seen the inside of a Paris prison in connection with his heretical book on anti-Christ. He came to Rome to appeal against his condemnation, but Boniface made no official comment on the curious new doctrine that anti-Christ would appear in the next few years.

Arnold proved to be a better physician than prophet, and Boniface was prepared to overlook a spiritual heresy if he could but find a physical cure. The cardinals, at least, thought that Arnold was exclusively responsible for saving Boniface's life—and were singularly unprepared to thank him for it. "Rumor has it, and truly, that the Pope would already have been dead and buried if the master had not come—and what curses they mutter against him I don't think fit to write," [21] Gerald dutifully told his master. Like everybody else he put down Boniface's cure to magic, and certainly part of Arnold's prescription was the wearing of a special loincloth in which cabalistic seals were sewn. Rumor later seized on this and exaggerated it—Boniface was supposed to carry a seal or ring in which an evil spirit dwelled, and to which he sacrificed hair and nails.

But whether it was an evil spirit or commonplace gout which goaded him on, he was intolerable at close quarters. Humiliating his intimates and social subordinates, enraging his distant equals with his soaring claims, of all men Boniface VIII was the architect of his own destruction.

In the year 1299, however, no man could have prophesied his fall. He was at the pinnacle of a unique power, his enemies the Colonna vanquished, his friends in Florence holding their own, the Romans utterly cowed. It was appropriate that in the following year he should launch the first great Jubilee of the Roman Church, when Christians in tens of thousands came to Rome as to their natural home.

In proclaiming Jubilee, Boniface was for once speaking as the mouthpiece of inarticulate Christians, even though he was thus able to trumpet his glory to the world.

Throughout the closing weeks of the dying century, more and more little groups of pilgrims had been entering Rome. Unconsciously, they were performing a Christian version of an ancient ceremony, for the pagans too had flocked to the mother city of Europe to mark the turn of the century with appropriate solemnity. Boniface found good enough precedent to transform a pagan into a Christian centennial ceremony; and on February 22, 1300, he proclaimed the bull that launched the Jubilee.

The official blessing of the instinctual urge created a fantastic, continent-wide enthusiasm. For the last time, Rome appeared again as the center of Europe, its ancient splendor as the seat of all authority deepened by its Christian significance. Jerusalem was lost to the infidel, the crusades were dying in bitterness and disillusion; Rome therefore became the chief goal of all pilgrims. The population of the city expanded by some thirty thousand. The Romans themselves estimated that two million people entered their gates during the year, and though doubtless they exaggerated, it seemed to observers in the cities that lay on the pilgrim road as though all Europe were on the move.

The land for once was at peace. The harvest that year was good: Bread and wine, meat and fish, were so cheap and plentiful that even the habitual rapacity of the Roman shopkeepers could be kept under control. The city fathers established good order, a fact that deeply impressed those who had had personal experience of this Mother of Europe. At the city gates, committees from their own nations awaited pilgrims, shepherding them through the complexities of what was still the greatest city in Europe. In the first chaotic weeks, people were crushed to death by the milling crowds, particularly in that stretch of road which ran over the bridge of Sant' Angelo and approached St. Peter's. The magistrates instituted a species of one-way traffic over the bridge, and the endless, shuffling throng passing docilely beneath the brooding castle vividly struck the imagination of at least one pilgrim. Years afterward, Dante's mind turned back to Rome in the Easter of 1300, and the memory of that procession became transferred into the vision of lost souls dolefully but obediently shuffling across the infernal bridge into hell.

Villani too came to Rome that year, and moved by the city's past glory, was inspired to write the history of his own. All the world was there, he thought. Every European tongue could again be heard in the streets, every variation of national costume could be seen, from the rough furs of Tartars to the silks and brocades of Venetians. Passing through the gates, each was caught up in the slow, inexorable current that took the crowds through the narrow streets, over the bridge, up the great flight of steps that led to the basilica and brought them at length to the tomb of Peter. There, crushed in a solid human mass, they prayed as best they might, and before leaving, cast their offerings before the altar.

"Day and night two clerics stood in front of the altar of St. Peter, holding rakes in their hand with which they gathered in an infinite quantity of money." [22] The sight of the servants of the Fisherman netting not men but gold provided excellent ammunition for the enemies of Boniface. The entire Jubilee was merely a moneymaking device, they gibed, yet another method to gain gold for the Gaetani. But the money gathered in was the copper of the poor rather than the gold of the rich, and probably barely covered expenses.

For, not quite all the world was there. The bull had specifically excluded the enemies of the Church, among whom were numbered the Colonna and all who aided and cherished them. But absent, too, were the great ones of Europe. No monarch came to pray at the tomb of Peter and kneel at the foot of his splendid successor—and thereby confess not only his spiritual but his temporal superiority. In the person of Boniface was again combined—at least on his own showing—the twin attributes of priest and king. He, Gaetani, was Pope-Caesar.

The long-drawn battle between pope and emperor had ended in

the total debasement of the empire. The vast potential had wasted away, dwindling now to a tedious squabble between two rival claimants in Germany. One at last overthrew the other and assumed the style of Holy Roman Emperor—but deemed it prudent to get ratification from Pope Boniface. The imperial envoys were met with scorn. "Emperor? I—I am the emperor," the pope replied. Or so his enemies said, and went on to give details of the charade that followed: how Boniface clad himself in the imperial purple, wearing the red buskins of imperial office together with the gilt shoes and spurs, with the great sword in his hand and the cross on his breast. Again, the enemies of the man probably overelaborated the tale. But the thronging thousands in the city took it as gospel, seeing nothing inherently improbable in the playacting of a self-consciously splendid pope, and took home with them the news that the Lord of Europe was to be found again in Rome.

Challenge and Response

But even while the endless processions of pilgrims to Rome seemed to betoken a golden age for the Papacy, the final challenge to its predominance was being framed in France. The clash came over the exacting of gold, not over some deeply held matter of faith or some aspect of affronted pride. But it served to topple Boniface.

The king in France was Philip IV—le Bel, his flatterers called him, for he possessed great physical beauty though seemingly little else. Villani summed up Philip's character accurately enough with that cool, Florentine insight of his. He granted that the king had virtues as a knight, "but he was inordinately pleasure-seeking. He loved the chase above all, and allowed others to use his power to rule his realm. He was generally swayed by ill-counsel, to which he lent a too ready credence whence many perils came to his reign." [23] On his deathbed, looking back over his stormy and disastrous life, Philip endorsed the Florentine's verdict: "Bad counsel has been my ruin." [24]

Money was the origin of the trouble between him and Boniface because Philip needed money to maintain supremacy in a land still torn by feudal struggles. He needed money to finance wars against barons almost as powerful as himself, money to fight the endless war with England. He tried every expediency, from debasing the coin to outright increase of taxes. The nobles were exempt. It was the little people of France who were called upon to pay, to yield a tenth, a quarter, a half of their pitiful earnings or produce to finance an extravagant court and a war that was bleeding the land dry. The lawyers who surrounded the king devised ever more ingenious means of extracting wealth, and to enforce their decrees, a ferocious body of tax collectors created more hatred than did the soldiers of the enemy king.

Inevitably, Philip turned to the immense reservoir of wealth that the church in France possessed. Boniface had provided him with a useful precedent by diverting crusading funds to a private war; and Philip could claim, with justice, that the money obtained from French priests was to be used for the defense of France. He began to milk the enormous wealthy Cistercian order. As monks, the Cistercian abbots had no other superior but the pope himself. By-passing the bishops of France, they were therefore able to protest directly to Boniface.

Boniface responded with his favorite method, a resounding bull in which his vast legal knowledge could be deployed to its greatest effect. The bull openly admitted what everyone had known for years—that the laity cherished a deep and increasing hostility for the clergy. It was therefore his duty to protect his servants, and he forbade, under threat of excommunication, any attempt whatsoever to extract any form of money from any of the clergy without direct permission of the Holy See.

Philip struck back promptly. The day before the bull was due to come into operation, his lawyers promulgated a decree forbidding the export of money in any form or for any purpose whatsoever, and at the same time forbidding foreigners to reside in the country. It was a double blow at Boniface: The rich revenue from the French church was immediately dried up and officials of his curia in France became technically illegal residents.

But behind the wrangle over money was a far deeper issue. Europe was emerging, for good or ill, from the sleep of centuries, but the form it was taking would be totally different from that it had worn before. The last of the great emperors had been in his tomb for over a century, and the land mass that had once been an empire was breaking up into permanent nation-states. Some, such as England, had already found their center, and with it, their identity. Others, such as France, were still seeking theirs. The war with England was one expression of the new French nation seeking to define and defend its own. The struggle with Boniface was another and deeper expression of that nationalism. The struggle was framed for the most part in arid, legal terms as Boniface, the great lawyer, fought the lesser but still formidable lawyers grouped around Philip. To the common people it must have seemed an incomprehensible warfare, its weapons composed of polysyllabic Latin terms, but its result was to affect them deeply. The question it sought to answer was simple: Was there but one lord in Europe?

After the launching of the bull, both Boniface and Philip hesitated from taking irrevocable action. In successive letters, the pope reduced the impact of his bull and the king did not pursue the question of the export of money. But the natures of the two men were far too similar to allow a permanent settlement based on compromise. Over the next three years, Philip again and again acted in French affairs that touched upon the affairs of Rome—the arresting of a treasonable bishop, the sequestering of French funds that happened to have passed through ecclesiastical coffers. "Thereupon a great controversy now sprung up between the lord king and the lord pope, increasing each day as each side hurled thundering letters one at the other." Papal and royal messengers, struggling through the Alpine passes during the winter of 1301, must have had cause to regret that both their masters had chosen this form of warfare.

In December, 1301, Boniface activated the dormant bull that forbade taxation of the clergy, and followed it up with a summons to the French bishops to appear before him in Rome "to take counsel touching the excesses, crimes, and acts of violence committed by the king of France and his officers" on the body of Holy Church. The bishops, torn between king and pope, their loyalties already inclining to the nationalist side, pleaded with their furious superior to abate, if possible, his demands.

It was not possible. In the same month, Boniface dispatched another bull, with the deceptively mild opening, "Listen, my son," in which he restated the papal claims. It was couched in moderate language, but the sentiment remained unchanged: The Papacy held power over all and defiance invited interdict—economic, social, and spiritual death. Philip replied with a remarkably childish series of insults. "To Boniface, who calls himself pope, little or no greeting. Let your stupendous fatuity know that in temporal matters we are subject to no man." [25]

Boniface, no man to accept insult without interest, retorted: "Our predecessors have deposed three kings of France. Know—we can depose you like a stable boy if it prove necessary." [26] He summoned the bishops again, this time under threat of excommunication. Philip, in his turn, called a council in which the crimes of Boniface, real and imaginary, were held up for all France, all Europe, to see: simony, sodomy, parricide, nepotism, heresy—a vile

Dante. Bronze, 16th century. National Museum, Naples.

Avignon. Palace of the Popes and Cathedral.

Left: — Philip IV of France. Abbey, St. Denis.

Facing page: — *St. Catherin*, Andrea Vanni. Church of *, Domenico, Sien*

Below: — Joanna of Naples. Church of the Incoronata, Naples.

Gregory XI Returning
from Avignon. Vasari.
The Vatican, Rome.

Sarcophagus of Pope
Urban VI. The Vatican,
Rome.

catalog whose compilation was not excused even by the violent emotions of the contest. Boniface, it was said, smiled at the charge of heresy. "We were good Catholics as long as we favored the cause of King Philip." [27]

Swiftly, the quarrel grew. Philip widened his appeal, turning from the lawyers to the people, making his personal battle a national cause. The States General was summoned in April, 1302, the first effective meeting of the Three Estates, the French nation in council. The clergy, responding to the current, aligned themselves with the king and from the pulpits of their churches the attack on Boniface was mounted. Not all thought it prudent to sever themselves from Rome. In November forty-five bishops and abbots attended the much postponed council. And from that council emanated the last trumpet call of the papal monarchy as conceived by Boniface—the great bull *Unam Sanctam*.

It was Boniface's supreme effort as lawyer. It stated nothing new, for ever since the Papacy had become a power independent of both emperor and Rome, the popes great and small had acted on the assumption that they now held both the sword and the keys. But *Unam Sanctam* made explicit what had been implicit: "It is necessary for salvation that all human creatures shall be subject to the Roman Pontiff." [28] Temporal power throughout the earth lay in the hands of the pope; he could, and did, delegate it to monarchs and princes but he could, and would, withdraw it as he chose.

In February of the following year, 1303, while the battle between king and pope raged publicly, a group of Frenchmen met in considerable privacy to prepare, at the king's request, certain plans. The leader of the group was a self-made lawyer, William Nogaret, who had climbed to his present position largely by virtue of his dedication to the king's financial health. He claimed the honor of having already crossed swords, in person, with the formidable Boniface. According to his account, he had gone on the Jubilee pilgrimage, obtained a private audience with the pope and there exhorted him to mend his ways. If the story was true, the interview must have been well worth witnessing.

It was Nogaret who had been responsible for the remarkably foul attack upon Boniface made in the king's council in the previous year, for he had a gift for scurrility, a liking for the seamier side of the law. In that speech he had hinted at the possibility of violence, which was now being discussed in secret. The conspirators had invited an Italian expert to be present at their meeting—Sciarra Colonna, survivor of the holy war of 1298.

In the summer of 1303 Boniface had escaped the heat of Rome and was living in the little town of Anagni, some thirty-seven miles from Rome. Anagni could not claim the high antiquity of Tusculum or Palestrina, it could boast of no links with the great pagan names of the past, but it possessed, instead, a far more valuable connection with the present. It was the birthplace of Benedict Gaetani who, as pope, had showered many great favors upon it.

Boniface had no particular liking for Rome—few of Rome's great citizens actually lived there from choice. The most competent civil government would have now found it impossible to arrest, much less reverse, the process of decay, and competent civil governments in Rome were increasingly rare. Collapsing walls, blocked streets, nonfunctioning sewage systems, and scarcity of water made the great city a penance to be endured, quite apart from the risk of casual violence that was an everyday pattern of life. Boniface had therefore made a habit of traveling from one of the smaller hill cities to the other.

Anagni was his favorite town, and there a great papal palace had arisen to challenge the bulk of the cathedral. The town was the heartland of the growing Gaetani state, and as such, its citizens had grown rich. Here, of all places in Europe, Boniface felt at home, secure among a people whose well-being coexisted with his own. It was from here that the great bulls had been sent winging across the Alps to explode in France. It was here that he heard that the French parliament had met for the second time, on June 13 of this same summer, and had named him as heretic and called upon a council of the church to depose him. And it was at Anagni that he had drawn up his final bull, excommunicating Philip of France, declaring him expelled from Christian society, freeing all his subjects from obedience. He had even dated the bull—September 8,

1303—but it remained as yet among the documents of the chancery, a mere piece of parchment until it had been promulgated. It was to remain forever a mere piece of parchment.

Shortly before dawn on the morning of September 6, a large band of armed men entered the gates of Anagni. They were led by Sciarra Colonna, come at last to taste his dish of revenge served cold. Throughout that summer he and Nogaret had been in Tuscany, executing the plot that had been planned in Paris in February. Financed by the king, they had gone through Italy, seeking the enemies of Boniface, skillfully, swiftly, secretly drawing a net around him. They had found ample support from men eager, as Colonna was eager, for revenge; the gold was almost an irrelevancy. Even in Anagni itself, traitors had been found to open the vital gate.

Boniface was asleep in the great palace when he was awakened by the clatter and shouting of mailed men in the streets. The militia of Anagni were passive, believing—or affecting to believe—Nogaret's statement that they had come to invite Boniface to a council. But Boniface was not wholly helpless. The immensely strong papal palace, designed with just such a contingency in mind, was defended by his nephews. But the soldiers they commanded swiftly deserted, the nephews surrendered, and Boniface was alone, the cardinals present in Anagni having fled at the first uproar.

It seemed that Boniface was wholly immune to fear, for when at last Sciarra and Nogaret entered the palace, they found him as he always appeared at moments of supreme crisis. He was seated upon the throne, crowned with the great tiara, dressed in the splendid pontifical robes, awaiting his death in silence. The sight of him maddened Colonna, who strode across the chamber, raised a dagger, and would have plunged it into the old man if Nogaret had not caught his arm.

For three days Boniface was kept in close imprisonment. Both Nogaret and Colonna seemed to be at a loss, as though they had not expected this sudden success. They talked of dragging their prisoner in chains to Lyons to be tried, but while they debated, the citizens of Anagni underwent a tardy repentance and fell upon the invaders. Nogaret and Sciarra escaped, and Boniface was freed and taken back to Rome.

But his power was utterly broken during the three days that he remained prisoner. Enemies of the Gaetani arose, occupying the lands that had been stolen from them. In turn, the Gaetani collected allies and fought back, and faction took the place of the calm that had been enforced by the old man's iron will. For that will was now as broken as his power. During the remaining month of his life he locked himself away in the Lateran, suspicious of all visitors, planning insane revenges. "He was out of his mind," a contemporary recorded. "He believed that everyone who came near him would take him a prisoner." [29] Rumor spread that he gnawed the flesh from his arms, ultimately killing himself by beating his head against the wall. But rumor lied. He died in utter despair, but of natural causes, not by his own hand. And with him died the last true Roman emperor.

"Know that thou art the father of princes and kings—the ruler of the world." So had run the formula at Boniface's coronation; he had taken it literally and to its logical end, and—as logically—had been destroyed. But even those who had writhed under his arrogance pronounced themselves appalled at the manner of his going. Dante, who had hated Benedict Gaetani with all the hatred that one man could feel for another, yet shared the sense of outrage that all Italians—all Europeans—felt for the sacrilege that had been committed on the person of Pope Boniface.

> I see the fleur-de-lys Anagni enter
> And Christ in his own Vicar captive made
> I see him yet another time derided
> I see renewed the vinegar and the gall
> And between living thieves I see him slain.[30]

The elegy that Dante wrote for Boniface did not cancel the fierce indictments made of the same pope; and neither Dante nor his contemporaries were aware of any contradiction in the attitude. The Vicar of Christ and the papal monarch were two distinct beings. The fact that it was impossible to whittle down one to size without offending the other was the paradox that lay at the heart of papal power, and from which it drew its temporal strength so long as the greater body of Europeans acknowledged its spiritual supremacy.

Benedict XI, Boniface's brief-lived successor, roundly cursed the place that by its citizens' apathy had contributed to the outrage. "O, miserable Anagni—that thou shouldst have allowed such a deed to be committed within thee. May neither dew nor rain fall upon thee, for though thou couldst have defended him, the hero fell and he who was girded with power was vanquished." [31]

Benedict, though he did not know it, was also pronouncing the funeral oration for the heroic period of the Papacy. He survived for less than a year and then a Frenchman, Clement V, was elected in France, remained there, and so turned the universal church into a chapel for the French king. Philip, seeking to lay forever the splendid, arrogant ghost of Boniface, instituted a posthumous trial to have him condemned as heretic and therefore not pope. But Clement, pliant creature of the king though he was, cheated him of this last satisfaction. The trial never came to a verdict.

IV

The Wandering Pope

Bartolomeo Prignano

Pope Urban VI (1378–1389)

Avignon, September, 1376

Since the dark hours of the morning, a silent crowd had been gathering before the Palace of the Popes, the vast building that towered like a white mountain over the narrow, evil-smelling streets of Avignon. Within the palace officials were still scurrying about the last tasks imposed upon them by the sudden and astounding decision of Pope Gregory VII. For months—indeed, for years—there had been rumors that the Papacy would return to Italy, but the wise had long since learned to discount them. The Papacy could never return to that violent and treacherous land.

Then there had come the visit by the volatile, urgent, eloquent Sienese maiden, Catherine Benincasa, who had turned the full force of her personality on Gregory—threatening, urging, pleading with him to return. Yet even then the worldly-wise had had few misgivings. There was no reason why this curious, untutored mystic should succeed when giants like Dante and Petrarch had failed only too dismally. Skillfully, the Avignonese courtiers had set about discrediting her.

Gregory, after first welcoming her, had cautiously edged away and the rumors died down again. Then, almost overnight, the tormented pontiff had made his decision: The curia would return to Rome. Once made, the decision could not be rescinded; the heavy baggage had already gone ahead and now, on this morning of September 13, the court itself was leaving.

By midmorning it seemed that all of Avignon and most of the surrounding county was packed into the square and the streets around the palace. The departure of the curia spelled financial disaster for the scores of thousands of merchants and artisans who had earned good livings from the munificent popes. Inexorably, Avignon would return to that provincial status from which it had been so unexpectedly elevated seventy years before; and the wealth of Europe, channeled through the multifarious agencies of the universal church, would again bypass it. The crowd had come to witness the end of a glorious period—or perhaps to hope for a miracle which would change the mind of Gregory.

Late in the morning Gregory came out of the palace, a man still young in years for he was not yet forty-five, but a man already bowed, wracked, and almost broken after months as the target of conflicting parties. Every political and personal consideration inclined him to remain in this safe and luxurious city upon the Rhône. His cardinals regarded the departure with a mixture of rage and despair—and he knew too well the fragile loyalty of an Avignonese cardinal. He wanted to stay, for staying was rational; he was being propelled, and with him the whole vast apparatus of the curia, by a wholly irrational force. Standing on the steps he looked out over the crowd for a moment, then he moved forward; at that, his aged father threw himself to the ground at Gregory's feet in a last melodramatic gesture. "My son, where are you going?" he cried out. "It is written," Gregory answered heavily, "that thou shalt trample on the asp and the basilisk," [1] and he stepped over his father's body. There was another delay a moment later when the mule he attempted to mount reared and refused to accept him. He stood woodenly, ignoring the muttering of omens and signs, until another mule was brought. This proved tractable and he mounted it; followed by his court, he rode out of the city on the first stage of the long and perilous journey to Rome.

Bartolomeo Prignano, archbishop of Bari and assistant to the vice-chancellor of the curia, was a member of the cortege. The most vital part of the curia, indeed, could not have moved without him, for in his care were the seven offices of the chancery, each with its scores of scribes, lawyers, engrossers, bullatores; its tens of thousands of parchment documents, its seals, its ribbons—the physical expression of the spider's web that Avignon had woven around Christendom. "The little bishop" they called him—mockingly, not affectionately, for there was nothing in this Neapolitan lawyer to inspire affection. He was a short, plump man, heavy-featured, his naturally sallow complexion muddied by years of indifferent food and confinement in airless, cluttered offices.

Unlike the majority of the high officials of the Avignonese curia, Prignano had come up the hard way, not eased into high office through his family's princely connections. He was indeed a living example of the principle that only through the church could a nonmilitary man make any kind of a career. Born in a Naples slum, still speaking with a thick Neapolitan accent, he was now an archbishop. But it was a hollow enough honor, given to him only because a bureaucrat at his level had to have a title. Even his office was ambiguous: There was no chancellor—business of that importance was handled by the pope himself—and he was merely assistant to the vice-chancellor, an arrogant Frenchman who treated him with contempt. The possibility that Prignano would make the final jump and become cardinal was extremely remote. It needed more than dedication to clerical duties, legal skill, and financial integrity to become a prince of the church, a member of that tiny Sacred College in whose hands lay the gift of the Papacy. It needed both influence and money and Prignano had little of either. It needed, too, a powerful monarch behind a candidate to bribe or threaten the pontiff, and Prignano's monarch, Joanna, queen of Naples, could afford to do neither. She was still indebted to Avignon for the little matter of absolution for her husband's murder and was unlikely to jeopardize her position by exerting herself unduly for her archbishop.

At fifty-eight, therefore, Bartolomeo Prignano had probably reached the highest level he was ever going to reach. True, the work of the chancery was far more complex and potentially important than ever before in the history of the curia. After the tremendous fall of Boniface, the curia had abandoned much of its position. Canon lawyers still poured out treatises which established, to the writers' satisfaction at least, the temporal supremacy of the pope. The curia still interfered where a timid monarch or a confused situation allowed the Papacy to exert temporal rights—the endless war in Italy that engulfed over half the revenue was there to prove that fact. But, for most practical purposes, the Avignonese Papacy had been content to withdraw from the world in order to amass not merit but gold.

The fiscal machinery of the church, with its lines passing through the greatest monarchs down to the humblest country priest, was perhaps the most efficient system ever devised for a continent-wide extraction of gold. And with these extractions went their records—the enabling bulls, the reports of legates, letters, petitions—the rustle of parchment inevitably accompanying the chink of gold. All these documents, circling through Europe, passed at some stage through the hands of Bartolomeo Prignano. Sitting passive in his dusty office he probably knew more about the activities of the curia than any of the cardinals peacocking their way through the gorgeous chambers of the palace.

Savage, dictatorial to his inferiors, taciturn toward his superiors, a bitter, frustrated man—this was Avignon's opinion of Prignani when it bothered to have an opinion. Apart from reasons of personal ambition, there was ground enough for Prignani's bitterness. Buried deep within him, almost strangled by the legal web in which he moved, was a very genuine piety that was offended by the gross luxury of the Avignonese court. He was by no means alone in his opinion of Avignon as a corrupt and corrupting center—the "Babylon of the West." It had been Petrarch, the great scholar and poet, who gave it that vivid name which its many enemies seized upon. Prignano may have suspected the man and been puzzled by the adulation accorded to this spinner of words, this exponent of a new-fangled scholarship; as he was later suspicious of, and puzzled by, that other word-spinner—Catherine of Siena with her supernatural voices and very earthly nagging. But though he might disapprove of their manner, he could not possibly disagree with their matter—the indictment of Avignon as a sink of all that was luxurious and offensive to his puritan nature.

He, who treated food as a fuel, could not be astounded by the fantastic banquets with which the pope and cardinals regaled each other and visiting potentates—banquets in which each of the endless courses, served in massive gold, were heralded and overwhelmed by a profusion of gifts ranging from jewels to horses. He, who habitually wore the coarsest and plainest of clothes, could not but be contemptuous of the silks and furs that caressed the tender skins of French prelates—cloth of gold from Damascus, silks from Tuscany, brocades from Venice, East and West contributing their exotica for the adornment of pope and cardinals, all paid for from the gold of the church.

There was little wonder that Avignon had constant need of

money. "Whenever I entered the chambers of the ecclesiastics I found brokers and clergy engaged in weighing and reckoning the money which lay in heaps before them." [2] So his predecessor at the chancery, Alvaro Prelayo, had written—himself as staunch a defender of the Papacy as Prignano but, like him, filled with foreboding as to where this golden dance of pleasure must end.

But in the end, it was not the luxury of Avignon that offended Prignano so much as the character of these French popes. There had been six of them at Avignon, some good if weak men, some miserly, some jovial hedonists—all of them disastrous. "Our two Clements have destroyed more of the Church than seven of your Gregories could restore," [3] a French prelate confided to Petrarch.

First there had been Clement V, the timorous pope who had brought the Papacy to Avignon and cowered beneath the French king. Then had come John XXII—the Banker of Avignon they called him. He destroyed the little friars who had arisen with their terrible heresy that Christ and his disciples had been poor men, that the amassing of wealth was contrary to his teaching. It was John who had created the fantastically complex financial system, making church preferments a kind of chess game, at every move of which a shower of gold fell into Avignon. There had been a smell of heresy about him but a deathbed confession had expunged it, and perhaps better evidence of orthodoxy, he had left the treasury richer by four million florins.

The whirling dance had been briefly halted by John's successor—Benedict XII, the burly, hard-drinking son of a carpenter, a great persecutor of heretics but an honest man with an astonishing hatred of nepotism. The relatives who flocked to Avignon on the golden news of his election were turned away with pithy apothegms. "As Jacques Fournier I knew you—as pope I know you not." And, "A pope should be like Melchizedek—without father, mother or genealogy."

Europe knew a brief cessation from the rapacities of tax collectors, for Benedict, as competent as he was frugal, was able to run the church on less than a quarter of what his predecessors had demanded, and still had enough left over to finance the Italian wars and to found the great palace in Avignon. He died, and his epitaph was the hatred and mockeries of the court. "He was a hard, obstinate, avaricious man," one of the papal courtiers wrote, trumpeting after the man's death what he had not dared to whisper during his life. "He loved the good overmuch, and hated the bad. He was remiss in granting favors, and negligent in ceremonial matters. He was more addicted to unseemly jests than to polite conversation. He drank heavily so that the phrase *Let us drink like a pope* became current in his lifetime. He was a Nero—a viper to the clergy." [4] The cardinals, anxious to forget the taste of enforced austerity, with remarkable unanimity elected a man after their own heart: Pierre Roger de Beaufort, son of the lord of Rosiers, kinsman of the French king—a happy, splendid priest with a vast taste for the table, considerable culture, and an indiscreet love of women. He called himself Clement VI and was all that the cardinals could have asked for. The indiscriminate largess which he scattered at the opening of his reign made heavy inroads in Avignon's accumulated wealth, alarmed the treasury officials. "My predecessors did not know how to be popes," Clement lightly returned to their protests. "A prince's only duty is to send his subjects away contented." [5]

It was an excellent principle for the nearby subjects in Avignon, less attractive for the more distant subjects who ultimately did the paying. "The Apostles were commissioned to lead the sheep into pasture, not shear them," Edward of England snarled and his parliament set about creating some form of barrier against the steady drain of gold. But gold continued to pour into Avignon, the fiscal system keeping pace even with Clement's demands.

And the demands were huge. Artists were summoned to cover the bare walls of the palace with glowing frescoes. Goldsmiths, furriers, mercers, embroiderers, every type of worker in precious fabrics and metals, every merchant who could bring rare products found a ready market in the court of this splendid pope, precursor of the Renaissance. But it was not so much the extravagance that aroused the rage of moralists, as another more dubious channel through which the gold of St. Peter was diverted.

Clement made no secret of his liking for feminine company. Villani, the sober Florentine merchant, noted disapprovingly that

. . . when he was an archbishop he did not keep away from women
but lived in the manner of young nobles, nor did he as pope try to
control himself. Noble ladies had the same access to his chambers
as did prelates and, among others, the Countess of Turenne was so
intimate with him that, in large part, he distributed his favors
through her.[6]

Villani, living in distant Italy and citizen of a city ever at odds
with the Papacy, might have been prejudiced, but Petrarch, living
in Avignon, was more explicit and considerably more venomous.
Clement had done much for the young poet, and according to
Petrarch's own story, was anxious to do more. Nevertheless, in that
terrible series of letters in which he attacked Avignon—letters he
was careful not to publish—it was Clement whom Petrarch held
responsible for the scandal of Christendom: Clement and his countess, "this ecclesiastical Dionysius with his obscene and infamous
artifices and his Semiramis, soiled with incestuous embraces." [7]
Courtiers came to know that the beautiful countess of Turenne
held the keys to high office; she and her family grew rich on that
knowledge.

With Clement's death the woeful story began to end, excess
bringing about its own correction. And no longer was it a mere
academic point as to whether or not the true seat of the Papacy was
in Rome: Unless the Papacy returned, it would lose the vital States
of the Church on which the monarchy was founded. All Italy was
on the brink of revolt, exasperated beyond endurance by the incompetence and cruelty of the Avignonese legates. The mild and
virtuous Urban V, who succeeded Clement, at last yielded to the
growing demands and took the curia back to Rome. But throughout
his brief sojourn he had been under constant pressure from his
cardinals who pined for the comforts of Avignon, and under constant military attack from the Italians for whom the Papacy was
now a French power. Urban sadly came back to Avignon and his
cardinals rejoiced. The experiment, it seemed, was at an end.

But when Urban died and Gregory took his place, the pleas from
Italy were renewed. Petrarch, an old man now but still fiery in his

passionate love for Rome, his passionate hatred for Avignon, had taken up his pen again. And finally, four months earlier, in June, 1376, there had come the strangest and most powerful of all Italian advocates: Catherine Benincasa, the daughter of a dyer from Siena, a woman whom Italians already regarded as a saint.

Prignano had already met Catherine. She had come as an envoy from the city of Florence to plead its case before Gregory. The Florentines had been the leaders of the recent revolt in Italy against the Papacy, and in consequence their city was under an interdict. For months they had seen their dead buried without ceremony, their newborn ushered into the world without baptism, the churches closed, themselves treated as outlaws. They had rebelled again, forced the priests to continue their duties, known even greater penalties, and at last accepted Catherine's offer to go to Avignon on their behalf.

It was a stormy path that she took: The Florentines changed their minds and disavowed her while she was still in Avignon. But though she had failed in her political mission, she adopted with even greater passion her spiritual mission—the joining of the shepherd to his flock. Prignano had not been present at the first meeting between saint and pope, but he knew all about it —as did all Avignon. He knew Catherine had begun the interview with a vigorous denunciation of Avignon—here, where the heart of the church lay, she said, she had expected paradise and found instead a filthy hell. When Gregory asked, reasonably enough, how she could know this in the few hours she had been in the city, she retorted: "In the name of God, I tell you that while living in my own city where I was born I have seen more filthiness of sin committed in the Roman curia than they themselves have seen who actually live here, and do commit such sins here." [8] Gregory had nothing with which to counter this psychic claim and wisely kept silent. She withdrew from that first interview the victor.

Such stories swiftly developed into legend. The gossips of Avignon gleefully repeated the tale of the cardinal's mistress who attempted to approach her and how Catherine drew back in actual physical disgust. "If you but knew how she stank of sin," Catherine protested to a companion who reproached her for the tactless gesture. These manifestations of a saint were little likely to appeal to the worldly court of Avignon; even less likely when the cardinals knew that Catherine's whole object was to root them out of their comfortable lives and plunge them into the caldron of Italy. A dedicated campaign of denigration was put in motion, and Gregory was buffeted on both sides—urged forward by Catherine, pulled back by his cardinals.

As far as Prignano was concerned, Catherine represented all that he most distrusted: the mysticism that had given birth to innumerable heresies over the past century; the interference of women in ecclesiastical politics; the bubbling enthusiasms. Everything that was rational in him, everything that loved order, was repelled by her. Originally he had belonged to the band of her traducers, but gradually he too fell victim to her eloquence and passed from hostile neutrality to passive support. He did not come out into the open— partisanship was foreign to him. But in his molelike manner, working deviously behind the scenes, he contributed to that hidden but powerful current which suddenly swept Gregory and the curia out of the shelter it had known for seventy-three years. Catherine left Avignon on the same day that the court did, but she traveled separately, intending to return to her private life. But she and Prignano were to meet again, under very curious circumstances, in the very heart of the caldron—Rome.

Schism: Rome, 1378

Eighteen months after he had left Avignon, Gregory lay dying in Rome, bitterly repenting, so a Frenchman said, that he had listened to the prophesies of visionaries and brought the Church to Rome, and to the edge of disaster. There had been a brief honeymoon with the city during the first few days after his arrival, the Romans welcoming the apparent return of their wealth and glory. But now Rome no longer spoke for Italy. Throughout the peninsula, cities were rising in national rebellion against the appalling papal mercenaries who were the heralds of the Vicar of Christ.

Gregory had placed little faith in Catherine's assurance that Italy waited like a child for its father and had sent ahead one of the princes of the Church to prepare his path.

Robert, cardinal of Geneva—a lame and squinting man with an unquenchable thirst for blood, whose preferred costume was a suit of armor, whose preferred companions were ruffianly mercenaries— descended into Italy at the head of a horde of Breton mercenaries who were feared and loathed even by their colleagues in the trade. Hostile and friendly cities were subjected to the same treatment.

The little city of Cesena, which throughout had remained faithful to the pope, was goaded into rebellion by the Bretons quartered in the city. Robert of Geneva thereupon loosed another gang of mercenaries upon the citizens, and during a night and day of massacre, four thousand citizens were murdered and the rest thrust into exile. The news spread rapidly and the massacre acted as a catalyst throughout northern Italy, transforming sporadic mutiny into national rebellion.

It was against such a background that the wretched Gregory attempted to reestablish the Papacy in Italy. Like Urban, he was subjected to the protests of his cardinals as well as the missiles of Italians; like Urban, he would have abandoned his project, but death came for him in Rome. In his last days' illness he saw clearly enough what lay ahead. The iron law of the conclave decreed that a pope had to be elected in the same place where his predecessor died, and an election under the present conditions was going to place a great, perhaps an intolerable, strain upon the machinery of the conclave.

In an attempt to forestall the inevitable, he issued a bull decreeing that the conclave should meet without waiting for the five cardinals who had remained in Avignon as caretakers; that a two-thirds majority only would be needed; and, significant of where his fears lay, that the elected pope should be recognized even if there were a dissenting minority. He also ensured that Castel Sant' Angelo should remain in the hands of a French garrison. He died on March 27. Eleven days later the conclave met, the first that Romans had seen, or that Italians could influence, for seventy-four years.

The only thing that was known for certain about the coming conclave was that there was going to be trouble, for the tumultuous Roman mob was abroad. The city magistrates did what they could. A block and ax were set up in St. Peter's Square as public warning, influential nobles were banished, and the gate garrisons reinforced. But the magistrates also thought it worthwhile to warn the cardinals that their lives would be at stake if a Roman, or at least an Italian, pope were not elected. The mob pressed around the cardinals as they made their way to the Vatican, bellowing, "Roman or Italian, we will have a Roman or Italian!" Jean Froissart, the French chronicler, giving a characteristically confused account of the affair, recorded the picturesque threat: "Give us a Roman pope—or we will make your heads redder than your hats." [9]

There were sixteen cardinals in Rome at the time, ten of whom were French and only four of whom were Italians. But the French were themselves divided into two factions—the Limousin and the French, so-called—each as jealous of the other as of the Italians. The Limousins had already engineered the election of three of the Avignonese popes and were determined to maintain their lucrative hold. Their compatriots and rivals were so determined to prize that hold from them that they might even throw in their lot with the Italians. Robert of Geneva, the Butcher of Cesena, belonged by birth to none of the national groups but had thrown in his lot with the French. The sixteenth cardinal, the Spaniard Pedro de Luna, was neutral.

In the late afternoon of April 7, the cardinals were enclosed in an upper chamber of the Vatican, for the ancient Lateran Palace was a burned-out shell. Throughout the evening until far into the night the mob seethed outside. Drunken rioters forced their way into the lower room, piled up inflammable material, even attempted to thrust lances through the ceiling into the room above. Dawn was signaled by the great bell of the Capitol suddenly ringing out in the alarm called *a stormo,* the universal Italian signal for a call to arms. It was answered immediately by the bells of St. Peter's, and though both alarms were rung unofficially by rioting groups, it was a reminder to the fear-stricken French that they were in an enemy city. They had come at length to a realization that an Italian would have to be presented as pope—but each of the four Italians present was disqualified by circumstances: The cardinals of Milan and Florence came from cities recently at open war with the Papacy; the cardinal of St. Peter's was too old; Cardinal Orsini was too young and too ambitious. It was he who first made the dangerous suggestion that they should elect a temporary pope and later choose another in a place of safety. The suggestion was rejected then but remembered later, with embellishments. Listing the disadvantages, the cardinal of Limoges voiced the growing feeling that the candidate must come from outside the Sacred College. He therefore proposed Bartolomeo Prignano. After a moment's silence, the others agreed and Orsini went to the window to announce their choice.

The noise outside had grown steadily and Orsini's words were misinterpreted, leading to a bizarre scene. He apparently called out, "Go to St. Peter's," and the crowd assumed that it was the cardinal of St. Peter's who had been elected. A French prelate tried to correct the error, calling out "Bari, Bari," whereupon the Romans believed that they had been tricked, that the Limousin, Jean de Bar, had been elected.[10] At this, all restraint was dropped, and armed and murderous the leaders of the mob forced their way into the Vatican. In fear of their lives the cardinals forced the unfortunate cardinal of St. Peter's to don the papal robes and seat himself on the throne. The old man was an invalid, and worn out by the hours of fatigue and fear, seemed to become hysterical, raving of devils, cursing those who knelt for his blessing. It was a long while before the deception was finally eradicated. In Pisa, his election was officially celebrated, and in France, Froissart actually recorded that the old man was pope for three days and died through the too demonstrative joy of the Romans.

Throughout the conclave, Prignano had been in the Vatican Palace. He had recently bought himself a house and vineyard in the city, but it had proved impossible to live in a private house during those tumultuous days. His status had increased considerably since the death of Gregory, for everyone knew of the dissension within the college. He had been invited to attend the secret meetings of the Roman civil government and tendered sound advice, firmly refusing to attempt to persuade the cardinals to elect an Italian. Even within the college itself there were those who had begun to look speculatively at the industrious bureaucrat, reminding each other that though he was an Italian he was also a Neapolitan—and the queen of Naples was a very good friend of Avignon.

When the news came, therefore, Prignano was not utterly surprised. He made the routine disclaimer—routine, but in his case, sincere: "I am not worthy but will not contradict the Divine will."

But any pride he might have felt at the result was swiftly diminished by the lackluster method of announcing the news. The cardinal of Florence came to tell him informally, but there was no proclamation. Instead, the scurryings and arguments and interviews went on, not merely as though the conclave had not yet reached a decision, but as though it had not yet met. Some of the cardinals had hurriedly left the city, others had hastened to Sant' Angelo and the protection of its French garrison. Throughout the second night Prignano waited for the accustomed deputation from them, the deputation that would kneel at his feet, accept his blessing, ask his favors. But no one came.

Early on the following morning a Spanish prelate reported a most curious incident to his principal, Cardinal de Luna. He had gone to visit the new pope and found only two cardinals with him, those of Florence and Milan. Prignano, the Spaniard reported, was agitated, depressed. Was he or was he not pope? He had sent for the cardinals but they had given excuses—humiliatingly thin excuses: The roads were dangerous; they had no suitable clothes. They would come later—perhaps.

But Prignano had the backing of the city magistrates. They knew better than anyone else what was likely to happen if the Romans were again disappointed. Armed messengers were sent to the cardinals demanding their presence at the Vatican, and, gradually the confusion was sorted out. The cardinals might have been unenthusiastic about their new pope but they too knew the dangers well enough. On the morning of Friday, April 9, Prignano was formally proclaimed pope, received the homage of the Sacred College, and took the style of Urban VI. The European powers and the cardinals still in Avignon were informed that there was a new pope, and members of the college sought the customary spiritual and temporal favors from him. Nine days later Urban was crowned with all due ceremony and it seemed as though the conclave of 1378 was passing into history as one that had been violent but of no unusual significance. So indeed it might have done, had it not been for the character of the new pope.

According to his secretary, Dietrich von Niem, the absolute power so suddenly thrust upon the man actually turned his brain, transforming him from a short-tempered bureaucrat into a raging tyrant. Dietrich was probably right. Throughout his career, Prignano had been in a subordinate position. Socially, he lacked the graces that would have enabled him to mix at the higher levels of the curia. He was highly intelligent and learned but he lacked a sense of humor, was incapable of giving way in small things in order to obtain greater. There were many excellent qualities about him. Dietrich von Niem, the only man he trusted, who knew him both as bureaucrat and pope and was to record the most appalling details about him, remembered him as "a man humble and devout, keeping his hands free from every gift, a foe and persecutor of simoniacs, a lover of justice and charity—but one that relied too much on his own prudence and over-readily believed flatterers." [11] Prudence was the one vital thing that Pope Urban VI did not possess.

In the first few weeks of his reign Urban was laboring under a very real sense of grievance, a very human desire to put those gorgeous creatures, the Avignonese cardinals, in their place. He knew very well that they had elected him at best as a stopgap, at worst as a temporary pope. The first consistory in any reign was a delicate meeting, the moment when a man faced those who had been his equals or even his superiors and were now immeasurably his inferiors—but who could still make or break him by giving or withholding their support. Urban's first official meeting with his cardinals was utterly disastrous and from it all the subsequent evil flowed.

The cardinals of the Roman Church were princes in every sense of the word. Their numbers had dwindled steadily over the past century, declining even more swiftly over the Avignon period when the popes, inhibited by their connection with the French crown, had been reluctant to create non-French cardinals. French cardinals had therefore elected French popes, who in turn, mindful of the need to maintain the approval of the French king, created French cardinals, producing a closed circle of power in which the popes were utterly dependent upon the goodwill of the Sacred College. The power of the cardinals was as great outside the curia as within. All the great powers of Europe were alert to the need to keep a friend at court, and were prepared to pay heavily for the privilege.

The cardinals' wealth was enormous. In addition to the gifts from European monarchs, the cardinals were directly connected to that elaborate system which sucked gold from all over Europe. Half the revenue of the Holy See was theirs by right—half of Peter's Pence, half the income from taxes, from gifts. At every election the pope, by custom, gave each cardinal handsome gifts in specie. Each held a plurality of benefices by right—a church in an English town, a canonry in a Scandinavian city, a bishopric in Italy. All over Europe, peasants and merchants, fishmongers, dukes, prostitutes, kings, contributed their great or little to the twenty-odd streams of gold, each of which found its destination in a cardinal's coffer.

It was gold that counted—gold not in the form of a symbol, but as actual metal. Between them, the cardinals disposed of a vast weight in bullion. When Cardinal Hugh Roger died, his executors found in his house a hoard that represented almost every currency in Europe. In a red chest there were twenty-one bags of gold, each containing mixed coins. Elsewhere they found—in bags, purses, boxes, or wrapped in cloth: 5,000 Piedmontese gold florins; 5,000 old gold crowns; 2,000 Aragonese gold florins; 4,500 gold crowns of England; 855 gold francs; 500 gold angels; 97 gold ducats; 1,000 gold papal florins; 363 of the pure florins of Florence; 511 Sicilian florins; and 900 gold florins of the mint called du Grayle.

This was the hoard of but one cardinal, not particularly important, not particularly miserly. In the Avignon for which they now pined, they had lived in splendor, their palaces and gardens forming a separate pleasure city, Villeneuve, on the farther bank of the Rhône. Their progress through Avignon itself had been not so much like princes as kings, for their long trains of attendants would not have disgraced a monarch of France or England. Some of the onlookers reveled in the glory brought to the city; others raged at it. Petrarch marked these princes down for his especial scorn.

> Instead of the Apostles who went barefoot we now see satraps mounted on horses decked with gold and champing golden bits and whose very hoofs will soon be shod in gold if God does not restrain their arrogant wealth. They could be taken for kings of the Persians or Parthians, who demand to be worshipped and into whose presence must no man come empty-handed.[12]

These were the men who faced the ex-assistant to the vice-chancellor, now supreme pontiff, in Rome in April, 1378. It is just possible that they might have accepted the position, might even have resigned themselves to staying in Italy, had Urban acted with even elementary courtesy. But Urban's opening address to them was not merely violent but personally abusive, spitting out the bile accumulated over years of inferiority. Each cardinal was singled out for attack—his lust for power, his scandalous wealth based on simony, his immorality, his neglect of duties—each was upbraided in language drawn from a slum. Most of the charges were justified but the manner in which they were couched would have offended the mildest man. He yelled at one to shut up, called another a liar, another a fool and described the soldier-cardinal of Geneva, accurately enough, as a bandit. At the end of the consistory, as the sullen men were making their way out of the chamber, Geneva crossed over to Urban. "You have not treated the cardinals today with the respect that they received from your predecessors. I tell you in truth, if you diminish our honor we shall diminish yours." [13]

It was not only the cardinals who began to think that they had to deal with a madman. "I can do anything, anything!" he yelled at an adviser who had ventured to doubt his powers to excommunicate for the mildest misdemeanor. No one knew what his mood might be when they came into his presence. Sometimes he appeared reasonable, almost gentle; at others, the least opposition would send him into paroxysms of rage, his language rich with the studied insults of the Neapolitan.

His compatriots did not escape. Ambassadors from Queen Joanna, sent to congratulate him, returned furious at the insults offered both them and their queen. They met a friend of St. Catherine's on the way back to Naples and unburdened themselves to him. All Italy, all Europe knew the character of Queen Joanna, but was it fitting, they demanded, that the Holy Father should say such terrible things about her? And why had he gone out of his way to insult her husband Otto—in public at the great state banquet? Otto had knelt to offer, as customary, the ewer of water—and had been kept on his knees while Urban pretended not to see him.

"This Holy Father of ours is a terrible man and frightens people fearfully with his words and conduct," a correspondent wrote to Catherine who was watching the incredible affair from her home in Siena. "However," he went on cautiously, "it is all for the best. He seems to have a great trust in God and is manifestly striving to abolish the simony and great pomp that reigns in the Church of God." [14]

The disciples of a saint might approve the abolition of pomp and simony even if they were doubtful about the means; the cardinals emphatically did not. Throughout the summer Urban's behavior grew steadily worse, culminating in a physical attack upon the cardinal of Limoges in consistory. One by one, the members of the college found excuses to drift from Rome, and by Septem-

ber most of the Frenchmen had assembled at Anagni, that city
with its ominous associations for the Papacy. Discreet messages were
passed between them and the other cardinals, inviting them to
discuss the position. Could Urban be deposed? Was he indeed pope
at all, considering that the election had been held under duress?
They remembered Orsini's suggestion made during conclave that
they should elect a temporary pope. If the "temporary" pope had
proved to be a rational man, all would have been well. But in the
circumstances. . . .

Urban heard of the conspiracy and acted with both courage and
dignity, offering to submit the validity of his election to the test
of a council, even sending three of the Italian cardinals with peace
proposals. Shortly afterward, the already tiny Italian faction
suffered a loss with the death of that aged cardinal of St. Peter's
who had been forced to play the part of mock pope. He died declaring that Urban was indeed true pope, but his declaration was
ignored. The three surviving Italians did not attempt even the
little they might have accomplished but remained neutral throughout. There were well-founded rumors that each of them hoped
that he might be elected in a new conclave, but the passive treachery of each was unrewarded. On September 20, the Sacred College
elected Robert of Geneva as pope; obedient to the Avignonese
tradition, he took the name of Clement VII. Far too late, Urban
did what he had often threatened to do, creating a number of
Italian cardinals—in effect erecting another Sacred College to take
the place of that which had abandoned him. Two distinct curias,
each self-generating, were thereby established.

It might have been Urban's violent nature that sparked off the
conflict, but it was French policy that maintained it. "Now I am
pope," the king of France said, mockingly or gleefully, on news
of Clement's election, and he spoke truly. Throughout he had encouraged the rebellious cardinals, even overriding the clergy of
France who had sensibly decided that the situation in Italy was
too grotesquely confused for them to commit themselves to either
party at this stage. The schism was being created on national, not
religious, lines, as the lineup which followed clearly showed for it
was occasioned almost entirely by alliance with, or hostility for,

France. Thus England automatically recognized Urban, while Scotland, England's enemy and France's friend, as automatically recognized Clement.

Italians made it very clear where their sympathies lay. As soon as she heard the rumors Catherine wrote a series of blistering letters to the cardinals.

> O men—not men but rather demons visible, how does the inordinate love that you have set upon the dunghill of your bodies, and on the delights and states of the world, blind you so that, when the Vicar of Christ—he whom you elected by canonical election—wishes to correct your lives you now spread poison and say he is not true Pope.[15]

Urban recognized in her the voice of Italy, and after Clement's election summoned her to Rome, where she gave much sound advice. It was she who, when the inevitable clash of arms became imminent, roused by her eloquence a military champion for Urban and for Italy. Alberico da Barbiano, a young Italian nobleman, had raised a company of purely Italian mercenaries, and Catherine appealed to him for help in one of those astonishing letters of hers which could persuade the most reluctant person to her way of thought. Barbiano hastened southward with his company, intercepted Clement just outside Rome, and utterly destroyed his army.

It was an immensely heartening omen: For the first time in generations a purely Italian army had met in open battle and destroyed the foreigners who were fastened upon the vitals of Italy. Barbiano entered Rome in triumph where Urban presented him with a handsome silken banner, inscribed with the words "Italy delivered from the Barbarians." The French garrison in Sant' Angelo surrendered, Clement fled to Naples, and despairing of gaining support in Italy shortly afterward took ship for Avignon. The first round had ended decisively in Urban's favor.

The Long March

With the flight of Clement just six months after his schismatic election, Urban had no major enemy left in Italy. This was the moment when, had a normal man been in control, the Great Schism could have become a thing of the past. Lawyers would have continued to argue the finer points of the matter for decades, but the Avignonese curia would have dwindled into a shadow court very rapidly once Europe became aware that Urban held the sacred city itself, secure in the support of Italians. The support had nothing of warmth or affection in it— the dreary bureaucrat still remained, side by side with the violent pope. But Urban had one great advantage over his enemy: He was an Italian. He had but one basic policy—he intended to remain in Italy. Italians could forgive him much else.

But there was one other factor that ultimately destroyed all Urban's advantages: He was not merely an Italian but a Neapolitan. The treachery of Queen Joanna in giving refuge to Clement came as a personal affront. Insofar as Urban ever had a home, a *patria*, it was Naples. He had dragged himself out of the stinking narrow alleys that had given scant shelter to his childhood and youth, mounted step by painful step out of the squalor that was the lot of most Neapolitans. His desire to return to his native city in all his papal pomp was very human. It was also to prove fatal.

But quite apart from his personal feelings, Urban could not have avoided involvement with the endless "Neapolitan question" which touched every pope. Naples was more than a place—it was an idea. The great, squalid, beautiful city upon its superb bay was the heartland of the largest state Italy was to know for six hundred years. The "Kingdom of the Two Sicilies" was its curious and resounding title, a vast tract of land that included Sicily and all southern Italy almost as far as Rome, where its frontiers touched the Papal States. Over this area Byzantines and Saracens, Normans and Teutons had, one after the other, swept in from the Mediterranean or down the long spine of Italy. Each wave of invaders had first dominated and then become absorbed, each contributing its characteristics to create a culture no less foreign to Italians from the north than that of any non-Italian race. It shared the same land mass, its dialect was just discernible as Italian; beyond that the kingdom had nothing particular in common with its neighbors on the peninsula.

A little over a century earlier the last foreign conquerors had settled in the kingdom. They were Angevins, members of that incredible House of Anjou whose tentacles spread from France to England and now groped from Naples eastward to Hungary. They had established themselves first in Sicily, where they exercised that curious tyranny which the French ever seemed to impose when they had dominance over their southern neighbor—a tyranny that went beyond the exercise of power and became the infliction of personal humiliation. The islanders rebelled in the terrible "Sicilian Vespers" when thousands of French—men, women, children— were slaughtered in an ecstasy of racial hatred. But the Angevin system of dynastic marriages spread their power throughout southern Italy and across the Adriatic, and sons of the house ruled in Sicily and Naples, Taranto, Durazzo, and Hungary. In each generation, one or another of the branches would attempt to dominate the others. Naples was the chief prize and the ferocious dynastic struggles for it made Neapolitan politics highly lethal, even according to Italian standards.

Urban's troubles began with the reigning monarch of Naples, Joanna. "La douce reine," the French called her, and even now, in her fifties, she possessed a rare charm, a compound of sensuous beauty and unaffected majesty, of considerable learning and easy wit. Both Petrarch and Giovanni Boccaccio, in their different ways, paid tribute to her and the polished court she had inherited and maintained. Petrarch—perhaps the greatest living European scholar —considered himself honored to be given a high seat at one of those courts of love over which Joanna loved to preside, where the art of conversation was valued as much as that of flirtation. Boccaccio, as good a judge of women as Petrarch was of learning, thought her "fair and comely to look upon," dedicated his stories to her, enshrined her in his gallery of great women—but cautiously refused to say whether he believed her guilty or innocent of her husband's murder.

For this was the cloud that hung over Joanna during her days of triumph, the tragedy that dogged her throughout her life and brought her at last to a violent and shameful death. As a child of five, Joanna had been married to her cousin Andrew, the seven-year-old heir to the Hungarian branch of the house. It was a desperate political attempt to weld together the sundering branches and failed completely. Andrew was a dull, lumpish fellow—virtually a moron—surrounded, and completely influenced, by his savage compatriots who flocked into Naples on his marriage. In the permissive atmosphere of Naples it was natural enough that Joanna—gay, intellectual, laughter-loving—should in maturity find a lover among her own people. Andrew was murdered, victim of a political battle; but he was murdered by Joanna's lover, indeed, was lured from Joanna's bedroom to his death. All Europe took sides on the matter of the girl's guilt or innocence. She took her case to Avignon, pleaded in person before Clement VI and was judged innocent. But Clement, it was well known, was susceptible to women, and a more than easy judge for this beautiful, eloquent woman with the blood of a great French house in her veins. Italy, as a whole, reserved its judgment, but Andrew's relatives in Hungary swore to be revenged as soon as circumstances permitted.

The relationship between Joanna and Urban was curious. She had been genuinely delighted to hear of his election, and despite the stupid insults offered her, had even sent him military aid during the first days of the schism. Why she suddenly decided to recognize Clement, pay him money she owed to Urban, and offer him shelter in Naples, no one really knew. She may have been the victim of her courtiers, most of whom were working for France; she may have believed genuinely that the line of papal succession ran through Avignon; or she may have acted from pure caprice, for Joanna was ever as much woman as queen. From whatever cause, Urban found that his native city was closed to him.

Urban, on his side, had been glad to accept Joanna's support, and when she began to cool toward him, even contemplated sending Catherine to Naples to bring her back to the true path. But then a new scheme emerged from his fevered brain, a scheme based on nepotism of a peculiarly shabby kind. It is perhaps an indication of

Urban's essentially isolated, lonely condition that he, the genuine opponent of simony in any form, should have fallen victim to that dreariest of papal sins, destroying all that he had worked for in order to advance his nephew, Francesco Prignano. Unlike many papal "nephews," the younger Prignano was not a son of the elder, for Urban's virtue in this sense was unassailable. But that was all that could be said in favor of Francesco. "Butillo," the Neapolitans called him—"Fatty"—a heavy, stupid man of gross pleasures who had spent his life waiting for other people to do something for him. This was the man for whose sake a great kingdom was to be tormented and an unfortunate woman murdered.

Moved by a variety of causes—a desire to shine in his native city, nepotism, a desire, too, perhaps, to reverse that dubious judgment made in Avignon twenty years before and thus put down the ungodly—Urban sought a champion to overthrow Joanna. He found him in the person of Charles of Durazzo, a relative of both the murdered Andrew and of Joanna. Charles agreed to undertake the crusade against Joanna in return for the crown of the kingdom, and in 1380 he came to Rome where he and Urban hammered out the details. Urban would proclaim and finance a holy war, obtain mercenaries, then crown and anoint the pretender. In return, Charles agreed to confirm Butillo in his possession of the richest areas of the kingdom with which Urban had already endowed him—Capua and Amalfi, Salerno, Fondi, Caserta, Sorrento. Whether or not Charles really intended that these vital cities of the kingdom should go to Butillo, there is no knowing. But he satisfied Urban, was crowned king of Naples, and left Rome for the campaign in the summer of 1381. In order to finance him, the churches of Rome were again plundered of their negotiable wealth.

Joanna recognized her extreme danger and in despair she too sought and found a champion. She adopted a member of the elder branch of the family as her heir, inviting Louis of Anjou, brother to the king of France, into Italy, weaving and reweaving that tangled Angevin net which was strangling southern Italy. Louis came but his advance was slow, and Charles was able to besiege Naples without interference. In characteristic generosity and improvidence, Joanna gave shelter to all who desired it in her castle, and as a result, food failed. She surrendered at last to Charles, throwing herself upon his mercy.

It was not an idle hope, for Charles was a brave and gallant man, much loved by those who knew him, and had Joanna's surrender brought about the end of the conflict, her life would probably have been spared. But Louis of Anjou, having delayed long enough to cost Joanna her liberty, now hurried to help her and so ensured her death. Charles forestalled rebellion in Naples by the assassination of Joanna. She was murdered, some said, by the same means that her first husband had been murdered—strangled with a silken cord—and her body exposed in the marketplace.

It is difficult to understand what Urban really thought Charles was going to do next. It should have been obvious to any experienced politician that Charles of Durazzo had not undertaken a long and dangerous campaign in order to create great estates for Francesco Prignano. But Urban had little experience of either politics or war. All he could see was that Charles was dragging out the war and that his beloved nephew was as far away as ever from his estates. A series of peremptory demands and impossible instructions had been met first with evasion and then with something approaching mockery. In his mind, there was only one thing left to do—go in person to Naples. His cardinals were appalled when he told them of his decision, for he had no intention of leaving them behind to brew more conspiracy. The entire curia was to set out on yet another pilgrimage.

The cardinals' protests were not necessarily based on a selfish reluctance to leave the comparative safety of Rome for the wilds of southern Italy. They knew that only Urban's physical presence in Rome kept the Romans in some sort of obedience—and so they told him. He ignored protests and arguments. If Catherine had still been alive she might have been able to persuade him from his mad course, or at least prevented some of the excesses which were to attend the Neapolitan war. But she had died, burned out at the age of thirty-three, shortly after Charles had left the city in 1380. Urban issued his orders, collected a raggle-taggle army of mercenaries, and in April, 1383, the curia left Rome. Five and a

Leo X and Cardinals Giulio de' Medici and Luigi
de' Rossi. Raphael. Palatine Gallery, Florence.

Castiglione. Raphael.

Clement VII. Sebastiano del Piombo. National
Gallery of Capodimonte, Naples.

Above: — Charles V.
Titian. Munich.

Left: — Martin Luther.
Lucas Cranach. Uffizi
Gallery, Florence.

Right: — Guicciardini.

Francis I. Titian. Louvre, Paris.

Niccolo Machiavelli. Santi di Tito. Palazzo Vecchio, Florence.

Tomb of Giuliano de' Medici. Michelangelo.
Medici Chapel, Florence.

half years were to pass before it returned, demoralized, its members depleted not by the privation it had endured but by murder.

Four months after leaving Rome, Urban entered Naples. If anything, things were worse than he had feared. On arrival at Aversa, a few miles from the city, Urban had been virtually imprisoned for five days while Charles beat down his demands. Raging but impotent, he was at last freed, granted the empty honor of a ceremonial entry into Naples, and thereafter ignored. He had not sufficient troops to make his displeasure felt and the Neapolitans, from whom he had hoped for so much, received him with something less than enthusiasm. He had taken the precaution of sending ahead his legate Cardinal Sangro to cleanse the city of its Clementine followers. The fact that Sangro carried out his task with a dedicated cruelty meant nothing to the Neapolitans. They were largely indifferent to the fate of a number of French prelates but they resented deeply the end of the carefree days under Joanna. Butillo came in for a large share of the hatred, for he conducted himself—as far as his pleasures went—as though he were already king. He touched a new depth in his career when he abducted a noblewoman from a nunnery, shut himself up in a house and enjoyed her while protected by papal swords. Her enraged relatives went off in a body to protest to Urban, demanding action against Butillo. "He is but a youth," replied Urban, dismissing their protests. His nephew was then in his fortieth year.

After an uneasy spring and summer, during which relations between Urban and Charles grew steadily worse, Urban left Naples. He did not, as the curia hoped, turn to the north, to civilization and sanity, but instead continued a few miles south to the town of Nocera, not far from Pompeii. It was a pleasant enough little place, close to the sea so that the breezes rendered bearable the stifling heat of a southern summer. But in the eyes of the cardinals it was the end of the world, an outpost of hell. The castle was not big enough to hold all the court, and servants and officials were scattered about the town itself, adding grounds of domestic discomfort to the cardinals' larger complaints.

Many of these cardinals were Neapolitans, pliant creatures who did what they were told, accustomed to the ways of this curious country. But there were also a number of non-Neapolitans and even a handful of non-Italians in Urban's college, among them Cardinal Sangro and an Englishman, Adam Easton. Both men had attempted to persuade Urban to return to Rome, but finding that reasoning was useless, that the Papacy was apparently to be buried indefinitely in a small hill-town, they began a conspiracy.

They were remarkably inept plotters. Indeed, the extent of their action seems to have been a largely academic debate with sympathetic colleagues as to whether or not Urban could be canonically deposed. Some of them went as far as to discuss the possibility of having Urban burned as a heretic—a good example of selling the lion's skin while the beast still lived. But none of them actually did anything, to their subsequent remorse. One of the debaters thought it prudent to make the matter known to Urban. On the night of January 10 the six ringleaders were arrested and lowered into a cistern until Urban had decided what to do with them.

Dietrich von Niem is the unimpeachable witness for what happened next. Dietrich was a German, thirty-five years old at the time, rather earnest, rather stolid, well read but utterly without imagination—and totally devoted to Urban. He had been with him in the Avignon days, stayed by his side throughout the tumultuous days of the conclave and the beginning of the schism. Urban trusted him as he trusted no other man, treating him like a son—a son of whom he was fond in spite of his limitations. Dietrich never presumed to advise his master, but in the diary he kept he recorded his misgivings, his conviction that the whole curia was sliding to disaster.

A few nights after the arrest of the cardinals Urban sent for Dietrich. By then, Dietrich was pretty certain that he had to deal with a madman and he was deeply frightened, though he obeyed the summons. Urban's rage, however, was not then directed against Dietrich, who with four other officials was instructed to "examine" the cardinals forthwith. Butillo Prignano went with them to ensure that the examination was conducted with sufficient vigor. The cardinals had been transferred to separate cells in the castle and the interrogators went from one to the other, seeking the origins of the conspiracy by comparatively humane means, Butillo in particular promising leniency if they confessed. They learned nothing of much value, for there was nothing much to learn.

Later that night Dietrich went to see Urban. He had a strong suspicion that the interrogation was not going to stop at verbal means, and taking his life in his hands, he actually dared to warn Urban that he was alienating loyal servants, and pleaded with him to be lenient with the cardinals. Urban nearly had a stroke on the spot. He screamed till he was hoarse, his face "blazing like a lamp," thrusting "proof" of the cardinals' guilt in Dietrich's face. The young man wisely shut up and left the room. His had been a brave action but a useless one.

Three days of "examination" followed and then Urban gave orders that the cardinals were to be "put to the question," the formula for torture. The interrogators obediently set to work. Dietrich was particularly distressed by the treatment of Cardinal Sangro: The corpulent old man was hoisted to the ceiling three times by the strappado and each time was dropped heavily to the floor. Dietrich tried to persuade him to confess, to say anything, but Sangro was forced to reply that there was nothing to say. Butillo, meanwhile, stood by laughing, as though at a comedy.

The morning's work did not satisfy Urban. He had been unable to hear Sangro's screams, he told Dietrich and the others. They had better improve their methods—or else. When work began the following day on the next victim, Urban paced up and down in the garden outside the cell, reading his breviary aloud so the reluctant torturers could hear his voice and thus be stimulated in their task. At the end of the session Dietrich had had enough. Even his loyalty could not include the torture of elderly and foolish clerics, and he quietly slipped out of the castle and made for Naples. The work went on without him.

By now, Charles and Urban were at open war. Urban excommunicated his erstwhile champion, laid Naples under an interdict, and announced his intention of crowning his nephew king of Naples. Charles replied by sending an army to besiege Nocera, giving its command to another erstwhile champion of Urban's, the condottiero Alberico da Barbiano. Neapolitan heralds proclaimed outside Nocera that ten thousand florins would be paid to whoever surrendered the pope—dead or alive. Urban never lacked courage and his response to the sacrilegious proclamation was to appear at one of the windows of the castle with bell, book, and candle, raving curses at the army below, excommunicating every man in it. He did this, an onlooker reported, three or four times a day, miraculously escaping the shower of arrows that greeted every appearance.

Nocera fell but the great castle held out, and on July 5, help arrived. It was tardy and insufficient but it ended an impossible situation. One of the local lords, for some reason of personal hatred, broke with Charles, fought through the Neapolitan lines, and escorted Urban out of the castle. Charles was glad enough to see him go; indeed, the escape may have been prearranged, for Urban was not pursued even though the countryside swarmed with Neapolitan soldiers. He managed to get word to one of his few remaining supporters in Italy, the doge of Genoa, who promised to send a fleet of Genoese galleys if the papal party could make its way to the coast.

Under a blazing sun the dwindling curia trailed dismally back to Naples, destination of the galleys. The tortured cardinals were dragged with it, though most of them were scarcely able to keep their seats on their half-starved horses. Urban had not yet finished with them. One of them, the bishop of Aquila, managed even in his enfeebled state to excite Urban's suspicions. He was murdered on the spot in sight of his horrified companions, his body was dumped casually by the roadside, and the party moved on. Most would have long since fled but they were hemmed around by mercenary soldiers. Urban had been unable to pay the soldiers and they now looked upon him and his court not as paymasters but as material for ransom.

The curia arrived at the coast to find that the galleys had not arrived. Somebody had overlooked the fact that Naples was in the hands of Urban's enemy, and the fleet had then been rerouted to the Adriatic coast. Wearily the party turned about yet again and struggled across the entire width of Italy to a port on the Adriatic.

There the Genoese found them, took them on board, and brought them to Genoa.

Urban remained eighteen months in Genoa—and long before the visit ended, the doge bitterly regretted that he had ever offered asylum to this madman. Urban was obsessed with one idea—the gathering of an army for another attack upon Naples. Everything else was subordinate to this. The activities of his rival in Avignon seemed to pass unnoticed; the protests and pleas from Rome, again in a state of anarchy, were ignored. He and the Genoese almost immediately came into conflict. The city was a republic, prepared to accept Urban as true pope but definitely not prepared to accept his autocratic interference with its constitution. The citizens made it very plain that in their eyes the terrible Urban was a refugee and should conduct himself with gratitude and prudence. The city fathers refused to let his gang of mercenaries roam the city, imperiling the delicately balanced peace. But, more than anything else, the Genoese were scandalized by his treatment of the cardinals.

Part of the price he had paid for Genoese help, in addition to the 130,000 florins that the hire of the galleys cost, was a promise to release the cardinals as soon as he was in Genoa. This he refused to do, becoming ever more truculent as the Genoese became ever more insistent. Some of the citizens made a gallant but ill-timed attempt to free the prisoners. Five of the six were immediately murdered: buried alive according to some reports, tied in sacks and thrown into the sea according to others. The sixth, Adam Easton, owed his life to the persistence of his king, Richard II, who had never ceased his attempts to obtain Easton's freedom. Urban had just sufficient political sense left to stop short at needlessly alienating the support of the powerful English monarch, and not long afterward he released Easton.

The murders were committed on the night of December 15; early the following morning Urban left Genoa. There is little doubt that had he remained, the Genoese would have taken matters into their own hands and eliminated one of the two popes of the schism. From Genoa he sailed to Lucca and then marched inland to Perugia where his agents had been gathering together a mercenary army for the attack on Naples.

The last crusade against Naples ended in humiliating failure before the so-called army had even crossed the frontier. The mercenaries which Urban's agents had been able to obtain for him were the dregs of their profession, for Urban had a bad reputation as a tyrannical employer and a very tardy paymaster. Even this indifferent company had been hired only because cash had immediately been paid and more was promised en route. The march started bravely enough. Urban led the army in person from Perugia in August, carrying the baton of command. "Saint Peter in person," some flatterer or satirist called him. But the troops were unimpressed and the march ended a few miles south where the main body, citing an obscure clause in their contract, announced through their leaders that they were abandoning the campaign.

Urban raged in vain; no money was produced or could be produced, and the mercenaries went off to seek a better paymaster. A few hundred men alone remained with Urban and the ragged band trailed onward through Umbria. For the first time in his career, doubts and fears beset the usually courageous pope. They were probably the result of a fever he had contracted in Naples, for they were accompanied by hallucinations in which the apostle appeared to him and sternly pointed the way to Rome. Substance was given to the visions by the apparition of one of the innumerable hermits who haunted the Italian countryside. "You will go to Rome, willingly or not," he told Urban. "For in Rome you must die." It speaks much for Urban's demoralization that the hermit was not speared on the spot.

Even Urban could admit defeat. Supernatural warnings apart, the idea of an attack on Naples with the force at his command was preposterous. He was sick now, in body as well as spirit, and the last few miles of his journey were made in a horse litter. Still short of the Neapolitan frontier, he made the decision to return to Rome and entered the city, still in his litter, in September, 1388.

Urban had before him just one year of life, a year spent in violent conflict with the Romans. Gone was the dream of glittering kingdoms, thrust out by the reality of exercising power in a city that had tasted independence. In spite of his fever-wracked body, he reduced the tumultuous people to order, imposing his will upon the most anarchical of cities. Here, at least, he was king, and though the powerful families hated him, he brought peace of a sort for the common people and earned a cold respect. He died on October 15, 1389. Dietrich von Niem, who had come back to him in Genoa, was at his deathbed. It may have pleased Urban.

Urban's intransigence had in great part created the schism, but his death did not end it, for the two self-perpetuating, mutually exclusive, colleges of cardinals in Rome and Avignon each continued to elect a unique pope. The brief but violent reign of the Neapolitan bureaucrat had posed an unanswerable problem as to the nature of spiritual power, counterpart to the problem that Boniface VIII had posed. Boniface's claim to universal temporal power had been answered—brutally and finally. Urban's claim to universal spiritual power was inherited by his immediate successors in Rome, but the Avignonese counterclaim was never refuted, only ignored. Twenty years after his death the cardinals in Rome and Avignon, despairing of any other solution, united in council, deposed both popes, and elected a successor—but the problem was merely postponed.

As a result of the council, three popes now ruled where hitherto there had been but two. Which was the true pope? He elected in Avignon, he elected in Rome, or he elected by the council? What, for that matter, was an anti-pope? One who had not been canonically elected, the canonists replied. But what was a canonical election? Three hundred years earlier, in the dark days of the tenth century, a certain priest called Boniface Franco had murdered the reigning pope and had himself elected as Boniface VII. He then fled, returned, murdered the current occupant of the chair, and being of a legalistic turn of mind, carefully dated his reign from the first, not the second murder, thereby thrusting into legal oblivion the two popes who had reigned in the interim. Surely, of all popes, his election had been canonically suspect. Nevertheless, that great lawyer Benedict Gaetani had taken the style of Boniface VIII, thus tacitly recognizing the legality of Boniface VII. If such a man could be duly entered in the legitimate succession, on what grounds could the austere Benedict XIII, the Avignonese pope who succeeded Urban's rival, be excluded?

Benedict saw no such grounds, and for twenty-seven years he held his own while seven rival popes elected by Rome or a council came and went. The French, as weary of the scandal as the rest, withdrew their obedience together with their financial support and he withdrew to Spain, ultimately ruling over a few square yards of territory. Staunchly convinced of his legitimacy to the end, he appointed four cardinals, who, entering into the spirit of the game, elected a successor on his death.

But long before Benedict's death Europe had revolted, forcing the Papacy to bypass the obstacle that it could not surmount. At the Council of Constance in 1415, six European nations sat in judgment on the Papacy and forcibly deposed the reigning three popes: Benedict XIII; the "Roman" pope Gregory XII who saved his face by abdicating; and the bizarre figure of Baldassare Cossa— ex-pirate, ex-condottiero—who had somehow emerged as the choice of a previous council and taken the style of John XXIII.

But deposition was not enough unless there was unanimous choice of the successor. The council vested its powers in what was virtually a committee elected by the nations of Europe; and this committee in turn elected a member of the house of Colonna, who took the name of Martin V. The indomitable Benedict refused to recognize the election and other anti-popes appeared at odd times and places over the next generation. But none gained serious backing and the name of Martin V was duly slotted into place as the legitimate successor of St. Peter. The council made no pronouncement on the legitimacy of the Avignonese and conciliar popes, with some odd results in the styles chosen by later popes. Rodrigo Borgia chose the style of Alexander VI, thus recognizing the legitimacy of the Alexander V elected by the first council in Pisa, but Giulio de' Medici called himself Clement VII, thus extinguishing Urban's rival who had begun it all. And it was not until 1958 that the seal of oblivion was placed upon John XXIII, when Angelo Roncalli courageously took the style and so restored a great name to honor.

V
The Spanish Bull

Rodrigo Borgia
Pope Alexander VI (1492–1503)

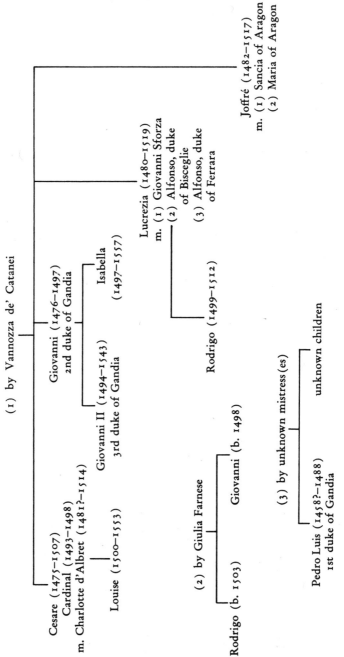

THE DESCENDANTS OF ALEXANDER VI
(born during his lifetime)

(1) by Vannozza de' Catanei

Cesare (1475–1507)
Cardinal (1493–1498)
m. Charlotte d'Albret (1481?–1514)

Louise (1500–1553)

Giovanni (1476–1497)
2nd duke of Gandia

Giovanni II (1494–1543)
3rd duke of Gandia

Isabella
(1497–1557)

Lucrezia (1480–1519)
m. (1) Giovanni Sforza
(2) Alfonso, duke
of Bisceglie
(3) Alfonso, duke
of Ferrara

Rodrigo (1499–1512)

Joffré (1482–1517)
m. (1) Sancia of Aragon
(2) Maria of Aragon

(2) by Giulia Farnese

Rodrigo (b. 1503)

Giovanni (b. 1498)

(3) by unknown mistress(es)

Pedro Luis (1458?–1488)
1st duke of Gandia

unknown children

Cardinal Rodrigo Borgia

Beloved Son,

We have heard that, four days ago, several ladies of Siena—women entirely given over to worldly frivolities—were assembled in the gardens of Giovanni di Bichis and that you, quite forgetful of the high office with which you are invested, were with them from the seventeenth to the twenty-second hour. With you was one of your colleagues whose age alone, if not the dignity of his office, ought to have recalled him to his duty. We have heard that the most licentious dances were indulged in, none of the allurements of love were lacking and you conducted yourself in a wholly worldly manner. Shame forbids mention of all that took place—not only the acts themselves but their very names are unworthy of your position. In order that your lusts might be given free rein the husbands, fathers, brothers and kinsmen of the young women were not admitted. . . . All Siena is talking about this orgy. . . . Our displeasure is beyond words. . . . A cardinal should be beyond reproach. . . .[1]

So the sober Pius II wrote to the young Rodrigo Borgia, cardinal and vice-chancellor of the Roman Church, in the June of 1460. It required a lot to shock Pius. In his unreformed days as the worldly-wise Aeneas Piccolomini, he had been as great a rake as any, and even now he was prepared to overlook many of the peccadilloes of the brilliant young Spaniard who could charm men as easily as he charmed women. But the affair in Siena, it seems, went beyond the bounds of even that city's permissive society and Pius recorded his displeasure in no uncertain terms—incidentally providing posterity with the first sketch of the private life of the future Borgia pope.

Rodrigo Borgia was then twenty-nine years old. Just five years earlier, his uncle had become pope as Calixtus III—and immediately flooded Rome with his Spanish kinsmen and friends. "Catalans," the Romans called them contemptuously, and watched with rage as the lucrative offices of the church and the city found their way into Spanish hands. Calixtus was generous to his compatriots but fatherly to his kinsmen. He adopted the two sons of his sister—

Rodrigo and Don Pedro Luis—and heaped the greatest possible honors upon them. Rodrigo was created cardinal at the age of twenty-six, and the following year the highest office that a pope could bestow fell into his lap: the vice-chancellorship of the church. It was a position where it would have been difficult to avoid making money and Rodrigo made the most of it.

Don Pedro Luis, a year older than his brother Rodrigo, seems to have been intended as the founder of a dynasty. The titles his uncle gave him were both sonorous and potent: duke and count of Spoleto, lord of Civitavecchia, governor of the Patrimony of St. Peter, generalissimo of Holy Church, and prefect of Rome. It was perhaps fortunate for Rodrigo that these temporal plums went to his brother and not to himself, for they drew upon Pedro the rage of the Romans. With that savage, insatiable hunger for wealth which characterized the Spaniards in Italy, Pedro set about the destruction of the great families of Rome. While Calixtus lived he was safe and all-powerful, but when his protector died in 1458, the Romans rose in rare concert and chased him from the city and he died not long after in exile. It was a curious parallel to the career of his brother's son Cesare.

Rodrigo survived the transference of power. Indeed during the lifetime of his uncle he seems to have conducted himself with a discretion lacking in later years. Piccolomini, who later had to reproach him, remarked: "Our Chancellor, Rodrigo Borgia, the Pope's nephew, is young, it is true, but his conduct and his good sense make him seem older than his years." [2] During the conclave it was the young Borgia's vote that gave Piccolomini the necessary majority, a fact that doubtless contributed to the new pope's warmth toward him. But with the new pontificate the manner of his life changed, his private debaucheries displayed to public amazement with a cynical indifference to scandal. Among his many and lurid crimes Rodrigo Borgia did not number hypocrisy; it left him wide open to his enemies, in whose pay were some of the most venomous, most skillful writers produced by the Renaissance.

The closing decades of the fifteenth century saw the Papacy approaching its outwardly most brilliant, most splendid period.

The claim to universal temporal power was gone, buried with the humiliated corpse of Boniface VIII, and less than a century ahead lay the challenge of Luther to the spiritual supremacy. But superficially it seemed as though the Papacy had returned to its pre-schism solidarity, and with the threat of councils receding into the distance, it was free to develop a more limited, if more secure power as an Italian principate.

But during the century that had elapsed since Urban VI precipitated the schism, a fundamental change had come over Italy; it was in the new world of the Renaissance that the Papacy reestablished itself in Rome. Insofar as such a multiform culture had a date and place of origin, the first flowering of the Renaissance took place in Florence about the year 1400, when the Florentines, under pressure of war, turned in on themselves, seeking to define just what it was they were defending. Their scholars found it in the past through the newly discovered letters of Cicero. The principle they were defending, they now could claim, was liberty itself—liberty as enshrined in the ancient Roman republic before the corruption of the Caesars.

In its immediate origins, perhaps, the Renaissance was essentially a propaganda movement, the means whereby the Florentines sought to justify their actions by citing the maxims of the great classical writers. But the arrival of the new culture was inevitable, Florence being merely the immediate cause of its flowering. Knowledge had been dormant not dead, and now in a more established, wealthier society, a handful of scholars had time to spare to prospect in the great rubbish heap of the past. The search for manuscripts became an obsession with some, and they beggared themselves to contribute to the slowly accumulating treasure of salvaged learning.

The accumulation snowballed, each discovery providing clues to others, so that by the middle of the fifteenth century, a great part of the body of Latin learning was again in circulation. It came as a revelation to men whose minds had been conditioned over centuries to accept Christian theology as the total horizon of learning. They accorded it an almost superstitious veneration, a reverence that hitherto had been reserved solely for the Scriptures. The ability to write elegant Latin became the touchstone of pure scholarship, and each surviving element of classical scholarship, whether a treatise on architecture, a poem, or a moral discourse, was regarded as the highest form in which the human intellect could express itself and was faithfully used as model.

The new culture became a fashion, pursued almost to mania. In 1485 the discovery of the body of a beautiful maiden of ancient Rome sent the whole city into a kind of hysteria. The body, in an astonishing state of preservation, was brought from its grave on the Via Appia to a public building where men in their thousands passed by it to—adore? So it would seem, from the extravagant language in praise of the maiden's beauty; and so it would seem, too, from the reaction of the reigning pope, who, fearful of a new heresy, ordered the body to be secretly reburied. The worship of ancient Rome permeated the higher strata of society. Parvenu princes bankrupted themselves to rebuild their villas in the classic mode, or at least provide them with fashionably accepted facades. A new industry arose in Rome as laborers discovered that the nobility were prepared to pay enormous sums for the broken bits of statuary that for centuries had been regarded only as supply for the limekilns. Scholarly snobs laced their letters and conversation and even their prayers with classical allusions: God again became Jupiter, Christ was transformed into Apollo, saints into gods, nuns into vestal virgins. Even the magistrates of the city became conscript fathers, and the theoretically Christian carnivals that heralded Lent became the Lupercalia.

The spirit of the Renaissance entered Rome during the 1450's under the pontificate of Nicholas V. A modest, honorable man, he was by inclination a scholar, and though he directed the affairs of the church with energy and skill his first and last love was the new learning. He sent emissaries throughout the world in quest of precious manuscripts, and effectively founded that mother of libraries, the Vatican Library. Around him he gathered the foremost humanist scholars of the day, encouraging the spread and growth of that questing spirit which, inevitably, turned upon its patron. Rome itself he saw as a vast laboratory in which the eager new breed of architects, drunk with the rediscovery of the classical world, could make its experiments. Mean buildings and great palaces alike were swept away, the ancient Leonine City was redesigned and fortified. The venerable basilica of St. Peter's, which had loomed over Rome for more than a millennium, fell victim to the rebuilding fever. Years were to pass before the vast edifice disappeared entirely, and when finally Michelangelo's dome crowned the new St. Peter's, it was in a different world.

But there was a reverse side to this splendid new coin of the Renaissance. Earlier popes had looked dubiously at the frankly pagan aspect of this rebirth, the adulation of the great pagan poets at the expense of the fathers of the church. But the pagan aspect was a passing wonder. Far more dangerous to the Papacy was the new-born knowledge of the past which was beginning to put papal claims in perspective. The most devastating attack came from Lorenzo Valla, one of the new tribe of wandering humanist scholars. His favorite literary topic, as with so many of his colleagues, was pornography: His treatise *On Pleasure,* a recitation of the sensual possibilities available to man, was a libertine's *vade mecum* only thinly disguised as a scholarly treatise on hedonism. Other scholars were to call the culture that produced this kind of obscene frivolity the "False Renaissance"; but such a condemnation drew an artificial distinction between two aspects of the expression of the same energy—as Valla demonstrated. In the 1440's he produced a more conventional work of scholarship, an examination of the so-called *Donation of Constantine*—the basis of the papal claim to temporal dominium. Over the centuries other men had suspected this too-convenient gift, but even as late as the time of Boniface VIII a scholar of the status of Dante could accept the forgery. He might deplore it—

> Ah, Constantine, of how much ill was mother
> Not thy conversion but that marriage dower
> Which the first wealthy Father took from thee[3]

but the *Donation* was a fact of life. Valla, using the tools that the new learning placed in his hands, damned the *Donation* for the forgery that it was. "Even if it were genuine," he declared, "it would by now have been rendered void by the crimes alone of the Papacy, through whose avarice Italy has been plunged in constant war." [4]

Valla called upon Rome to rebel against its priestly tyrants, and a decade afterward a Roman heard the call. Stefano Porcari, the last republican, ironically was a protégé of the liberal Nicholas V. He was more a fanatic than a patriot, hankering after some cloudy revival of a nonexistent Golden Age when priests would again be subordinates, not masters, in the city. He carried around with him a golden cord with which to bind the pope after the curia was overthrown, but the papal grasp on Rome was too firm to be prized loose by a band of scholarly rebels. The rebellion was put down bloodily, but it was a foreshadowing. Less than a century later a German general, professing the new faith called Lutheran, marched on Rome with a golden cord not to bind, but to hang, the pope.

By his early forties, Cardinal Borgia was reckoned to be the second richest man in the college of cardinals, a group which included the richest men in Europe. Although he owed his initial advancement to nepotism, in the jungle warfare that existed in the higher reaches of the Church it required considerable native ability not merely to maintain but actually to expand wealth and power as he did. "Intellectually, he is capable of everything," a contemporary wrote.

He is a fluent speaker, writes well—though not in a literary style, is extremely astute and very energetic and skillful in business matters. He is enormously wealthy, and through his connections with kings and princes, commands great influence. He has built a beautiful and comfortable palace for himself between the Bridge of Sant' Angelo and the Campo di Fiori. His revenues from his papal offices, his abbeys in Italy and Spain, his three bishoprics of Valencia, Portus and Cartagena, are vast. His office of Vice-Chancellor alone yields him 8000 gold ducats annually. His plate, his pearls, his stuffs embroidered with silk and gold, his books are all of such quality as would befit a king or pope. I need hardly mention the sumptuous bed-hangings, trappings for his horses and similar things of gold, silver, and silk, nor the vast quantity of gold coin which he possesses. Altogether, it is believed that he possessed more gold and riches of every sort than all the cardinals put together, excepting only Estouteville.[5]

That vast hoard of wealth was required for purposes other than vulgar display. Gone were the days when a papal election could be decided by the swords of faction. Matters now were far more orderly. True, the mob sacked the palace of the successful cardinal, but that was merely according to custom. The issue was decided by gold, not steel, by bribery, not force. To that end, Rodrigo Borgia devoted himself to amassing specie as well as benefices, an activity in which his office of vice-chancellor gave him particular advantage over his colleagues. When someone protested at his wholesale distribution of pardons for the most heinous crimes—one of which included the murder of a daughter by the father—he retorted easily, "It is not God's wish that a sinner should die, but that he should live—and pay." [6]

But in the conclave of 1484 he was cheated of the tiara, although he entered the conclave in high hopes, having already prepared the ground. But, "he who enters the Conclave a Pope leaves it a Cardinal," [7] the Ferrarese envoy wrote later to his master, giving Rome one of its enduring proverbs. Nobody trusted Borgia. Instead, the cardinals accepted the paper promises of Cardinal Cibo. John Burchard, the papal master of ceremonies who organized the conclave, gives a vivid picture of the new pope signing promises without reading them, kneeling casually as he did so. The news spread to the cubicles where other cardinals were undressing for the night. So fearful were they of being overlooked that they rushed out, half-dressed though they were, to present their own petitions. Cibo, now Innocent VIII, blandly signed them all—and later repudiated the lot.

Rodrigo Borgia was fortunate in that he had been temporarily passed over, for the nature of the pontificate of Innocent VIII ensured that his own would appear as the reign of an honest man, at least during its first few weeks. It can only be assumed that Cibo was indulging a fine sense of irony when he chose his pontifical name. There was some scurrilous gossip about his sex, which was squashed by one of the vicious satires which passed for wit in contemporary Rome. "Why do you seek witnesses to prove whether Cibo is man or woman? Look at the number of his children—sure proof. Justly may Rome call this man 'Father.' " [8] With Innocent, the last shred of discretion was torn from the Papacy, for no longer did he insult his children by referring to them as nephews. "He was the first of the popes to acknowledge openly his illegitimate children and, setting aside all established usage, to load them with riches." [9] Despite the epigrams he boasted only two children —a daughter, and a son named Franceschetto.

Good-natured, lethargic, indifferent to everything but the acquisition of gold and the well-being of his children, Innocent left most of the day-to-day business to the man who had secured his election, his fellow Genoese, Cardinal Giuliano della Rovere. His son Franceschetto became enormously wealthy. Offices and pardons of every description were frankly and openly for sale. Young Franceschetto arranged a mutually beneficial system with the vice-chancellor in which the pope's son would receive the revenue from all fines above 150 ducats and the treasury would get the rest—from which the vice-chancellor took his share. With each transaction, a few more pieces of gold found their way into Borgia's already bulging money-bags. But while Borgia was looking to the future, young Franceschetto was quite content with the present. He lost 14,000 ducats gambling one night with one of the cardinals, but his father listened to his complaint that the cardinal had been cheating and ordered restitution. A papal heir was notoriously a bad gamble; nevertheless, even such an astute politician as Lorenzo de' Medici thought it a worthwhile investment to give his daughter as wife for young Cibo.

The Medici family ultimately got back their investment. Innocent VIII survived for eight years. Again and again his natural lethargy seemed to herald death—on one such occasion his devoted son plundered the treasury and made off, to return unabashed when his father recovered. But in 1492, at the comparatively early age of sixty, Innocent died. His legacy to the Papacy was the Holy Lance, obtained from the sultan Bajazet, an empty treasury, and the establishment of the principle that anything could be sold. Franceschetto, who had no desire for the dangerous struggle for power, promptly sold the vast possessions his father had given him, and with the proceeds, retired to safe obscurity.

During the last week of July and the first of August, John Burchard, papal master of ceremonies, was in the element which he loved: the organization of an elaborate ceremonial of the Roman Church. Over the years the rules governing the conclave had developed from casual, *ad hoc* decisions into a complex body of laws that decreed everything from precedence to the minutest details of toilet. It was a task that precisely suited the pedantic German mind of Burchard, for the master of ceremonies needed an encyclopedic knowledge of hierarchy in order to deal with a body of men each of whom looked upon himself literally as a prince and was fiercely jealous of his rights. He needed, too, the qualities of a superior butler to anticipate the most unlikely demands of twenty-three men who would be in enforced seclusion for an indefinite period. Burchard had supervised the last conclave, and turning to his invaluable diary would find the most detailed notes for setting everything out for each cardinal.

A table, a chair, a stool. A seat for the dischargement of the stomach. Two urinals, two small napkins for the table of the lord [cardinal]. Twelve little table napkins for the same lord and four hand towels. Two little cloths for wiping cups. Carpet. A chest or box for the garments of the lord, his shirts, rochets, towels for wiping the face and a handkerchief. Four boxes of sweets for provisions. One vessel of sugared pine-seeds. Marzipan. Cane sugar. Biscuits. A lump of sugar. A small pair of scales. A hammer. Keys. A spit. A needle case. A writing case with penknife, pen, forceps, reed pens and pen stand. A quire of paper for writing. Red wax. A water jug. Salt cellar. Knives. Spoons. Forks. . . .[10]

The regulations were designed to resist pressure from without and Burchard efficiently saw they were applied. It was not his duty to point out that they were quite useless to prevent corruption from within.

Even before the conclave met on August 6, the trafficking in votes had achieved impressive proportions. It was well known that the king of France had paid into a bank 200,000 gold ducats to ensure the election of Giuliano della Rovere and the republic of Genoa had followed up with another 100,000 for the same candidate. The French action was fatal to della Rovere's chances: His fellow cardinals were quite prepared to sell him their votes, but not at the price of French interference. The field was clear for the next buyers.

No one man dominated during the first week of the conclave. The Florentine envoy reported to his masters that the situation was far from clear, obscured by undeclared motives and allegiances. An observer from Ferrara listed the four most likely candidates: Rodrigo Borgia was the last. Nevertheless, thought this shrewd observer, Borgia's vast wealth might bring about his election. Had he not boasted that he had sacks of gold enough to fill the Sistine Chapel? True, he was a Spaniard and the Romans still cherished a bitter memory of the pontificate of his uncle, but the conclave now was free from outside interference.

By the evening of the tenth of August, Borgia had bought the votes of thirteen cardinals. They included members of the oldest and noblest Roman families, but once assured that their price would be met, none hesitated to sell his vote to the hated foreigner. He deployed his vast wealth with skill, overcoming the suspicions of his fellow cardinals, all of whom had been cheated by the paper promises of Innocent VIII. Later, a bitter epigram winged its way round Rome. "Alexander sells the Keys, the Altar, Christ Himself—he has a right to for he bought them." [11] It was precisely true. Throughout the first four days of the conclave he bargained hard and obtained solid support. Among the neutrals, Ascanio Sforza alone remained as a potential rival. He too was enormously wealthy and unlike Borgia could count on the wide-ranging support of his family, the ruling dynasty of the great duchy of Milan.

On the evening of the tenth of August, Borgia took him on one side for a private discussion. Who could outbid the other? Sforza was offered a dazzling range of bribes. An archbishopric? An abbacy? Hard cash? The vice-chancellorship itself? Sforza was a good bargainer and extracted from Borgia not only the lucrative office of vice-chancellor but a payment in cash as well. Borgia immediately honored the cash commitment. A note was sent to his palace, and before dawn four mule-loads of bullion—gold according to some reports, silver according to others—were on their way to Sforza's own palace.

Eight cardinals proved obdurate, but Borgia needed only one more vote. Its sale was perhaps the most debased of all the sales of that conclave, for its seller was the ninety-six-year-old cardinal of Venice. The gold fever, it seemed, had struck even this man, who could not, in the nature of things, hope to enjoy the price of his simony for very long. He received a contemptuously small price among the astronomical sums—five thousand ducats—but his vote gave Borgia the necessary majority. The college went through the motions of election, praying to the Holy Ghost for guidance—to the annoyance of Sforza who protested that the whole thing was a charade—and shortly after daybreak on the morning of August 11 the name of Cardinal Rodrigo Borgia was taken from the urn.

"I am pope, I am pope," he cried excitedly and hastened to robe himself in the gorgeous vestments. He made none of the modest disclaimers which tradition demanded. Instead, Burchard was immediately ordered to prepare slips of paper, bearing the legend, "We have for pope Alexander VI, Rodrigo Borgia of Valencia," to scatter among the crowd outside. Again, Borgia was having no business with hypocritical modesty. Not for him were the Piuses or the Innocents or the Clements: He took for his name that belonging to the greatest pagan conqueror of antiquity.

The Borgia Family

It is now thirty-seven years since his uncle Calixtus III made him a cardinal and during that time he never once missed a Consistory —except when prevented by illness and that was most rare. Throughout the reigns of Pius II, Paul II, Sixtus IV and Innocent VIII he was at the center of affairs. Few understood etiquette as he did. He knew how to dominate, how to shine in conversation, how to appear dignified. Majestic in stature, he had the advantage over lesser men. He was just at that age, sixty, at which Aristotle says men are wisest. He was robust in body and vigorous in mind and so was perfectly suited to his new position.[12]

This favorable portrait by Alexander's secretary, though colored by the self-interest of the courtier, on the whole reflected Italian opinion accurately enough. Those outside the closed circle of power knew only the handsome, generous prelate who delighted in providing lavish spectacles on public occasions. Some of those nearer the vortex held rather different opinions. The young cardinal Giovanni de' Medici, who had refused to sell his vote, thought it prudent to leave Rome immediately. But the majority of the Sacred College, sated with gold, was complaisant; and the other Italian powers, looking back over the two most recent pontificates, reasonably supposed that this third one could not be as bad.

To those Christians who still cared about the nature of the occupant of the throne of Peter, Alexander gave immediate hope. On the morning after the conclave he addressed his first consistory, giving solemn warning that he intended to reform the college and purge it of its sins—purge it above all of simony. Fourteen cardinals, even then assessing their gains from the simoniacal election of this pontiff, must have been rendered exceedingly thoughtful. For the ordinary Romans, whose delight in circuses remained a constant from century to century, Alexander planned the most gorgeous of coronation ceremonies. Even as a cardinal his theatrical displays for the great *Corpus Christi* processions had outshone those of all others. Now, as pope, he scattered the hoarded wealth of decades to witness the splendor of the advent of the Borgia dynasty. The Borgia arms, the great Spanish bull *passant,* appeared at every street corner. Near the Palace of St. Mark a gigantic figure of a bull was erected from whose forehead wine gushed in a never-ending stream. Naked youths, gilded over, formed living statues; flowers cascaded from every house along the processional route; triumphal arches brought their blaze of ephemeral color to the summer streets. Antiquity was reborn, the splendor of the classic world charged with the energy of the new.

> Rome was great under Caesar—but greater far under Alexander.
> The first was only a mortal man—the second is a God.

So the triumphal arches proclaimed and the blasphemy passed unnoticed.

The eulogies of Alexander referred to the honeymoon period of his pontificate. As the true character of the reign developed, as Alexander displayed his true nature, so contemporaries began to picture him as a man little removed from a monster. The partisan hatreds of the Renaissance inevitably exaggerated, for the same hysteria that could worship the dead body of a girl would not be content with hating an ordinary man. But among the chorus of shrill invectives remain the judgments of sufficiently sober men to give solid grounds to the accusations.

A major Florentine scholar, Francesco Guicciardini, who later served Alexander's successors, granted him his eloquence, his industry, his administrative skill:

> But these virtues were bound up with far greater faults. His manner of living was dissolute. He knew neither shame nor sincerity, neither faith nor religion. Moreover, he was possessed by an insatiable greed, an overwhelming ambition and a burning passion for the advancement of his many children who, in order to carry out his iniquitous decrees, did not scruple to employ the most heinous means.[13]

The nepotism of Innocent VIII had been of a shabby, squalid, but essentially harmless, nature. Franceschetto had hungered after gold to purchase the grosser lusts of the flesh. But the Borgia clan hungered after power, and in grasping it, nearly destroyed the Papacy in the process.

Some time about the year 1460 the young Rodrigo Borgia had begun an association with a certain Vannozza de' Catanei, a member of one of the lesser noble families of Rome. Over the next twenty years Vannozza bore him four children: Giovanni, Cesare, Lucrezia and Joffré. Borgia had had at least three other children by other women before he met Vannozza and for one of these, his eldest son Pedro, he obtained the dukedom of Gandia in Spain. The young man was destined for a high secular career but he died before his father became pope, and his title—together with his father's ambitions for him—were transferred to the next in line, the fourteen-year-old-Giovanni.

In any other walk of life Borgia would have passed as the ideal husband: generous, affectionate, and, according to the casual standards of the day, reasonably faithful. Vannozza herself presents a contradictory picture as mistress to one of the more bizarre figures of the Renaissance. She must have possessed some special quality to attract and keep such a lover over decades—and maintain both his affection and protection after her beauty had gone and a younger woman at last had taken her place in his bed. But this quality is not apparent in any of the few records that bear directly upon her. She lived discreetly, as any respectable Roman matron ought, efficiently administering the properties that fell to her. In her later life she seemed keenly aware of her anomalous position, devoting her declining years to conventional good works. In her letters to her daughter she was in the habit of signing herself, "Your fortunate and unfortunate mother."

Borgia provided her with three successive husbands, each of whom gladly gave her the cloak of his name in exchange for the comfortable living provided by her lover. In 1486 when she was in her mid-forties, she married for the third and last time; immediately afterward, Borgia broke off the relationship that had lasted nearly a quarter of a century. The two eldest children, Giovanni and Cesare, had long since left the maternal home and now the six-year-old Lucrezia and her young brother Joffré were removed from Vannozza's care and placed in the home of Borgia's cousin and lifelong confidante, Madonna Adriana. And it was there, three years later, that Borgia met the beautiful Giulia Farnese —*La Bella Giulia*—to whom the wits of Rome were to accord the title of "Christ's Bride." Giulia came to Adriana's house as her future daughter-in-law. In 1489, when Giulia was perhaps sixteen, she was married in the palace of Rodrigo Borgia to Adriana's only son, and about the same time was added to the lengthy score of Borgia's mistresses.

Madonna Adriana was a widow, so there was no husband to raise difficulties about the curious situation. The Farnese family, who might possibly have objected to the debauching of a daughter, were easily satisfied from the papal cornucopia. One of Borgia's first acts as pope was to make young Alessandro Farnese, Giulia's brother, a cardinal. The Petticoat Cardinal, the Romans called him, mildly enough, and he bore the title until he too became pope in his turn, as Paul III. Even Giulia's relatives by marriage benefited. Her sister's brother-in-law came in for his share: "You will have received letters from Florence before mine reaches you and have learned what benefices have fallen to Lorenzo and all that Giulia has secured for him," Girolama Farnese wrote to her husband. "You will be greatly pleased." [14]

Borgia was forty years his mistress's senior, but it was not the obvious story of a family pandering their daughter to an elderly roué for the sake of gain. Giulia was a willing partner even after she had matured and could, within limits, make her own decisions, for her lover was an immensely attractive man. "He was a comely person of cheerful countenance, full of honeyed discourse, who gains the affection of all the women he admires and attracts them as the lodestone attracts the iron." [15]

Despite the obvious temptations, gluttony was not one of Borgia's crimes; indeed, so frugal was his normal table that his colleagues disliked dining with him. He kept his large and dignified body in good condition: Even in his late seventies he could complete a long and arduous journey by riding into Rome on horseback in the cold of an early spring night. His delight in magnificence, his uninhibited pleasure in balls and spectacular entertainments, though they might shock the sober, must have been powerful attractions for a flighty young girl just stepping into life.

Vannozza had been kept in the background while Giulia sparkled in the foreground of his life. Lorenzo Pucci, that fortunate brother-in-law of Girolama Farnese, paid a visit on Christmas Eve, 1493, to the house in Rome which sheltered the three women whom Pope Alexander loved above all other creatures. Pucci found a domestic and happy scene. "Madonna Giulia had just finished washing her hair when I entered. She was sitting by the fire with Madonna Lucrezia, the daughter of our Master, and Madonna Adriana and they all received me with great cordiality." The conversation turned to family affairs, Pucci gracefully thanked Giulia for her favors, had the compliments as gracefully returned and then was taken to see the new baby, Giulia's firstborn.

She is now well grown and, it seems to me, resembles the Pope. Madonna Giulia has grown a little stouter and is a most beautiful creature. She let down her hair before me and had it dressed. It reached to her feet—never have I seen anything like it. She has the most beautiful hair. She wore a headdress of fine linen, and over it a sort of net, light as air, with gold threads interwoven in it. In truth it shone like the sun. She wore a lined robe in the Neapolitan fashion as did also Madonna Lucrezia, who after a little while went out to remove it. She returned shortly in a gown almost entirely of violet velvet.[16]

Lucrezia, then in her thirteenth year, was herself a married woman of six months' standing. Legally speaking, it was her third marriage, for marriage contracts had been exchanged on her behalf twice before, on each occasion with noblemen in her father's native country. But that had been when he was still a mere cardinal— powerful, rich, but only one of a privileged group of rich and powerful men—glad enough to obtain even a minor member of a noble Spanish house for his illegitimate daughter. But after he became pope Lucrezia's value increased astronomically. The two contracts were repudiated and Alexander sought a more suitable husband. Cardinal Ascanio Sforza—the man to whom ultimately Borgia owed the tiara, and who now as vice-chancellor was one of the most powerful of ecclesiastics—spoke up on behalf of his kinsman Giovanni Sforza. Alexander welcomed the chance to ally himself with the powerful Lombard dynasty then controlling most of northern Italy.

Giovanni Sforza responded as eagerly to the invitation, for what heights could a pope's son-in-law not achieve? Lucrezia had not yet acquired the appalling reputation which her father's and brother's ambitions thrust upon her. In her early years, before she was moved as a pawn, and in her later years, when she was removed from the atmosphere of Rome, her true character was visible to those who cared to record it. She was generous, like her father, rather pliable and not particularly intelligent. Physically, she could not compare with Giulia but she was attractive enough. "She is of middle height and graceful in form. Her face is rather long, the nose well cut, hair golden—eyes of no special color. Her mouth is rather large, with brilliantly white teeth, her neck is slender and fair, the bust admirably proportioned." Young Giovanni Sforza might well count himself most fortunate.

On June 12, 1493, the marriage was celebrated at the Vatican, the first of those splendid family celebrations to give their own peculiar atmosphere to the legend-shrouded slopes of the Vatican Hill. Burchard, the papal master of ceremonies, brought the same painstaking efficiency to bear upon the preparations for the marriage of a pope's daughter as he would for a conclave, a funeral, or a coronation. The great *Sala Reale* and all its adjoining apartments were covered in tapestries and velvets, and upon a platform the Chair of Peter, decorated with brocade, dominated the room. Other lesser chairs were placed on either side of it, and over the wide expanse of the *Sala*'s marble floor were scattered velvet cushions in brilliant colors.

Burchard carefully recorded all details. No precedent was being established, for Innocent VIII had celebrated his son's marriage in the same place. Then, Burchard had been moved to protest, not because of the basic principle involved, but because etiquette had been broken by the presence of women at the banquet that followed. "I made a note of it because it was contrary to the prescribed rules of our ceremonies which expressly forbids women to sit at table with the pope." [17] But a lot of rules had been broken over the past twenty years and on this occasion he merely contented himself with recording what happened, not what should have happened.

> Don Juan Borgia, Duke of Gandia, the pope's son and Donna Lucrezia's elder brother, was commanded by His Holiness to escort Lucrezia. He brought her in as far as the last room, a Negro girl carrying her train, and she was followed by Donna Battistina—the granddaughter of Pope Innocent VIII of blessed memory—and her train too was borne by a Negress. Donna Giulia Farnese, the pope's concubine, and many other Roman ladies, numbering in all about one hundred and fifty, followed Lucrezia and Battistina.

The ladies forgot their manners in their excitement. As they passed the pope on his great throne, "none genuflected, despite my admonitions, except for the pope's daughter and a few beside her." [18]

After the ceremony, the festivities continued all night. All Rome who counted was there, including the ubiquitous ambassador from Ferrara who had already noted Sforza's good fortune.

> When the banquet was over the ladies danced and, as an interlude, we had an excellent play with much singing and music. The pope and all the others were there. What more can I say? My letter would never end were I to describe it all. Thus we spent the whole night, whether for good or ill I will leave your Highness to determine. [19]

Alexander VI had been on the throne for just ten months: The authentic note of his pontificate had been struck.

Vannozza was not present at her daughter's wedding, nor was the eleven-year-old Joffré. But Cesare was there, overshadowed by his brother Giovanni. Cesare naturally had benefited from the golden shower, for his father had given him a cardinal's hat on the very first consistory in August the previous year. But that was an inevitable honor, for he had been destined for the church even as a tiny boy. The reigning Sixtus IV had obligingly dispensed the four-year-old child from his canonical impediment—"being born of a cardinal and a married woman"—and thereafter his upward path was clear. Now, at the age of eighteen, Cesare was cardinal, bishop of Pampeluna, archbishop of his father's old diocese of Valencia and held numerous lesser benefices in addition. He was well on the way to being as rich as his father had been as cardinal. But all this was the mere by-product of being a Borgia. It was upon Lucrezia that Alexander lavished his love, and upon Giovanni that he built his hopes for a Borgia dynasty. Giovanni was already duke of Gandia and had only delayed his departure to Spain, and his own brilliant marriage to a Spanish princess, in order to be present at Lucrezia's wedding. Three months afterward, in August, 1493, he left for Spain and in the same month Alexander married off his last child, Joffré, to Sancia, daughter of the ruling house of Naples. Within a year of his election, Alexander had linked his family to the three dominant houses of Italy and Spain: Only France remained to be brought into the net.

Invasion, 1494

In the same month of August, 1492, that first saw Rodrigo Borgia seated on the throne of Peter, Christopher Columbus set sail across the Atlantic. It was the dramatic demonstration of a hidden process, the growth of a new world from an old. Just a generation before, the Byzantine Empire crashed in utter ruin with the fall of Constantinople to the Turk in 1453. The great rival of Rome, the great Christian bastion in the East, had been tottering for centuries, betrayed by Christians though besieged by Turks, and when it had gone, a more deadly rival had arisen. Islam now dominated the greater part of the Mediterranean, stretching its fierce arm even up the Adriatic, the fingers groping toward the heart of Europe.

In the north, nation-states had arisen out of the ruins of the empire. Spain had been among the last to find itself but since achieving unity with the marriage of Ferdinand of Castile and Isabella of Aragon in 1469, it strode upon the European stage. Italy was encompassed and menaced by giants, but Italy found itself totally incapable of adapting. It had changed the form but not the direction of power. The republics had gone, save only Venice, and she was a despotism in all but name. In their place arose the princes, men who had grasped power illegally and maintained it with strength and cunning: Medici in Florence, Sforza in Milan, Este in Ferrara, Baglioni in Perugia, Malatesta in Rimini. Some were great men, some were small, but all were committed to maintaining the earlier disastrous policies of the republics: autonomy within the narrow limits of their tiny states. They maintained their petty power by a series of shifting alliances, each heralded by treachery, for in the narrow confines of the peninsula there was neither space nor time to establish long-lasting treaties. Once, the emperor brooded over all, theoretically impartial and ready to exert his weight upon this side or the other. But now that the emperor had, it seemed, passed into history, all were now equal. To gain ascendancy it would be necessary for any one prince to summon into Italy one of the kings of the new nation-states of the north. So far, that final treachery had not been committed.

It was Ludovico Sforza, regent of Milan, who at last opened the gates to the flood. One of the more engaging of contemporary villains, a sly, humorous, cultured, and treacherous man, he ruled illegally in Milan. His young nephew, the true lord, languished in semi-imprisonment; in despair, the young man's wife appealed to her grandfather, Ferrante, king of Naples. To forestall trouble, Ludovico made certain attractive overtures to the empty-headed Charles VIII of France. Ferrante of Naples was a descendant of the house of Aragon that had overthrown the Angevin dynasty. Now if Charles, himself an Angevin, were to claim Naples. . . . So the complex, bloodstained tangle of Neapolitan affairs again began its throttling of Italy.

Charles was interested. He was even more interested when Alexander's deadly enemy, Cardinal Giuliano della Rovere, hastily left Rome and made his way to France with more news and propositions. Ferrante had died and Alexander VI, totally ignoring the claims of France, had crowned Ferrante's son Alfonso as king of Naples. Borgia had received good returns, for his own son Joffré was made a prince with a vast income, and many other Neapolitan honors had been given to the male Borgia. But pressure could be brought to bear upon Alexander.

He, della Rovere, knew better than any man that Borgia's election was the result of simony. His own hands happened to be clean and he was therefore both willing and able to aid Charles in cleansing the church. A council should be summoned, this simoniac pope deposed and replaced by, say, della Rovere, and an attack could then be made on Naples to restore the rightful Angevin dynasty. As good measure, the prospect of a crusade against the Turk was also dangled before Charles. With one vigorous campaign he could become king of Naples, king of Jerusalem, deliverer of the holy places from the Muslim and deliverer of the Papacy from the debauches of the Borgia. Ludovico Sforza would aid and cherish him during the vital entry into Italy itself.

It was an attractive proposition for a young man whose brains were stuffed full of the more lunatic fantasies of chivalry. "From infancy he had been subject to illness and was weak in constitution," Francesco Guicciardini remarked in his scathing portrait of Charles, king of France—the new savior of Italy.

> His stature was short and his face very ugly—if you except the dignity and vigor of his glance. His limbs were so disproportioned that he had less the appearance of a man than a monster and not only was he ignorant of liberal arts but he was virtually illiterate. Though eager to rule, he was in truth made for anything but that. Hating business and fatigue, he displayed in such matters as he took in hand a want of prudence and a lack of judgment. His desire for glory sprang rather from impulse than from reason. His liberality was inconsistent, immoderate, promiscuous. When he displayed inflexibility of purpose it was more often an ill-founded obstinacy than firmness.[20]

Such was Charles of Valois—but he was also king of France, able to gather together an army larger than Italy had seen in centuries. In the late summer of 1494 that army made the passage of the Alps and began the southward march.

The Papacy achieved true temporal power in the fifteenth century, but it was the power of an Italian prince wielded over Rome and the Patrimony of St. Peter. Perverted by nepotism, the vast dream of universal monarchy for which Boniface had fought and died, had become nothing more than the desire to hold on to the wedge of territories in central Italy. Alexander was in real danger, for the threat of deposition for simony was real. To counter it, he had to use the same methods as any other Italian prince, for in pursuing the goal of family aggrandizement he had reduced the Papacy to the status of an Italian family. And no European power saw any particular reason to come to the aid of the Borgias.

He turned outside Christendom, appealing for aid to its archenemy, the sultan Bajazet. Alexander had one strong card to play, for in his keeping was the bizarre figure of Djem, Bajazet's younger brother. Years before, Djem had fled after an abortive rebellion and found refuge of a sort in Christian Europe. Thereafter he had been passed from monarch to monarch as a kind of living mortgage, for Bajazet was paying a fee of 40,000 ducats a year— so long as Djem was kept in confinement. Innocent VIII had acquired him and bequeathed him to Alexander. Djem was treated as though he were a member of Alexander's intimate family group. Giovanni Borgia became particularly fond of him—even to the extent of aping his dress—and when Pinturicchio came to paint the Borgia family portrait, under the guise of *St. Catherine Disputing,* Djem found a prominent place in it.

But Djem's official position was that of hostage, and at this moment of crisis Alexander had no scruples in exploiting the unfortunate young man's value. He warned Bajazet that the French expedition was a crusade designed to depose him and place Djem upon the throne—should the "crusaders" succeed in detaching him from Rome. Urgently, therefore, Alexander requested that Bajazet should forward immediately the current 40,000 ducats due, and at the same time persuade his good friends the Venetians to launch an attack on Charles.

Bajazet had a better idea, and promptly replied to his opposite number in Rome. The simplest thing would be to kill Djem, and on receipt of his body Bajazet would hand over 300,000 ducats "with which to buy possessions for your sons." Thus the matter would be concluded to the benefit of both parties.

But Djem's execution was postponed, for both the letter and Alexander's messenger fell into the hands of the French. The knowledge that the high priest of Christendom was plotting with the sultan against the Most Christian King merely underlined what had gone before. It was high time that Christendom was relieved of this particular high priest.

Charles's army swept down the peninsula unopposed. In Florence the fanatical monk Girolamo Savonarola welcomed him as the sword of God whose coming he had long foretold. Rome itself was in a state of utmost confusion. The great family of the Colonna had long since gone over to the French; now the Orsini followed—the Orsini who were connected to the Borgias by marriage.

Alexander was in an agony of indecision. First he was going to fight, and then taking a closer look at his Neapolitan allies, decided to fly. Burchard was instructed to pack everything portable, even down to bedding. Then the pope changed his mind again. The Romans would not defend him, but the foreigners might. He sounded out Burchard as to the possibility of the large German population volunteering to serve as militia. They too declined. Then came the bitterest, most personal humiliation of all. A French patrol, sweeping ahead of the main body, captured Giulia Farnese and Madonna Adriana outside Rome while they were fleeing to Viterbo. On learning the nature of his prize, the captain of the band first informed his king, and when Charles refused to have anything to do with the matter, thriftily offered them to Alexander for a ransom of three thousand ducats. With his state toppling around his ears, Alexander yet had time to arrange the ransom, dress in a handsome suit of black velvet, and ride out to meet the distraught women. Ludovico Sforza was furious when he heard the news. To let such a prize go for three thousand ducats. . . ! "They were the heart and eyes of the Pontiff. They would have been the best whip for compelling him to do everything that was wanted of him for he could not live without them." [21]

The French army entered Rome late in the afternoon of December 31. To the last, Burchard was preoccupied with questions of etiquette and precedence. He complained to Alexander that French envoys were occupying places reserved for high ecclesiastics—what should he do about it? "Let them alone!" Alexander cried. "Do you want me to lose my head? Let the French go where they please."

Burchard perforce gave in, but he had no intention of allowing his own property to suffer. When he found that some soldiers had requisitioned his house, he complained to the king himself—and received satisfaction. Charles made a great show of keeping his troops in order: "They would not take a hen or an egg or the smallest item without fully paying for it," [22] and a number of thieves were duly strung up to encourage the Romans. But Alexander took small comfort from the protestations. He retreated into the impregnable fortress of Sant' Angelo, taking Djem Sultan with him and from there began the bargaining.

It was an anticlimax after all. Once more, the vast, undefinable, intangible power of the supreme pontiff and universal pope came to the aid of the Italian prince. All Charles's counselors and advisers agreed that Borgia should be deposed for simony—none pressed it more enthusiastically than that same Ascanio Sforza whose vote had been bought at such an enormous price—but could the rest of Christendom be persuaded that they were acting from love of Holy Church and not from plain politics? How would Charles's deeply religious subjects take it? And, in any case, who would then fill the vacant throne? In the last analysis, the decision was Charles's —a decision which the weak young man did not dare to make. Instead he exacted a cardinal's hat for one of his favorites, demanded the custody of Djem Sultan, and as surety for Alexander's good behavior, Cesare Borgia was to accompany the army in its march on Naples. Ultimately, Charles kept only the hat. Cesare Borgia escaped shortly after the army left Rome, and a few days later Djem Sultan died "from something he ate which disagreed with him," as Burchard recorded with a discretion that achieved irony.

The attack on Naples too came as an anticlimax; a corrupt foreign dynasty, cordially hated by its subjects, collapsing at a touch. For a brief while, young Charles strutted in splendor, towering schemes of conquest passing through his addled brain. But yet again, Italy, like some bottomless morass, sucked down yet another triumphant army. While the French were dissipating their strength in the luxury of Naples, behind their backs their late allies in the north realigned themselves. Charles was too successful—therefore he must be brought low. Treachery, the northerners called such grossly amoral conduct; practical politics, the Italians retorted. Their dealings with each other were based, after all, on a precisely similar code. Alexander suddenly found new friends. Too late, Charles found himself outwitted and isolated and was forced to retreat up the peninsula, this time fighting all the way. In Tuscany, Savonarola came out to nag and upbraid him. "You have incurred the wrath of God by neglecting that work of reforming the Church which, by my mouth, He had charged you to undertake." But Charles had had enough alike of glory and prophesying monks; all he wanted now was to get home in one piece. He succeeded, but at terrible cost. At the battle of Fornuovo the French barely escaped annihilation and were forced, moreover, to leave behind the colossal booty they had accumulated during the triumphant days.

Alexander was in a stronger position than before. The looming threat of deposition had been dispersed; his opposition was in the open and could be attacked not simply as enemies of the Borgia family, but of the Holy See itself—indeed of Italy—for having aligned themselves with the French invader. Now he could begin to crush the last elements of resistance, beginning with the Orsini. His son the duke of Gandia was summoned from Spain for the glorious cause.

This "stage prince, bedizened with ornaments and tinsel," was made legate of the Patrimony of St. Peter, legate of Perugia, commander-general of the papal forces and then sent south to win glory for the Borgia. He failed completely. Alexander propped him up with the great Spanish general, Gonsalvo di Cordoba, under whose veteran leadership the task was accomplished. Alexander dispensed fitting rewards. Gonsalvo was thanked, and large areas were carved out of the States of the Church and granted to Giovanni, duke of Gandia, and his descendants in perpetuity. There was only a thin protest at the theft of Church property, for the college of cardinals was now dominated by Spaniards, eight of whom were blood relations of Alexander's.

Murder of the Duke of Gandia

On the evening of June 14, 1497, just a week after Giovanni Borgia was established as an Italian baron, his mother Vannozza gave a family dinner in the vineyard of her home in the suburbs. The evening passed decorously, and toward dusk Giovanni and his brother Cesare, together with some servants and friends, rode back to the papal palace. At some distance from it, Giovanni bade his friends good night, and accompanied by only a groom and an unknown man in a festive mask, rode into the darkness. A few minutes later he dismissed the groom and continued his mysterious journey with the masked man. It was the last time he was seen alive.

Late on the following morning his servants reported to Alexander that Giovanni had not returned. "His Holiness also became very anxious, but continued to hope for the Duke's return during the rest of the day, having persuaded himself that his son had spent the night with some girl and did not want to be seen leaving her house in daylight." [23] It was a reasonable assumption, knowing Giovanni's habits as he did, but at nightfall the groom was found, terribly wounded, and unable to give information as to his master's whereabouts. Alexander, now thoroughly alarmed, ordered a massive search to be made.

On the following day—June 16—the searchers questioned a wood dealer who plied his trade on the banks of the Tiber. He was asked if he had seen anything unusual on the night of the murder and replied with a circumspect tale. On that night he had been in his boat moored alongside the bank. At about midnight two men cautiously appeared and surveyed the river. Obviously they had not seen him, for they retraced their steps, and shortly afterward there appeared a rider on a white horse with the body of a dead man slung over it. The two men whom he had first noticed were walking on each side of the horse, keeping the body from falling.

Near the sewage outfall, the horse was backed into the river and the two men then picked up the corpse and threw it as far as they could into the river. The body disappeared, but the cloak floated and stones were thrown at it till it sank. The horseman and his companions then disappeared again into the night.

On completion of his story the wood dealer was asked a reasonable question: Why had he not reported the crime to the city fathers? He replied, equally reasonably, that during the time he had worked on the river he had seen at least a hundred bodies thrown in. No inquiries had ever been made about them, therefore he had seen no particular reason to report this one incident out of so many.

Some three hundred watermen were immediately assembled and the river was dragged. "Truly, now, was Alexander VI a fisher of men," the wits of the city mocked. At about midday the body of Giovanni, duke of Gandia, was brought up from the liquid filth. He was still dressed in all his finery, down to a pair of gloves under a belt that contained thirty ducats. His throat had been slit and nine other terrible wounds had been hacked all over his body.

According to Burchard, Alexander went out of his mind with grief. "From Wednesday evening until the following Saturday the Pope ate and drank nothing whilst from Thursday morning to Sunday he was quiet for not one moment of the day," the master of ceremonies recorded with his cold exactitude, betraying no hint of compassion for the tormented man. Vannozza Catanei, the discarded mistress, came forward to comfort Alexander, soothing his grief with the reminder that he had other children—in particular Cesare—who would sustain the Borgia glory as adequately as the slaughtered Giovanni.

The murderer was never discovered, though suspicion rested upon many people: the Orsinis, who had been dispossessed to give Giovanni his estates; the Sforzas, particularly young Giovanni; any one of a number of personal enemies, including an unknown cuckold; and finally, the dead man's brother Cesare. That particular accusation was not made until a year after the murder, when Cesare threw off his priestly robes to emerge as a prince. But once made, it mushroomed until it overshadowed all other accusations and passed at last for fact. His main motive was supposed to be jealousy of his brother's secular glory and a desire to obtain the titles and honors for himself. Cesare was probably innocent of this crime at least.

There was no particular animosity between the brothers and

Cesare stood to gain nothing from the murder, for Giovanni had a son to whom, in fact, his title passed—as Cesare must have known it would. The motive for the murder was almost certainly, as Cardinal Ascanio Sforza speculated, "something to do with a love affair." The frenzied, brutal hacking of the body, its tied hands, and the attempt to dispose of it argued some such cause. Moreover, a political assassination would have been cleanly and swiftly done and the body left where it had fallen—Romans were accustomed to finding corpses in the morning streets.

After the first passion of his grief was spent, Alexander's reaction was characteristically extreme. On June 19, 1497, five days after Giovanni's murder, he addressed a consistory in a speech of considerable dignity:

> The blow which has fallen upon us is the heaviest we could have possibly suffered for we loved the Duke of Gandia more than anyone in the world. We would give seven tiaras to recall him to life. God has given us this punishment for our sins, for the Duke has done nothing to deserve such a death. Therefore, we are resolved to amend our life and reform the Church. We renounce all nepotism. We will begin the reform with ourselves and so proceed through all levels of the Church till the whole work is accomplished.[24]

At the time, Alexander meant exactly what he said. The Church was to be cleansed of the accumulated filth of centuries, and a commission of six cardinals was immediately appointed to draw up a draft bull to cover the whole field of reform. It speaks much for both Alexander's energy and sincerity that the notoriously lumbering curia was goaded into such a burst of activity that in a little over six weeks the complex draft was laid before him for approval. It did not spare either the reigning or the previous popes. Simony, above all, was condemned in all its forms, whether it were the open simony of the sale of votes at elections, or the alienation of Church territories by the creation of such hereditary barons as the late duke of Gandia.

The morality of the clergy came in for special scrutiny, and if the provisions had been made operative, the lives of the entire hierarchy—from parish priests to pope—would have been immediately affected. The clergy were not to involve themselves in worldly affairs, whether of politics or pleasure. All concubines were to be dismissed within ten days of the publication of the bull. Frugality was to be enforced upon the cardinals: The numbers of their household servants were to be limited, strolling players and musicians were forbidden their palaces. So the great plan of reform unrolled itself, touching even minor details of the civil government of Rome.

The draft bull of July, 1497, is one of the great "ifs" of history. Alexander was genuinely, if briefly, sincere, and to avoid the obvious accusations he had ordered his youngest son, Joffré, to leave Rome with his wife immediately. He even contemplated sending Lucrezia to live in Spain. Other popes had made dramatic changes in their lives on achieving the Papacy—he had the example of his old patron Pius II to follow. Even the contemptible Petticoat Cardinal abandoned his more lurid habits on becoming Paul III.

Alexander was not particularly gifted as a statesman, for most of his policies were shortsighted except where they affected his children. But he did possess an immense enthusiasm, an almost limitless ability to charm and persuade. It would have been impossible to enforce morality by a godlike decree from above, for the cardinals, those hinges of the Church, had long been immovable save as they desired. But it might well have been possible to accomplish a basic change if only by making immorality unprofitable. That, Alexander could have done; and Luther, then a neurotic fourteen-year-old, would probably have lived and died a faithful Augustinian monk.

But Alexander's very enthusiasms told against him: He lacked the moral stamina to undertake a long, hard, and dreary path when all around him was a glowing world to be enjoyed. The bull was never published, though it created one scapegoat. A month after it was drawn up, Alexander's secretary, Bartolomeo Flores, was arrested and charged with forging papal briefs. There was no doubt that Flores had pursued a lucrative sideline for years and his condemnation to lifelong imprisonment was richly deserved. But it was also observed that Flores had been privy to a great many dangerous secrets of his master's.

Cesare Borgia

On July 21, 1498, Alexander's daughter Lucrezia was married off for the second time, the first stage of a complex plan to place her brother Cesare upon the throne of Naples. There had been a certain impediment in that she was already legally married to Giovanni Sforza, but threatened alike by his father-in-law's spiritual menaces and his brother-in-law's dagger, the young man gave way. He did it reluctantly, ungracefully—but achieved a vengeance upon his wife far more effective than the casual stroke of a sword.

Sforza had been placed in an unpleasant position during the invasion of 1496 when his kinsmen had thrown in their lot with the French. He pointed this out forcefully to his uncle Ludovico:

> Yesterday His Holiness said to me, "Well, Giovanni Sforza, what have you to say to me?" I answered, "Holy Father, everyone in Rome believes that your Holiness has entered into an agreement with the King of Naples who is an enemy of the State of Milan. If this is so I am in an awkward position, as I am in the pay both of your Highness and of Milan. I don't see how I can serve one party without offending the other. I ask that your Holiness may be pleased to define my position. . . ." He replied saying that I took too much interest in his affairs and that I should choose in whose pay I would remain according to my contract. My lord—if I had foreseen in what position I would be placed I would have sooner eaten the straw under my body than have entered into such an agreement. Do not, I beg you, desert me but give me help, favor and advice. . . .[25]

Giovanni, the merest pawn in a giant and bloody game, got no help from his uncle—who had his own problems. Bitterly, now, Giovanni paid for his brief glory as son-in-law of Pope Alexander VI as his position daily became more intolerable. He was not to know it, but even had his uncle remained Alexander's devoted ally, his own position would not have been a whit the better. The Borgias had decided on another plan and Giovanni Sforza was in the way. He was asked outright to agree to a divorce, refused, and pressure was immediately put upon him. Lucrezia may have saved his life

—unless she and her brother had planned together to give him unequivocal warning. Cesare came to her room when Sforza's chamberlain was with her; she ordered the chamberlain to hide and he overheard Cesare's frank declaration of intent to murder Sforza. "Go and tell your master what you have heard," Lucrezia instructed him after Cesare left. The chamberlain did so, and Giovanni immediately fled.

The duke of Gandia was murdered a few days afterward and Giovanni was given a breathing space. But it did him little good. An obedient commission found that Lucrezia was a virgin after more than three years of marriage, accepted her declaration that Giovanni was impotent, and therefore established grounds for declaring the marriage null. Giovanni appealed to the head of his family, the sardonic Ludovico, who made the helpful suggestion that Giovanni should demonstrate his ability before witnesses. His nephew declined, and then in rage and shame cried out that the real reason why the pope wanted the divorce was in order to enjoy his daughter himself. The accusation fell on fertile ground, appealing as it did both to lovers of pornography and haters of the Borgia, and developed into a monstrous plant. The wild accusation that Alexander wanted to commit incest rapidly crystallized into assertions that he had. Both Cesare and the dead duke of Gandia were drawn in. They too were supposed to have been involved in an incestuous relationship with Lucrezia, and Cesare's jealousy was adduced as sufficient reason for the murder of his brother. Groundless though the charges were, the characters of all the males of the family only too easily gave them a color that was never wholly to be washed away.

Despite his protests, Giovanni Sforza was at length obliged to recognize his helplessness, and on December 20, 1497, Lucrezia was released from a marriage that her father no longer required. In July of the following year she was married, very quietly, to the duke of Bisceglie, son of the king of Naples. She brought with her a massive dowry, but part of that purchase price was intended to persuade the king to give his daughter Carlotta to Cesare. Sitting at the center of affairs, Alexander knew full well that the days of the present dynasty of Naples were drawing to a close. When it fell, he intended that his son would be established there to found a new and enduring dynasty. But the plan failed. The king declined to hand his daughter over.

The princess Carlotta was at that time in France, having been brought up at the royal court—a trivial fact that was to have profound consequences for Italy. The empty-headed young Charles VIII had died and was succeeded by the scarcely more practical Louis XII. In the same month that Lucrezia was preparing for her wedding, Louis sent envoys to his Holy Father humbly requesting that his marriage to an ailing and unattractive woman should be dissolved, leaving him free to marry a beautiful and wealthy heiress. Alexander received the envoys kindly. Yes, of course Louis could receive a dispensation, if he would agree to use his influence on the princess Carlotta and also grant some worthy honor to Cesare. Louis was delighted to agree to both conditions.

Alexander had received Cesare's request to relinquish his cardinalate with deep displeasure, but in the end had given way—the first stage of Cesare's ultimate domination over him. One of the problems that the renunciation would create was that Cesare would be stripped of his lucrative benefices, but now, with a wealthy and grateful king prepared to dispense honors, that difficulty was resolved. Cesare was offered, and accepted, the dukedom of Valentinois in the Dauphine, together with an income of 20,000 francs per year. The Spaniards protested at this transformation of a Spanish cardinal into a French duke, but Alexander replied smoothly that it was necessary for the salvation of Cesare's soul. In any case, Spanish interests would still be protected: Alexander's cousin Giovanni Borgia neatly filled the vacancy left by Cesare. On August 17, 1498, Cesare began his career as secular prince: He was just twenty-two years old.

That indefatigable gossip writer Andrea Boccaccio, the resident envoy from Ferrara, sketched a vivid portrait of his hero while Cesare was still a priest.

> I met Cesare yesterday in the house in Trastevere: He was just on his way to the chase dressed in a costume altogether worldly: that is, in silk—and armed. He had only a little tonsure like a simple priest.

I conversed with him for a while as we rode along—I am on intimate terms with him. He possesses marked genius and a charming personality, bearing himself like a great prince. He is especially lively and merry and fond of society. The archbishop never had any inclination for the priesthood but his benefices bring him in more than 16,000 ducats annually.[26]

It is an innocent picture, this first portrait of the man who in five short years was to loom on the Italian consciousness as a species of demon. He shared with his sister the Borgia charm and gaiety, but where she drifted with the wind, easily giving way to more dominant wills, behind his silks and perfume and easy conversation was an iron determination directed toward one goal—the acquisition of power. Even the easygoing discipline of the Renaissance Church had proved too irksome for him. "Either Caesar or nothing" a flattering smith later engraved upon his sword, and it was an appropriate enough motto. Had he been older, thus with a proportionately higher chance of succeeding his father, he might have carved his career in the Church, making the Papacy truly hereditary. One of the reasons he gave for desiring to relinquish his priestly role was that he wanted to marry. But women meant little to him. His awesome reputation as satyr rested on grounds as flimsy as that of the charge of incest, and he never saw his wife after the few weeks of their honeymoon in France. He perhaps had a genuine desire to found a dynasty but as a by-product of gaining power, not as its motive.

On the same day that Cesare formally renounced the priesthood, royal envoys arrived in Rome to escort him to France. Over six weeks passed before Cesare deemed himself ready to leave: Much of the time was consumed in gathering together a train brilliant enough to impress the French. On October 1 when the cortege assembled outside the Vatican it resembled more closely the state of an oriental monarch than the escort of an as yet uninvested duke. Cesare himself was dressed dramatically in black and white and gold, in the French fashion. His immediate companions were the highest prelates of the Church and young nobles of the foremost Roman families, all eagerly forgetting the Roman contempt for a

Spanish bastard in their desire to attach themselves to his rising star. A vast train of mules carried treasure computed at 200,000 ducats.

But the total effect of the pomp was vulgarity rather than splendor. Alexander, watching the procession from a window of the Vatican Palace, was utterly delighted with every detail. Louis, who also watched that procession from a window as it approached him at Chinon six weeks later, was openly contemptuous. The display "was too much for the petty duke of Valentinois." But the petty duke bore the king's precious dispensation and was granted all the honors he desired—save one. No one was able to persuade the young Carlotta to accept this dubious bridegroom. It was humiliating for Cesare and embarrassing for Louis and infuriating for Alexander. But even the high priest of Christendom could not dispense a bridegroom from the necessity of obtaining his bride's voluntary consent.

Nevertheless, Cesare had come to France for a royal bride and a royal bride was provided for him. There was another unattached maiden being brought up at the royal court, the seventeen-year-old Charlotte d'Albret, a princess in her own right. Louis offered her and Cesare equably accepted her in lieu of Carlotta. Their married life was happy for it lasted precisely four months. In September, 1499, King Louis left France to undertake the second invasion of Italy and Cesare hastened to follow, playing the part of jackal so that later he could himself be lion. Charlotte, already pregnant, never saw him again.

A decade after Alexander had descended to the grave and the bubble empire of Cesare was scattered to the winds, the disgraced Florentine politician Niccolò Machiavelli dispassionately surveyed their tumultuous career. They had done well he thought, all things considered, twisting circumstances to meet their desired ends. Lucidly he analyzed Alexander's purpose in welcoming those same French before whom he had trembled barely five years earlier.

Alexander, wishing to give his son a sovereignty in Italy, had not only present but future difficulties to contend with. He saw no means of making him sovereign of any state independent of the Church— but if he attempted to dismember the ecclesiastical state he knew full well that the Duke of Milan and the Venetians would never consent. Elsewhere, the military power of Italy was in the hands of those who had the most to fear from him—such as the Orsini, the Colonna and their allies. It was consequently necessary to dissolve these various alliances and to throw the Italian states into a confusion, in order to secure the sovereignty of a part.[27]

Pope Alexander, Machiavelli concluded, applied with skill and the necessary cynicism the ancient formula of "divide and rule."

The first part of the plan called for an attack upon Milan, the price for French aid in Italy. It went smoothly. Ludovico Sforza fled, the Milanese welcomed Louis, and he declared himself duke of Milan by right of inheritance. By October he was ready to help his ally Cesare to carve himself a principality.

The area chosen was Romagna, the northern section of the Papal States where they touched the Adriatic. Each of the Romagnol cities was in effect the personal stronghold of some warlord who recognized with infinite reluctance the authority of his overlord, the pope. Alexander was probably in his right when in October, 1499, he declared that the Romagnol lords had fallen behind in their feudal dues and their cities were therefore forfeit to him. Backed by French swords, Cesare immediately swooped upon the first of his prey, the cities of Imola and Forlì which had been granted to a nephew by a previous pope and were now ruled by the virago Caterina Sforza. The citizens immediately abandoned their mistress but she fought on with immense courage, spurred on as much by personal loathing and fear of Cesare as by political considerations. She had reason to fear, for when inevitably she surrendered, she found she was the personal possession of her conqueror.

The opening of the campaign in Romagna was not a very impressive performance after all, for Romagnol loyalty to Romagnol lords had never been particularly strong. Cesare's dependence upon the French was shown very clearly a few weeks later when a revolt in Milan forced Louis to withdraw the troops he had lent Cesare and the conquest of the rest of Romagna immediately came to a halt. But in Rome, Alexander heard of the news of his son's success with tears of joy. He was now seventy years old, "but he grows younger every day," a disenchanted Venetian recorded. "His cares never last the night through. He is always merry and does nothing except that which he chooses. The advancement of his children is his only interest—nothing else troubles him." [28] Cesare was not the only object of that incessant care.

The lands of the Gaetani, which old Boniface VIII had been at such pains to acquire, now fell to the Borgia hunger. The head of the Gaetani family was disposed of by the time-honored method of imprisonment, followed by either poison or starvation, and Lucrezia joined the thinning ranks of landed Roman nobility. A year later, the lands of the two other great Roman families—the Colonna and the Savelli—were carved up and shared between her little son Rodrigo and her stepbrother Giovanni, Alexander's child by Giulia Farnese. The unbridled nepotism did not go without notice or protest. The Portuguese threatened to call a council: There was real danger that Spain and Germany would withdraw obedience. But each could be bought off, or threatened with an enemy. The Italians themselves, as Machiavelli saw with the clarity of hindsight, were dazed and confused.

On February 26, 1500, Cesare entered Rome in triumph. He was dressed in his habitual black velvet, surrounded by a bodyguard dressed too in his somber colors. Caterina Sforza, the late Lady of Imola and Forlì, was dragged behind him in golden chains and, after being displayed to the mob, was imprisoned in Sant' Angelo. She would never again have seen the light of day had it not been for the French. They had greatly admired the gallantry of her defense, and under their pressure Alexander was forced to release her.

Cesare had a superb stage to display his first triumph, for 1500 was another year of Jubilee and Rome was crowded with pilgrims from every nation in Europe. It was during this year of Jubilee that Cesare at last emerged as the dominant half of the father-son partnership. It was from here onward that the reign of Rodrigo Borgia took on its lurid colors. Hitherto, the Vatican had been the scene of scandalous enough behavior; now, the court became actively criminal—curiously, deliberately, perverted. Not only the gossipmongering enemies of the Borgia recorded details, inevitably exaggerating as they did, but even the pedantic Burchard coldly described scenes which the professional pornographers of the day could not have bettered. Lucrezia was dragged in, with her fatal compliancy. Burchard merely recorded the fact that she was present upon the occasion when fifty Roman harlots coupled with fifty palace servants for prizes presented by Alexander. Others embroidered, making her promoter as well as observer. She stood with her father at a window in the Vatican while Cesare shot down a number of unarmed criminals who had been turned loose in a courtyard. It was as though Cesare was intent upon debasing her name totally.

Outside the Vatican, Cesare became undisputed lord of Rome. "The Pope loves his son—and has great fear of him," [29] a foreigner noted; and under Cesare's rule Rome knew a terror it had never experienced under Alexander. The pope could, and did, murder—but that was for political, not personal, reasons. Cesare murdered for both reasons. A drunken masquerader lost his hand and tongue for mocking him. A Venetian, accused of circulating a hostile pamphlet, was condemned to be drowned in the Tiber. The Venetian ambassador came to plead with Alexander but the pope could only shrug his shoulders. "The Duke is a good-natured man—but he cannot tolerate insults. I have often told him that Rome is a free city, and that everyone may write and speak as he pleases. Evil is often spoken of me but I let it pass. The Duke replied 'Rome is accustomed to write and speak—maybe, but I will teach such people to take care.' " [30]

"Evil is often spoken of me but I let it pass"—Alexander spoke the truth in this matter. As supreme pontiff he had launched the first censorship of printed books into the world—the *Index*, which was to survive over four hundred years. Yet never did he take official notice of the peculiarly vile personal attacks that circulated throughout Italy in pamphlet form. It was perhaps this very tolerance that allowed his son to gain ascendancy over him.

Cesare had come to Rome not only to display his triumph but for money to continue his conquests, and his father was quick to oblige. The Jubilee gifts of tens of thousands of pilgrims found their way into Borgia coffers, but even this was not enough. In September, nine new cardinals were created. "Most of them are men of doubtful reputation. All have paid handsomely for their elevation—some of them have paid 20,000 ducats and more, so that between 120,000 and 130,000 ducats have been collected. Alexander VI is showing to the world that the amount of a Pope's income is exactly what he chooses." [31]

Yet still Cesare was not satisfied. It seems that he was jealous of Alexander's generosity toward Lucrezia, not from any sense of personal affection for his father, but because he felt that these fat revenues should be devoted to his own campaigns. Lucrezia's second husband, the duke of Bisceglie, had lost his value. The French and the Spaniards had temporarily united to topple Bisceglie's family in Naples. Alexander had smoothly agreed to invest the victors with his son-in-law's inheritance, and the duke of Bisceglie was in exactly the same position as Giovanni Sforza had been three years earlier. He had already fled but foolishly returned at Alexander's command. Now, fearfully, he watched for the first hostile move from his wife's appalling family.

On the evening of July 15, 1500, the young man was set upon by a band of assassins in the Piazza San Pietro. He was badly wounded but escaped. Convinced that Cesare was behind the attempt, as soon as Bisceglie recovered he made a brave but inept attempt to shoot Cesare as he walked in the Vatican gardens. He missed and condemned himself to death.

There was considerable mystery as to exactly how he met that death. A Venetian report stated that he had returned to his invalid bed where he was nursed by his wife and sister, who for fear of poison cooked his food in the room. Cesare entered the room with one of his professional killers, forced the women to leave, and strangled the invalid. Burchard was considerably more discreet, remarking only that the dead man's physicians were examined, "but were soon released since the man who had entrusted them with the commission went unpunished—and he was well known." Normally lucid, Burchard's discretion led him to a probably deliberate incoherence. Bisceglie was strangled, not poisoned, so the examination of the physicians was irrelevant. But Burchard was following his master's lead. Alexander, while not planning the murder, did not deplore it: The whole thing was to be forgotten, and a veteran papal official like Burchard had learned not to trust even his own diary.

In September Cesare left Rome at the head of 10,000 men for his great sweep of conquests. He had only one dangerous enemy in Italy and that was time itself, for young though his father might be at heart, he was nevertheless an old man. "He had good reason to fear that a new pope would be hostile to him," Machiavelli considered,

> . . . and seek to deprive him of what had been bestowed on him by his predecessor. He therefore made four distinct provisions, in the first place by utterly destroying the families of all those nobles whom he had deprived of their states so that no future pope could reestablish them. Secondly, by attaching to his interests all the gentry of Rome in order to control the power of the Pope. Thirdly, by securing a majority in the College of Cardinals. Fourthly and lastly, by acquiring so much power in the lifetime of his father that he might be able to resist the first attack of the enemy. Three of these designs he had effected before the death of Alexander.[32]

Alexander's task in the grand design was to maintain the supply of gold and divide and confuse the enemy. Both tasks he faithfully discharged. As he had anticipated after agreeing to invest both the kings of Spain and France with the dismembered kingdom of Naples, the French and Spaniards quarreled over the spoils. Now, swiftly, Cesare arose from that subordinate position which he had been obliged to tolerate in his relationship with Louis. The French influence that had served to check his more outrageous activities declined and vanished: Louis needed Cesare in his struggle with the Spaniards. The slender black-clad figure seemed to have the ability to appear in a dozen places at once, now in Naples, now in Tuscany, in Romagna, Umbria—but always back to Romagna. Alexander heard with joy of the fall of city after city—Faenza, Cesena, Senigaglia, Urbino, Camerino. On news of the fall of Camerino, the Venetian ambassador Antonio Giustiniani happened to be with him.

"He could so little contain himself that, to give some relief to his feelings and mark the importance of the news, he got up from his chair and went to the window and there he listened as the letter of his Duke was read aloud." [33]

Nothing was too much for this wonderful son. He gave him the resounding title of "Cesare Borgia of France—by the grace of God Duke of the Romagna and Valencia and Urbino, Prince of Andria, Lord of Piombino, Standard-Bearer and General-in-Chief of the Church." The murder of Bisceglie now paid dividends, for Lucrezia, again free to marry, was offered to the son of the Este of Ferrara, whose dominions bordered Cesare's to the north.

Young Alfonso d'Este was extremely reluctant to be added to the ill-fated catalog of Lucrezia's husbands, but the rich bribes that were offered overcame his natural hesitation. He gained, in fact, a pious and virtuous wife, for Lucrezia, as adaptable as ever, conformed to the comparative respectability of the Ferrarese court as wholeheartedly as she had joined in the Roman saturnalia. Her father considerately postponed the start of Lent in Ferrara "so that the people there could lawfully eat meat and have festivals and thanksgiving when Donna Lucrezia arrived."

Shortly before her marriage Lucrezia had discharged an important task for her father, acting as a species of deputy-pope while he visited his son's encampment at Piombino. Burchard, who had once been shocked by the presence of women at a papal banquet had no comment to offer on this curious innovation.

The late summer of 1503 was unusually hot and sultry even for Rome. The stench emanating from the streets at the height of summer gave clear warning of the dangers of remaining in the city, and normally Alexander would have sought the coolness and health of one of his country villas. But the affairs of Cesare were approaching their climax—a massive expedition was being planned against Naples—and the pope therefore was obliged to remain at the center of affairs.

August began badly for him. His cousin, Cardinal Giovanni Borgia, had fallen victim to the Roman summer and his funeral took place on the first day of August. Alexander stood glumly at his favorite window in the Vatican Palace, watching the funeral of his cousin, a man who had been as portly as himself and much the same age. "This is a bad month for stout people," [34] he remarked, and had barely finished speaking when in broad daylight an owl flopped through the window and fell at his feet. He was terrified by the omen.

The occasion of the eleventh anniversary of his accession fell ten days later. There were no particular celebrations to mark it, and observers noted that the usually jovial pope was melancholy and downcast. On the following day, Saturday, August 12, he fell ill—desperately ill. So too did Cesare, and a certain Cardinal Adrian Corneto at whose villa Alexander and Cesare had dined a few days earlier.

Rumor made the most of the coincidence. It had long been believed that Corneto had been marked down by father and son as their next victim. According to the Venetian ambassador Giustiniani, their practice was to fatten their victims before slaughter, gorging the more powerful of the cardinals with ever richer benefices for which they received immense payment, and then dispatching them with a certain "white powder."

It was a demonstrably simple matter to show that the vast majority of the cardinals who died during Alexander's reign succumbed from natural causes: Cardinals tended to be elderly men. But the hatred in which the Borgia were held made the accusation universally acceptable. Italians, in addition, were morbidly preoccupied with the concept of poison as a political weapon, for it carried into effect that national taste for coldly planned vengeance which Machiavelli enshrined as a political philosophy. Any death not obviously attributable to violence or plague was simply accounted for by the theory of poison—it was axiomatic that every man had an enemy. Despite the fact that poison was notoriously difficult to administer to a man on his guard—Cesare himself preferred the surer method of open murder—the Borgia as archcriminals naturally became invested with the skill of archpoisoners.

Alexander employed poison as a useful adjunct to politics with about the same level of success as did his supposedly less gifted rivals. But the skilled pens of his enemies turned that modest ability into something approaching the supernatural. The "white powder" of the Borgia—a crude preparation of arsenic that was difficult to disguise and unpredictable in effect—became a magic potion employed at will by all members of the family; with it, they could strike down enemies far distant and at any fraction of time they desired. Everything that the Borgia did was larger than life, and it was too much to expect of the gossips of Rome that they would accept Alexander's fatal illness as a result merely of the prosaic, if lethal, fever of the Roman summer. Adrian Corneto thought that he himself had been poisoned, and from his natural suspicion a most elaborate story was built up. Cesare was supposed to have prepared a poisoned cup for him, but it had been switched and the unsuspecting Alexander and Cesare had drunk freely of it.

Cesare, though very ill, began to recover within a few days: Alexander was doomed. For a week, the seventy-three-year-old man battled with a fever that laid prostrate his tough young son; but on the same Friday that Cesare took a turn for the better, Alexander entered his death agonies. Rumors of supernatural activities made their rounds, for no man could believe that such a pope was making his exit in a natural manner. Servants swore that they overheard the dying man pleading with an invisible companion for a little more time—he had sold his soul to the devil who had promised him a pontificate of exactly eleven years and one week. "The devil was seen to leap out of the bedroom in the shape of an ape. And a cardinal ran to seize it and, having caught it, would have given it to the pope. But the pope said, 'Let him go, let him go. It is the Devil.' And that night he fell ill and died." [35] And long after his death water boiled in his mouth and steam poured out of the apertures of his body.

Burchard knew nothing of demonic visitations and the suspension of natural laws. The story he had to tell was not so much earthly as squalid. Alexander was still *in extremis* when Cesare's men forced their way into the Vatican and collected all portable treasure. The pope died, and his valets immediately plundered his bedroom unhindered, for no person of rank came near the corpse until Burchard, as part of his duties, came to dress it. It lay all that night unattended, and when in the morning the Office for the Dead was recited over it, the palace guards attacked the handful of priests, who fled, again leaving their late master's corpse unguarded.

Burchard feared that the Romans might break in and desecrate it in their hatred, and so it was moved to a chapel where it remained throughout Sunday. Still it had not reached the nadir of its humiliation. When Burchard came back to prepare it for its last resting place, he found the changes wrought by death had made it too large for the coffin. Coldly, meticulously as ever, he described the swollen, blackened appearance of what had been Alexander VI. "The face was mulberry-colored and thickly covered with blue-black spots: the nose swollen, the mouth distorted, the tongue doubled over, the lips puffed out so that they seemed to cover the whole lower face." The porters joked obscenely as they tried to stuff the corpse into its coffin. Eventually they succeeded but only by taking the miter off, rolling the body in a carpet, and then pounding it into the coffin with their fists. "No candles were lit, and no priest or other person of dignity attended the corpse."

> So died Pope Alexander, at the height of glory and prosperity about whom it must be known that he was a man of the utmost power and of great judgment and spirit, as his actions and behavior showed. But as his first accession to the Papacy was foul and shameful—for he bought with gold so high an office—so similarly his government was in agreement with its vile foundation. There was in him, and in full measure, all vices both of flesh and spirit. . . . There was in him no religion, no keeping of his word. He promised all things liberally, but bound himself to nothing that was not useful to himself. He had no care for justice, since in his days Rome was a den of thieves and murderers. His ambition was boundless, and such that it grew in the same measure as his state increased. Nevertheless, his sins meeting with no punishment in this world, he was to the last of his days most prosperous. In one word, he was more evil and more lucky than, perhaps, any other pope for many ages before.[36]

The judgment of Francesco Guicciardini, the great Florentine scholar, was written over a generation after Alexander had gone to his grave. But still the fierce hatreds aroused by the name of

Borgia were strong enough to distort the truth, so that Guicciardini could repeat, without qualification, the charges of incest and wholesale poisoning. Few would dispute his opinion that Alexander had been one of the luckiest of popes, even though that luck was created largely by the incompetence and mutual treachery of his enemies. But Guicciardini's confident moral judgment—that Alexander had been the most evil pope for ages—was a very large claim in the context of the Renaissance Papacy. The judgment of posterity was based on the opinions of contemporaries, and those opinions were luridly colored by the hatred of men who had been despoiled or threatened by the papal monarch, but who remained indifferent to the grotesque corruption of the priest except as it benefited them politically. Other popes had been solicitous for the advancement of their children: few had been as energetic or successful as Alexander. And every acre of land, every title gained for those children, earned just a little more hatred from those forced to yield their possessions to a Borgia bastard.

The true extent of Alexander's power was demonstrated by the total collapse of Cesare's empire on his father's death. Cesare himself put it down to bad luck. "He told me himself," Machiavelli remarked, "the very day that Julius II was elected, that he had foreseen every obstacle which could arise on the death of his father—except that, at the critical period, his own life would be in imminent danger." When Cesare recovered it was to find that the great enemy of the Borgia, Cardinal Giuliano della Rovere, had been elected pope as Julius II. *Il papa terribile,* the Italians called Julius, the "Awesome Pope," who lived by preference in armor but yet had diplomatic skill enough to outmatch Cesare. Lucrezia alone remained loyal to her brother, but there was little that she could do. Encircled by resurgent enemies, Cesare at length fled to Spain, and there, three years after Alexander's death, he fell fighting bravely enough but as a common mercenary.

VI
The Golden Age

Giovanni de' Medici
Pope Leo X (1513–1521)

THE HOUSE OF MEDICI
(The senior branch)

Giovanni di Bicci de' Medici (1360–1429)

Cosimo (1389–1464)
m. Contessina de' Bardi

Lorenzo (1395–1440)
m. Ginevra Cavalcanti

Pier Francesco (d. 1467)
m. Laudomia Acciaiuoli

Giovanni (1467–1498)
m. Caterina Sforza (1462–1509)

Giovanni delle
Bande Nere (1498–1526)

Maddalena (1472–1519)
m. Franceschetto Cibo

Piero (1416–1479)
m. Lucrezia Tornabuoni (1425–1482)

Lorenzo the Magnificent (1449–1492)
m. Clarice Orsini (1453–1487)

Giuliano (1453–1478)

* Giulio (b. 1478)
Pope Clement VII (1523–1534)

Giovanni (b. 1475)
Pope Leo X (1513–1521)

Giuliano (1478–1516)

Ippolito (1511–1535)*

Piero (1471–1503)
m. Altensina Orsini (1472–1519)

Lorenzo (1492–1519)
duke of Urbino
m. Madeleine of Auvergne
(1501–1519)

Catherine (1519–1589)
Queen of France
m. Henry III
King of France (1517–1559)

* Alessandro (b. 1510)
1st duke of Florence (1530–1537)

* = illegitimate

The High Renaissance

Julius II, *Il papa terri-bile*, died in 1513 and the college of cardinals awoke from a bad dream. For nine years he had scourged them and Rome and all Italy, purging the land of the Borgia dross. A violent, harsh, honest man who was rarely seen out of armor, he was capable of breaking such a man as Cesare Borgia and yet capable, too, of tying such another as Michelangelo to him. Under his fierce and urgent care, the Sistine Chapel emerged as one of the wonders of Rome while at the same time the Papal States were wrested from the hands of thieves and restored to the Church. The Roman gallows bore heavy fruit but the streets were relatively innocent of casual corpses. Within the Church he stamped out, if only during his reign, that simony which had become a normal source of revenue to the cardinals: On his very deathbed he issued a bull declaring any future simoniacal election invalid. And to make quite certain that the cardinals did not plunder during the interregnum, he placed the treasure he had won, in his manner, for the Church in the safe-keeping of the castellan of Sant' Angelo with strict instructions that it should be handed over only to his successor. It speaks much for his personality that his promise was honored even after death.

The twenty-five members of the Sacred College met in conclave on March 4, 1513. For once they were virtually unanimous as to the type of pontificate they desired—the exact opposite of that of Julius II. They were tired of marching and countermarching across the face of Italy and they did not want to be bullied or harangued anymore. They wanted a peaceful, easygoing pontiff who would lift irksome financial restrictions, rule in a civilized manner and die soon enough for some other member of the college to enjoy the tiara.

After a week, the choice had narrowed down to Cardinal Giovanni de' Medici. He was ideal in many ways—immensely wealthy, a son of the ruling family of one of the major city-states, cultured and tolerant. But he had one great defect: He was just thirty-seven years old; if he were elected, the older cardinals would almost certainly have disfranchised themselves of any chance of the tiara.

But, though young, the pudgy Giovanni de' Medici by no means enjoyed good health. For years he had been tormented by an open ulcer, and in order to allow him to attend the conclave, his physicians had been brought in with him. Whether by accident or design, they became increasingly troubled by his condition during the conclave and let it be known that there was a high probability that the young cardinal would not long survive his dangerous and painful illness. With that assurance, the older members of the college at last came over to the side of the younger. On March 11, Cardinal Giovanni de' Medici, son of Lorenzo the Magnificent, was elected pope and took the name of Leo X.

The cardinals were accurate in their assessment of Leo's character. "God has given us the Papacy—let us enjoy it," [1] he wrote to his beloved brother Giuliano. Pleasure was to be the keynote of the pontificate—but a civilized pleasure, not the gross orgies of the Borgia with their bullfights and murders in the Spanish mode. Leo was not merely an Italian but a Florentine. It was in his city that the mysterious alchemic change, wrought under pressure of war, had produced that phenomenon which later generations were to style Renaissance. Specifically, it had been his family, with their blend of business acumen and aestheticism, who had cherished the tender new plant, acting as patrons to scholars and artists, pouring out tens of thousands of the pure gold florins of Florence in their role of new Maecenas—and incidentally tightening their grip upon Florence.

The same causes which had extinguished the ancient republics of Italy, one by one, had produced the rise of the Medici in Florence. The city had been almost the last to succumb to the role of the *signor;* even now it was still, in theory at least, a republic, the Medici being merely the first among equals. Twice already the city had twitched off the cautiously descending yoke and chased them into exile. But each time they had returned, for Florence, as all other cities, had discovered that only under the rule of a single, powerful man could there be cessation from endless faction warfare. Lorenzo de' Medici was only twenty-one when,

On the second day after my father's death, the leading men of the city and the state came to my house to condole with me and at the same time to request that I assume charge of the city and the state as my father and grandfather had done before me. Owing to my youth, I accepted the responsibility with reluctance and solely in the interests of our friends and their fortunes—one lives very insecurely in Florence without control of the state.[2]

The reluctance to assume responsibility was sincere but once having undertaken it, Lorenzo discharged his task with vast skill, piloting his city through its most hazardous, most brilliant period with honor, even though he attended to the fortunes of his own family.

"I have three sons," Lorenzo once remarked. "One is good, one is shrewd and one is a fool."[3] It was Piero the fool, and unfortunately the elder, who precipitated the second expulsion of the Medici by capitulating to Charles VIII during the first French invasion. Giuliano the good remained in his brother's shadow. Giovanni the shrewd was destined for the church from his boyhood. He was only seven years old when he received the tonsure, and thereafter Lorenzo applied his talents as businessman and statesman to the acquisition of rich benefices for his son. In 1483 when the boy was only eight, he was made abbot of Font Douce in France; in 1484 he collected the abbey of Passigano; in 1486 the legendary abbey of Monte Cassino. By a continual pestering of Innocent VIII, Lorenzo got his boy made cardinal at the age of fourteen, but even Innocent gibed at the idea of a child exercising quite this type of power and insisted that he should wait at least three years before taking his place in the college of cardinals.

Lorenzo had to be content with that, but the moment that the period had expired, Giovanni entered upon his cardinalate and was sent to Rome to take up his new career. He already had family ties in Rome for his sister had married Innocent's son Franceschetto, and it was this brother-in-law who met him on the Milvian Bridge and escorted him in a grand procession to the Vatican. There he was handed over to Burchard to be briefed on the etiquette of presentation to the pontiff. "I remained with the Cardinal till nightfall," Burchard noted, "and I had his tonsure made larger. I showed him what reverences to make to the Pontiff and instructed him on all other points, as I had been commanded by our Most Holy Lord." [4] It rained all the next day and Burchard, as usual, worried that some detail of his beloved ceremonial might go wrong. But a Medici took to ceremonial as easily as he took to finances or politics and young Giovanni acquitted himself well.

Lorenzo was laid low by the sickness that ultimately killed him and so was unable to take part in any of the festivities which accompanied his son's assumption of the cardinalate. He contented himself with a long letter of advice and exhortation, a curious mixture of political shrewdness and religious sincerity designed to guide the inexperienced boy through the jungle at the heart of Christendom. Lorenzo ignored, or conveniently forgot, the fact that gold had purchased his son's rank.

> Today I have given you up entirely to God and to His Holy Church. Be therefore a worthy priest, and act so as to convince all who see you that the well-being and honor of the Church and the Holy See are more to you than anything else in the world. If you keep this constantly before you, you will not lack opportunities to be of service to our city and our family. To be united with the Church is advantageous to Florence and you must be the bond of union between the two—and the welfare of our house depends on that of the city.

Proudly, Lorenzo reminded his son that

> . . . you are the youngest member of the College, not only of the present College but the youngest that has ever yet been made a cardinal. Therefore, in all that has to do with your colleagues, keep yourself in the background, be observant and respectful. You will soon learn which among them are deserving of esteem.

Distant though he was from Rome, Lorenzo knew too well the kind of company Giovanni would henceforth be keeping. The "Sacred" College was composed for the most part of corrupted men, who counting on Giovanni's youth would seek to drag him down with them.

The College is at this moment so poor in men of worth. I remember the days when it was full of learned and virtuous men—and theirs is the example for you to follow. The less your conduct resembles that of those who now compose it, the more beloved and respected you will be.

And finally, in the authentic voice of Polonius, Lorenzo gave his son sound advice as to his personal conduct.

Spend your money rather on keeping a well-appointed stable and servants of a superior class than on pomp and show. . . . Silk and jewels are for the most part unsuitable for you, but you should possess some valuable antiques and handsome books, and your circle should be select and learned rather than numerous. . . . Entertain at home rather than dine out . . . take plenty of exercise . . . rise early . . . look after your health.[5]

Cardinal Giovanni de' Medici faithfully obeyed his father's good advice; Pope Leo X ignored almost every detail. The cardinal had declined to sell his vote to Rodrigo Borgia, even at some risk to himself; the pope found ways of making money that even the Borgia had not explored. The cardinal had worthily maintained the Medici patronage of scholars; under the pope, patronage degenerated into the fickle interest of the dilettante. It was as though the tiara were a catalyst which invariably exaggerated the dominant characteristics of the wearer. The hedonism which young Cardinal Giovanni had absorbed from the new learning was transformed by Pope Leo into a consistent mode of life.

Leo's actual coronation took place in incongruously mean surroundings. The ancient basilica of St. Peter was almost totally demolished and the new basilica arising from its ruins was little more than a shell. Paris de Grassis, the new master of ceremonies, was forced to improvise. It was unthinkable that the coronation should take place anywhere else but in the vicinity of St. Peter's and therefore a tent was erected in front of the dilapidated facade which was all that remained of the thousand-year-old building. It was in that temporary shelter that Leo X was crowned with the massive triple tiara that had been made for old Julius II—a gem-encrusted burden that sorely tried Leo before the end of the long day.

According to traditional usage, the master of ceremonies approached the newly crowned papal monarch and held before him a rod on which was tied a bunch of tow. He lit the tow and as it flared, intoned the ancient admonition: "So passes the glory of the world." The rite was older than Christianity, for during the triumphal processions in the days of the imperial city, it had been the custom for a slave to stand behind the victorious general in his chariot, uttering the warning "Remember—thou art but a man"—a well-meant but useless attempt to curb the swelling pride of a man at the peak of his career. Certainly the warning never had effect upon Leo, except perhaps to increase his desire to taste all pleasures before the darkness came. Paris de Grassis' next traditional warning, however, must have struck a responsive chord in the thirty-seven-year-old pontiff. "Thou shalt never see the years of Peter," the master of ceremonies chanted—no pope would ever reign as long as had the first. Considering that Peter's pontificate was supposed to have lasted twenty-five years, and that Leo could reasonably hope for at least another thirty years of life, the prophesy sounded uncommonly like a threat.

But if the coronation itself was a meager affair, with high dignitaries crowded in the pavilion like peasants at a market, the grand procession to the Lateran that followed was a fitting prelude to the Leonine Age. The Lateran had long since been eclipsed by the Vatican. During the long absence of the Papacy in Avignon it had been badly damaged by fire, and for nearly a generation was little more than a blackened ruin. Successive popes had restored it to something of its earlier splendor, but it was upon the vast palace beside St. Peter's that their wealth was lavished. Nevertheless, the Lateran held a peculiar sanctity and the ceremony of the new pope taking formal possession of the palace always came as a triumphant climax to the act of coronation.

Rome still remembered the *Sacro Possesso* of Alexander Borgia, but that of Leo's far surpassed it, the Medici talent for stage management giving a polished theatrical quality to the ancient

Petrarch. Andrea del Castagno. Convent of St. Apollonia, Florence.

Bridge and Castel Sant' Angelo, Rome.

The Disputation of St.
Catherine. Pinturicchio.
The Vatican, Rome.

Plaza of St. Peter's in the
Time of Sixtus V. 17th
century. Vatican Library,
Rome.

ft: — Alexander Adoring the Risen Christ. Pinturicchio. Rome.

View of Rome, 1490.

ceremony. In Leo's entourage was a Florentine physician, Gian-Giacomo Penni, one of the pope's many fellow citizens who had hastened to Rome on news that a Florentine was in the seat of power. Penni was an otherwise obscure man, but he did possess the Florentine gift for a vivid narrative style and in a long letter to Leo's sister he described in loving detail this Renaissance version of the *Sacro Possesso* which fittingly ushered in the Leonine Age. He concluded—naïvely, or, perhaps, ironically:

> In thinking about all the pomp and magnificence which I had witnessed, I experienced so violent a desire to become pope myself that I could not sleep or rest all night. No longer do I wonder at these prelates who desire this dignity so ardently, and truly I believe that every lackey would sooner be made a pope than a prince.[6]

The processional route from Vatican to Lateran had been decorated with literally priceless ornaments—"statues of marble, alabaster and porphyry worth a king's ransom"—the newly discovered art treasures of pagan Rome which the wealthy now eagerly outbid each other to possess. The wealthy banker Agostino Chigi had erected a magnificent arch on eight columns—a work of art in itself which was crowded with these treasures that had lain so long forgotten in the rubble of the imperial city:

> The time of Venus has passed: Gone, too, is Mars
> Now is the rule of Minerva

a golden inscription on the arch proclaimed—a delicate reference to the recent reigns of Alexander and Julius and a flattery of Leo's love of classical scholarship. Immediately beyond Chigi's arch, the goldsmith Antonio da San Marco had erected a beautiful Greek statue of Aphrodite with an inscription that subtly corrected Chigi's:

> Mars has gone and Minerva reigns
> But Venus still our worship claims.

The Florentines had gone to immense trouble to erect a suitable memorial for their illustrious fellow citizen. "To Pope Leo X, ambassador of heaven," the inscription on their arch ran, and upon the massive structure was crowded every possible symbol that related to the Medici: the three balls of the family, the ox yoke of Leo, the diamond of his brother Giuliano, the ring and ostrich plumes of their father. Altogether, it presented a medley more impressive for its size than its execution.

Every house on the route had its sprays and wreaths of laurel and myrtle, its banners and tapestries of velvet and gold. The streets were covered so thickly with box and myrtle that the endless procession passed in curious silence, raising as it went a cloud of aromatic perfume. Mounted spearmen led the column, followed immediately by the "families" of the cardinals, each such household dressed in its master's livery.

Leo was also lord of Rome, so immediately following the retinues of the princes of the church came the banners of Rome—the gonfalons of the ancient regions of the city. Behind them came the five gonfalons of the Holy See—the banners of the temporal church —led by Leo's illegitimate half-brother Giulio de' Medici in the insignia of a knight of Rhodes. Today, Giulio was only a prior, but on the morrow he was to be created archbishop of Florence, the first step on the brilliant career now opening to him, the fortunate relative of a Medici.

After the gonfalons came a string of white mules from the papal stables and behind them the young equerries of the court, all nobly born and clad in robes of red silk fringed with ermine. A cavalcade of Roman barons followed, men whose names were inextricably woven into the history of the Papacy—Orsini and Colonna, Gaetani, Savelli, Santa Croce—all now in apparent amity. On their heels trod the Florentine notables. Bankers and merchants, they could lay claim to no such splendid names as the Romans, but they possessed something rather more important: access to the stores of gold which paid for all this splendor and ensured them their place of honor.

And after the laymen had passed, after the soldiers and paymasters of the Holy See had bruised the thick carpet of herbs and gone on their way to the cheers—ironical or admiring—of the throng thousands, the clergy came, led by deacons and subdeacons with their silver wands of office. The white horse that bore the Sacrament walked alone, accompanied only by those who held a golden canopy over the great monstrance. But then, in a river of black and violet and scarlet, came the hundreds of lower clergy of the curia, the rustle of their flowing garments sounding like a soft wind. They were the lawyers and clerks who kept the immense machinery turning over; humble men, yet who in their sum disposed of more true power than the magnificent group of cardinals who followed. At the head of the Sacred College rode a handsome young man, Alfonso Petrucci, cardinal of Siena, another man whose fate was to be inexorably altered by the fact that a Medici was pope. His horse, like those of his colleagues, was clad in the jealously guarded symbols of senatorial power—the flowing white draperies that had been inherited from the senators of Rome. Immediately following the cardinals came those who, strictly, should have worn the sacred white—the conservators of Rome— the true descendants of the senate but now no more than humble officials of the papal court.

And finally came Leo himself, preceded by the Swiss Guard. These tough veterans, recruited by Julius, were incongruous in their gay uniform of green and white and yellow but formidable soldiers, as capable of keeping a mob at bay as they were of defeating an enemy on open battlefield. Leo was riding an Arab stallion, a huge white creature whom he loved as though it were human. Above his head, as above the Sacrament, officials held a great canopy of silk, but despite its protection the heat even of this early spring day badly affected the corpulent pontiff. Penni noticed that he was perspiring heavily, and borne down by the weight of the tiara and the heavy jewelled robes, Leo was undoubtedly in a state of acute physical discomfort throughout the procession. But he gave little sign of it. He rode well, despite the ulcer that must have given him excruciating pain at times, and majestically but affably bestowed his smiling benediction on the crowds. Behind him came two chamberlains, each carrying heavy bags of gold and silver coins from which at intervals they would take a great handful of coins, and like a sower broadcasting seed, cast it into the jubilant crowds lining the route.

The ceremony of the *Sacro Possesso* cost Leo some 100,000 ducats in all, one seventh of the reserve that Julius had gathered together being dissipated on a single festival in the first days of the new reign. It was an adequate index of the prodigal expenditure over the next seven years. Men were later to call this reign of Leo's the Golden Age, and for once the hyperbole of courtiers reflected a truth, the reign of Pope Leo X proceeding under a shower of golden coins that made Rome a treasure house only awaiting a plunderer.

Like his father before him, Leo was physically unprepossessing. His head was huge, almost deformed in its size, and his body too was so massive that seated, he gave the appearance of a very large man. Standing, he lost something of his majesty for his legs were ludicrously short and spindly so that he seemed to scuttle rather than walk. His protuberant eyes, set in a fat red face, were painfully shortsighted. A distinguishing feature of his costume was the beautiful eyeglass with which he quizzed his audience or deciphered his beloved manuscripts. Objects at a distance he could see only hazily, if at all: Throughout the ceremony of the *Sacro Possesso* an official had discreetly deciphered for him the flattering inscriptions that adorned the route.

But in contrast to his ungainly body was his attractive personality. He spoke clearly and lucidly in a soft, rather gentle voice and laughed often and spontaneously. He was genuinely interested in people, caring nothing for their social standing, demanding only that they should amuse him.

> It seems to have been his intention to pass his time cheerfully and to secure himself against trouble and anxiety by all the means in his power. He therefore sought all opportunities of pleasure and hilarity and indulged his leisure in amusements, jests, and singing—either from a natural liking for this kind of pastime or because he believed that by avoiding vexation and care he might thereby lengthen his days.[7]

Such was the opinion of Paolo Giovio, a writer whom Leo himself compared to Livy. Certainly Leo, while not a hypochondriac, went to extreme lengths to look after his health. His immoderate passion for hunting, which later scandalized the Germans, arose in part from his belief that it was good for his health. The sport was in fact an obsession with him. Specifically denied to him by canon law, in the early months of his reign he had wistfully attempted to put it behind him, but swiftly it regained its hold upon him. Thereafter, hunting alone could take him willingly from the delights of Rome.

Preparations for a hunting tour were on an enormous scale, for the court went with him and he made personal arrangements for the entertainment of the high officials, favorites, and foreign ambassadors who formed the inner core. He wrote to the castellan of the papal villa near Civitavecchia: "I shall be at Civitavecchia on the twenty-fourth day of this month with a large company. You must be sure that there is a good dinner with plenty of fish for me, as I am most anxious to make a display of state before the men of letters and others who will be my companions. . . . We shall be 140 in number and that will serve to guide you, so that there may be no mistakes through ignorance." [8]

At the beginning of autumn the papal party would make a leisurely tour of the most beautiful preserves in central Italy. First to Viterbo for the game birds, then to Lake Bolsena for the fishing and the sumptuous entertainment provided by Alessandro Farnese, the Petticoat Cardinal, in his superb pleasure grounds. Then slowly northward to Tuscany and the villa near Civitavecchia for the dangerous, exhilarating hunting of the wild boar and—the noblest sport of all—deer coursing. His hunting costume was a source of deep distress to Paris de Grassis: "He left Rome without his stole, and what is worse, without his rochet—and what is worst of all, he wore long riding boots which is most improper. How can the people kiss his feet if they are encased in long boots?" [9] The metaphysical problem as to whether or not his foot could be kissed through a boot left Leo unmoved. Clad in his gorgeous, if uncanonical, costume he spent many happy days during which the affairs of the Church were discharged in the intervals between hunts. His courtiers swiftly learned that the best moment to present a petition was shortly after the kill, when the natural good nature and generosity of the pontiff were raised to exuberant heights.

Leo liked people to be happy, liked to be liked, and never rejected a petition if he could possibly avoid doing so. His arrival at his favorite villa of Malliana, some five miles from Rome, was greeted with extravagant joy by the peasantry who lined his path as for some triumphal procession. Casual gifts of gold, grants of dowries, pensions, rights of one kind and another, came pouring from the papal cornucopia for great and small alike. And as the vast majority of petitions concerned the granting of income in one form or another, his careless generosity made heavy inroads on the treasury. But in the first carefree years of his pontificate the supply seemed endless. He had his own wealth as a Medici, and had inherited the vast treasure which his predecessor Julius had accumulated over nine years and faithfully handed on.

From the very beginning Leo had need of money, if for no better reason than to hold his own in the fantastic orgy of spending in which his fellow nobles in Rome indulged. The city now presented a curious contrast in public squalor and private luxury. To the eyes of the pilgrims who still flocked in their thousands it was a shabby, inhospitable city. The demolition begun a century earlier was achieving its climax but the new pattern was not yet apparent. Vast palaces arose out of derelict or festering streets. The gorgeous processions in which the hooves of horses ground countless blossoms to pulp passed by filthy alleys in which the debris of centuries was gradually lifting the whole level of the city. But within the palaces, designed by men whose names were destined to be immortal, an almost oriental splendor was maintained at a cost that might have made Nero look thoughtful.

The most conspicuous spenders were the Florentine bankers whose business skill had primed this golden pump. The Florentines had flooded into Rome on the election of a Medici, following the established pattern whereby nationals immediately hoped to profit by the election of a fellow countryman. And in Rome, the all-corrupting atmosphere seemed to have stripped them of their native caution. Lorenzo Strozzi, whose family's bank had once financed the monarchs of Europe, gave a banquet to Leo's relatives, the cost of which would have financed a small state for a year. His entire palace was altered for the occasion. The guests entered a vast somber apartment designed as a mortuary; after that shock they stepped into a brilliantly lighted, splendidly decorated hall to which the food was brought from below by complex machinery —fruits of the genius of yet another artist whose talents were sidetracked to the making of toys.

Agostino Chigi outshone even Strozzi at a banquet he gave for Leo in his villa near the Tiber. The menu was exotic enough to interest, if not please, the most jaded palate: The culinary value of parrots' tongues from Africa and live fish brought in specially from Byzantium must have depended largely on novelty. The food was served on gold plate, and after every course—with a great display of indifference—the ware was hurled through the window into the Tiber. Thriftily, Chigi had ordered that nets be suspended beneath the window so that the plate could be recovered, but the salvaged gold could only have been a tiny discount on the overall cost of a banquet that deliberately recreated the atmosphere of the banquets of classic Rome.

Even the hetaerae were present, the necessary feminine company to balance the exclusively masculine ranks of a celibate clergy. They were known now as courtesans, brilliant, cultured, beautiful women who maintained their own courts and did not disdain to have their profession inscribed upon their graves. They were ideal companions for such a man as Leo who delighted in feminine company but had no desire to become entangled with a demanding mistress.

"Now is the rule of Minerva," Chigi's inscription had proclaimed, and though it flattered Leo's accomplishments it indeed reflected his intentions. He was widely if not deeply read, accomplished in the newborn study of Greek, capable of turning out neat little poems and epigrams. His greatest intellectual love was that study of antiquity to which he had been introduced at his father's court, and which now, in the noonday blaze of the Renaissance, dominated Italian culture. Whoever could advance that study, no matter how slightly, no matter how artificially, was ensured of a welcome at Leo's court. The papal chancery, the administrative heart of the curia, was staffed almost exclusively with the new race of scholars. Their morals might be suspect, their Christian faith dubious, but they were able to reproduce the cadences of Ciceronian Latin; and for this narrow enough accomplishment they were awarded the highest titles that lay in Leo's power to bestow.

The golden shower fell capriciously enough. Pietro Bembo, the Venetian scholar who was closely associated with the great printing house of Aldus, was made a secretary of state. Paolo Giovio too got himself a bishopric for his neatly turned essays and elegant little histories. Pietro Aretino, the swashbuckling satirist with his endless fund of pornographic tales, did not quite qualify for Church preferment but had no other cause to grumble, for his purse was permanently filled from the seemingly inexhaustible source. He was perhaps Leo's true favorite, and continued in high prosperity in Rome until Leo's sober successor Adrian threw him out for a particularly obscene set of verses.

But other scholars were less fortunate. Niccolò Machiavelli found that his licentious comedies went down very well; but his gifts as political philosopher were totally ignored and he was forced to kick his heels in Florence while more fortunate fellow citizens filled their hats with gold. That other great Florentine, Francesco Guicciardini, the writer whose history of his own times pronounced enduring judgment on the Medicean rule, fared slightly better than Machiavelli: He at least picked up a governorship, but it was a hard and dangerous honor and not to be compared to that bestowed on poetasters for a happily turned verse.

Erasmus of Rotterdam, perhaps the most comprehensive scholar of his age, hinted broadly that he would not object to a post at Rome. But his hints were ignored—to the Papacy's later cost. Lodovico Ariosto, the greatest living Italian poet, came to Rome in hope but was disappointed. He was particularly bitter at his treatment, for he and Leo had been close friends in the old days "when the Lion had been but a cub: then he had fondled his playmate, the spaniel, but when he arrived at lion's estate he found so many foxes and wolves about his den, that he forgot his former playmate." [10]

So strong was Leo's love for classical scholarship, so totally did he appear to surrender himself to it, that it seemed to many that he cherished profane literature at the cost of the Scriptures, absorbing the skepticism of the humanists as well as their learning. "How very profitable this fable of Christ has been to us through the ages," [11] he remarked lightly to Bembo when the latter had occasion to quote from the Gospels. Pope Leo ever loved a jest, ever delighted in catching a passing thought and turning it into an epigram, and Bembo too was not above improving a quotation. But there was increasing speculation on what kind of a man would be uncovered were the courtly, cultured mask to be stripped away. Even the infamous Rodrigo Borgia, it was observed, had had himself depicted in the act of adoration before the resurrected Christ: Leo's favorite portrait showed him fingering a priceless manuscript, eyeglass at his side.

Leo had inherited the services of both Michelangelo and Raphael from Julius II. Michelangelo was perhaps too intractable a character to make a good court painter for the easygoing pope. Raphael adopted the role with ease, making himself a kind of propagandist for the Medici. The greatness and glory of Leo were to be antedated by centuries, and prophecy be given the benefit of hindsight. Raphael's first commission, therefore, was to immortalize the actions of Leo's great namesakes in history: Leo I who had halted Attila, Leo III who had crowned Charlemagne, Leo IV who had built the Leonine City—each was given the features of Giovanni de' Medici.

In the *Sala di Constantino*, the last of the series of rooms he decorated, Raphael intended to show the triumph of the church, and at Leo's behest, prepared the cartoon to emblazon a discredited myth in the most public place in Europe. Nearly eighty years had passed since Lorenzo Valla had demolished the *Donation of Constantine*. The debate had long since left the scholar's study and was now the common property of wits so that Ariosto could refer to it quite casually when he took his hero, Orlando Furioso, to the moon where

> Then passed he on to a flowery mountain green
> Which now smelt sweet, now stinks odorously,

> This was the gift (if truth you wish to hear)
> That Constantine to good Sylvester gave.

But Leo, indifferent to the mockery of scholars and wits alike in this matter at least, decreed that one vast mural should be dedicated to the perpetuation of the myth.

The *Donation* served a secondary, but ultimately more important, role in that it preserved for posterity an impression of the interior of old St. Peter's: By a curious, if artistically justifiable, anachronism, Raphael showed Constantine making his donation in the basilica—which arose as a result of that donation. The old basilica was coming down with a rush, for Julius II, impetuous in this as in all other matters, had at last put into execution the fifty-year-old dream of a new St. Peter's. The foundation stone had been laid on April 18, 1506—the last ceremony to be organized by John Burchard—and thereafter Constantine's basilica began to pass into history in a cloud of dust and endless bitter arguments. Michelangelo had been particularly vociferous about the destruction of the gigantic columns, legacy that they were of pre-Christian Rome, for Constantine's architects had plundered them from pagan temples. Far below ground, St. Peter's tomb again became the center of frantic building, and around it, the tombs of innumerable pontiffs were moved from their centuries-long rest. Some found alternative sites of equal honor, others were less fortunate. Urban VI was humiliated in death as he had been in life by ecclesiastical bureaucrats: His sarcophagus finished up as a watering trough.

By the time Leo assumed responsibility for St. Peter's the storm of controversy had died down; the destruction was a *fait accompli* and the only problem now was that of construction. Raphael temporarily succeeded Bramante as architect of the pharaonic work, and spoke in a letter not only of the excitement he felt, but also hinted at that problem whose solution was to make a mockery of that whole spirit of unity which the basilica symbolized.

I have taken over the construction of St. Peter's from Bramante. What city in the world is greater than Rome and what building greater than St. Peter's? It is the chief temple of the world—the largest building that has ever been seen. It is going to cost over a million in gold and I can assure you that the Pope is determined to spend 60,000 ducats on it during the coming year, and can think of nothing else.

St. Peter's was the major artistic charge upon Leo's purse, but there were a score of other similar channels to absorb the gold of a man of whom a Florentine remarked: "It would be easier for a stone to fly in the air than for this Pope to keep together a thousand ducats." [12] On the credit side of Leo's vast expenditure was his attempt to survey the ruins of ancient Rome and bring to an end the long and dismal history of Rome's depredation at the hands of Romans. Raphael was given the task of both recording remains and controlling destruction. In his brief of authorization Leo observed: "Great quantities of stone and marble are frequently discovered with inscriptions or curious monumental devices which are deserving of preservation for the promotion of literature and the cultivation of the Latin tongue. But these are frequently cut or broken, for the sake of using them as materials in new buildings." [13] The passion for discovering beautiful statues and objects of high intrinsic value had turned Rome into a treasure hunter's paradise. It speaks much for Leo's sophistication that he could recognize the value of broken inscriptions as well as more obviously valuable finds.

How far the Papacy had progressed from suspicion of the works of pagans, to worship of them, was well expressed in Raphael's report to his patron. "How many have there been who, having enjoyed the same office as your Holiness—but not the same knowledge, nor the same greatness of mind, nor in that clemency in which you resemble the Deity—how many have there been who have employed themselves in the demolition of ancient temples, statues, arches, and other glorious works?" Having thus dismissed the majority of Leo's predecessors as rapacious vandals, Raphael diffidently concluded that the pope's true role was "to leave the examples of the ancients to speak for themselves, to equal and to surpass them by the erection of splendid edifices, by the encouragement and remuneration of talents and of genius, and by dispensing among the princes of Christendom the blessed seeds of peace." [14]

Humanist rhetoric lent itself with embarrassing ease to unwitting irony. Even while Raphael was devotedly scrabbling among the ruins of Rome, His Holiness was sowing the seeds of peace in Italy by precipitating a war for the establishment of a Medicean dynasty.

Triumph of the Medici

Italy was held like a nut between the jaws of a pincer. In the south the Spanish were firmly in possession of Naples, having driven the French out after their brief unholy alliance. In the north the French dominated with their base fixed uneasily on Milan. Throughout his furious pontificate, Julius had had but one war cry—"Out—out with the barbarians!" He had hated the French just a little more than he had hated the Spanish and so had used the latter to dislodge the former. Dislodge, not destroy, for the French too could call upon complex alliances to regain their foothold in Lombardy. The almost forgotten expedition of Charles VIII had started a chain of events destined to run until the nineteenth century, the giant new nations of Europe inexorably, helplessly, sliding down into Italy to fight out their differences. Blood and ferocity came back into Italian wars. For generations the cities had maintained their precarious balances by the employment of mercenaries, and the aim of mercenaries was ransom, not victory. Now, abruptly, racial hatreds were added to the civilized game.

Spaniards and French, Swiss and Germans, alternately lorded it in Milan and Lombardy; they were expelled not by Italians but by massive groupings of other foreigners. After battles, the dead were counted in tens of thousands: A surrendered city paid for its defeat in blood as well as gold. Italian hopes and fears receded ever further into the background, became ever more irrelevant as the alliances of their oppressors and allies became ever wider and more complex. The hopes of an English cardinal, affecting the ambitions of a Spanish monarch, would have repercussions upon a German emperor—which would affect the French and so goad the Swiss . . . the permutations were endless, but Italy was affected by each one.

Leo's recognition of the fact that control of Italian affairs had passed out of Italian hands was expressed by his readiness to make treaties with either of the dominant contestants as and when it suited either one of them. Both French and Spanish professed themselves astonished at the flexibility of the pope's promises. The

Italians claimed that they knew this Medici trait only too well: "Certainly, the house of Medici has always had a peculiar disposition to this. It is said that Pope Leo used to say that having made a treaty with one party, there was no reason why one should not treat with the other." [15]

On balance, like Julius before him, Leo disliked the French more than he disliked the Spanish. But unlike Julius, he was tied to them, having married his brother Giuliano to the aunt of the dashing young Francis I, the new king of France. It did not prevent him entering into negotiations with Francis' enemies, but when Francis destroyed a combined Spanish-Swiss army at Marignano, and in his turn ascended the ducal throne of Milan, Leo gladly made peace with him and sought favors for his relatives. "It appears that His Holiness has been playing a double game," the enraged king of Spain wrote to his ambassador. "All his zeal to drive the French from Italy is but a mask." [16] Leo was in fact playing a consistently single game, the game that so many of his predecessors had played—the aggrandizement of his family.

Shortly after his election Leo had created his cousin Giulio a cardinal. It had been necessary to precede the creation with an act of perjury, for Giulio was illegitimate; to remove the canonical impediment a declaration was drawn up, stating that his parents were wedded. The new cardinal received the lucrative and important post of vice-chancellor. Giulio was a good choice: Modest, learned, honest, he discharged his duties excellently in a subordinate position. It was only when he inherited the supreme authority that his disastrous weakness was displayed. Leo intended the highest of secular offices for his beloved younger brother Giuliano. In February, 1515, Giuliano went to France for his marriage to a French princess, the first royal alliance in the Medici family and the precedent for others. Leo made over to him the revenues from Parma, Piacenza, and Modena—a total of some 48,000 ducats annually—and king Francis granted a dukedom to his new relative.

The arrival of the newly wedded pair in Rome was the occasion for celebrations of a Medicean splendor. At the end, when the last mound of sweetmeats had been thrown to the crowds, the hordes of jugglers and musicians and poetasters paid, the velvets and the damasks and the silks and the wines and the flowers all accounted for, something in the region of 150,000 ducats had been spent—more than three times the new duke's annual income. But that income was only a temporary arrangement. Leo had other, and greater, ideas for his brother: the kingdom of Naples, perhaps, or a duchy to be carved out of Lombardy—or one taken, yet again, from the States of the Church.

But Giuliano never benefited further from his brother's love. He died, not quite two years after his marriage, leaving a bastard son as sole heir. It was a personal blow to Leo, for he had genuinely loved his brother. Politically, Giuliano's death was probably fortunate, for it was doubtful if he would have had the strength to uphold Leo's boundless dynastic ambitions. Their father had called him his "good" son, and certainly Giuliano had done nothing to bring discredit upon the family name. But it was the negative achievement of a melancholy withdrawn man who had been content to let others plan his life.

The whole force of Leo's love and family ambition was now turned upon his nephew Lorenzo, the son of his dead elder brother Piero.

Lorenzo at least was positive—positive enough to poison one uncle to gain the undivided attention of the other, men whispered. Lorenzo had been barely eighteen when Leo, forced to relinquish his role as lord of Florence on his election to the Papacy, had sought another member of his house to rule the city in his stead. For all the love that he bore Giuliano, he could not see his brother as de facto lord of Florence. The Florentines were still only half-tamed: Their republican vigor could yet unseat such a gentle, nervous rider as Giuliano. Leo could discern far more clearly the necessary toughness and flexibility nascent in the young Lorenzo, and it was therefore Lorenzo who was installed in the splendid new Medici palace in Florence when Leo went to the Vatican. Leo kept firm control even from a distance, but during the three years that had elapsed since his election, he felt that Lorenzo had justified his choice. Now that Giuliano was dead, Lorenzo must become the founder of a Medicean ducal house.

Julius II had left only one independent prince reigning in the Papal States—his nephew Francesco Maria della Rovere, duke of Urbino. The *Papa terribile* had been no more exempt from the besetting papal temptation of nepotism than other occupants of the throne, but in this instance at least he employed it to good use by placing a man he could trust in a notoriously restless area. The duke now paid, tardily but in full, for his dangerous honor. Seeking a suitable duchy for his nephew Lorenzo, Leo directed his gaze to the beautiful little mountain city of Urbino with its scattered but wealthy towns. As feudal lord of the Papal States the pope had the right to depose any vassal he deemed unsuitable; it was not too difficult to find convenient evidence of della Rovere's unsuitability. Like most of his fellow nobles he had a past which did not bear too close a scrutiny. There had been the murder of a cardinal—for which, admittedly, della Rovere had received papal absolution. But murder was murder. Della Rovere had also been disgracefully lukewarm in support of Leo's military activities in Lombardy. Leo therefore declared him deposed.

Della Rovere reacted violently. First he sent his adoptive mother to Rome. She pleaded eloquently with Leo, reminding him forcibly of the benefits which the della Rovere had bestowed on the Medici after they had been thrown out of Florence. Had not she, herself, held the young Lorenzo in her arms? Now that the child had grown to a man, was he to despoil his protectors? The pope's own brother Giuliano had admitted the Medici debt and while he lived, had protected Urbino. Was Leo going to trample on his dead brother's wishes?

Leo did precisely that: Not content with degrading della Rovere he excommunicated him for refusing to come to Rome and make submission. The French obligingly supplied troops, even as they had supplied troops to Cesare Borgia for the same purpose a little over a decade earlier, Lorenzo de' Medici was made captain-general, and the state of Urbino fell. On August 8, 1516, Lorenzo was created duke of Urbino, the first hereditary title to fall to a

Medici. Leo insisted that the entire college of cardinals sign the deed of investiture. All obediently did so, with the single exception of the bishop of Urbino, who declined to be associated with a robbery. Prudently, he immediately left Rome, for while Leo the dilettante might laugh at a rebuff, Leo the politician would not.

Lorenzo, duke of Urbino, did not long enjoy his state unmolested. Leo had made the prime error of driving an enemy to desperation, declining even to lift the spiritual ban of excommunication from della Rovere even though his victim pleaded "for the salvation of his soul." In daily and imminent danger of assassination, the exiled duke saw that greater safety lay in attack than in flight and he gathered together an army to fight his way back. He found supporters readily enough. The French were already regretting the aid they had given Leo, for it was now widely rumored that he intended to make his nephew duke not merely of Urbino but all the Romagna—and launch an attack upon his late benefactors. Della Rovere even found tacit support for his action in the college of cardinals. The charm of the Medici was wearing thin and there seemed now little difference between the ambitions of Leo and the late unlamented Alexander VI.

Leo was enraged. In his capacity of supreme pontiff he called on all Christendom to aid him in his titanic struggle with this impudent rebel. War taxes were raised throughout the Papal States, the bankers of Rome and Florence were appealed to for funds and responded with huge sums of gold—at an interest of some forty percent. With considerable chivalry, della Rovere sent an envoy to Lorenzo, challenging him to single combat to decide the issue. Lorenzo contemptuously ignored the challenge, and breaking his oath of safe-conduct, sent the envoy to Rome for "examination" by his uncle. Leo acquiesced in his nephew's treachery and put the wretched man to the torture in order to find out his master's military intentions.

Throughout the spring and summer of 1517 della Rovere and the Medici battled for the sovereignty of Urbino. The Medici at length prevailed, but less through the military efficiency of Lorenzo or the offended majesty of the pontiff than through the dislike of the Spaniards and the French for the campaign. These two monarchs had brought their troops into Italy to fight out their own dynastic war, not to act as auxiliaries in a war for a petty duchy. In a strange and temporary alliance they prevailed upon della Rovere to withdraw from the contest, guaranteeing him his life and personal possessions. Without their support he was helpless, and knew it; reluctantly he agreed, but in his eyes it was not a defeat but a temporary exile. Time proved him correct.

Leo had triumphed, but at an enormous cost in gold and prestige. Italians, who believed that they had witnessed the ultimate in human depravity during the Borgia reign, could still profess themselves shocked by the cold-blooded breaking of a safe-conduct. If the sacrosanct person of an envoy could be mutilated to gain a temporary advantage, who then could be safe? Among the ceaseless intrigues of the apostolic palace the life and liberty of no person, in fact, could be guaranteed—not even that of the pope himself.

Conspiracy of the Cardinals

Paris de Grassis, the new master of ceremonies, had learned his trade from John Burchard. He did not display any particular gratitude, indeed hating Burchard as a German and envious of him as a superior, but he paid his master the compliment of continuing his diary. He had all Burchard's pedantry—the obsession with detail of precedence, the fussing over the correct colors of garments—but he quite lacked Burchard's objectivity. In Paris' eyes, Leo was almost superhuman, a demigod who declined to display emotion even on the death of his beloved brother Giuliano. Paris' diary, therefore, lacked the dispassionate sense of verisimilitude that Burchard was able, effortlessly, to give his own. But it was given to Paris to record, as with a camera, a common but rarely seen event: the precise moment when a victim extricated himself from a plot on his life.

On the morning of May 21, 1517, the cardinals were assembled in consistory. "The pope then sent for the Cardinal of Ancona, who continued with him for an hour. As we were surprised at this long interview," Paris afterward recorded,

> I looked through the opening of the door and perceived in the chamber of the pope the Captain of the Guard and two soldiers waiting fully armed. I was apprehensive of some untoward circumstances, but I remained silent. Seeing, however, the Cardinals Riario and Farnese enter the pope's chamber with great cheerfulness, I concluded that the pope had called them to consult with him on the promotion of cardinals, of which he had spoken that morning. But scarcely had Cardinal Riario entered than the pope—who usually walked with great deliberation between two of his chamberlains—scurried out of the room and, shutting the door behind him, left Cardinal Riario with the guards. Greatly astonished at his haste, I inquired from the pope the reason for it—and asked whether he meant to enter the consistory without his stole. We arrayed him with the stole. He was pale and much agitated. He then ordered me, with a more positive tone than usual, to send all the cardinals from

the consistory and afterward, with a still louder voice, to shut up the consistorial chamber. I obeyed, and no longer entertained a doubt that the Cardinal Riario had been arrested. The other attendants and myself began to form conjectures as to the cause of the proceedings but the pope soon afterward explained them himself.[17]

There was a plot afoot to poison him and nominate Riario as his successor.

The originator of the plot was an obscure young cardinal, Alfonso Petrucci, with a commonplace grievance. His brother, the flourishing tyrant of Siena, had been expelled by the pro-Medici party in the city and the Petrucci estates confiscated. Young Petrucci felt himself particularly aggrieved because he had been one of the foremost supporters of Giovanni de' Medici in the conclave that gave him the Papacy. Now, far from benefiting from the universal shower of gold, the Petrucci family had been ruined by the ungrateful pope. The fact that they deserved it was irrelevant; few men, in those days, were paid according to their deserts.

Petrucci first intended to model himself upon some classic hero and stab the pope in some sufficiently public place. But a tardy fear of sacrilege stirred within him and he decided upon a method that would leave his hands technically free from blood. Leo was still being treated for a dangerous and painful anal ulcer. During the timely indisposition of the pope's own physician, Petrucci planned to introduce a physician of his own choice who would mingle poison with the ointment intended for the treatment of the ulcer. The plan would have succeeded had not Leo, with a fortunate delicacy, declined to be treated by a stranger. The pope was still quite unsuspecting, but thereafter, Petrucci, becoming more and more careless in his confidences, betrayed himself. Hastily he left Rome but was induced to return on promise of a safe-conduct. Medici safe-conducts might have appeared to be devalued instruments but this one was guaranteed by the Spanish ambassador himself. As soon as Petrucci was back in Rome he was seized, and despite the heated protests of the Spaniard whose own honor was thus traduced, the foolish young man was thrust into Sant' Angelo.

So far the affair had been the routine suppression of a malcontent. There was some embarrassment over the matter of yet another broken safe-conduct, but Leo retorted to the ambassador that "faith need not be kept to a poisoner," and told the Venetians, who had also protested, that he had made no promise to the Spaniard and that Petrucci had received merely a general permission to come to Rome. On the whole Italy concluded that in this matter Petrucci had certainly got his deserts.

But the affair did not end with the imprisonment of Petrucci. Under torture he implicated more and yet more of his fellow cardinals—not junior members of the college but men of high seniority such as Riario, who had been a member of the Sacred College for more than forty years; Leo's own fellow citizen Soderini; the Genoese de Saulis; Leo's favorite, Adrian of Corneto—all these names were wrung out of the wretched Petrucci by the skilled attentions of the papal torture gang in Sant' Angelo. Leo had intended to confront the cardinals in consistory with a dramatic revelation of Petrucci's guilt, but terrified at the wide extent of the plot he decided immediately to eliminate only the man who was expected to succeed him—Cardinal Riario—who had been also his chief rival during the conclave.

Even Paris de Grassis was shocked by the arrest of Riario, for the doyen of the Sacred College was both popular and respected.

> We could scarcely believe that the Cardinal Riario, whose prudence and abilities were so well known, could have engaged in such a plot —or if he had been guilty, that he would not have made his escape. We were therefore inclined to suppose that this accusation was made by the pope as a pretext to revenge himself for former injuries.[18]

Others were to share the opinion, even though the "former injuries" had taken place before Leo was born when Riario had been involved in a plot against Leo's father. It seemed unlikely that even a Medici could harbor thoughts of vengeance for a lifetime—but even more improbable factors were to be disclosed.

On June 8, Leo summoned a full consistory. Throughout the intervening period, while his trusted servants had been unraveling the full complexities of the plot, he had shut himself up in Sant'

Angelo. Rome was kept quiet only by the presence of papal troops at every street corner, ready to crush the first sign of rebellion. But the Romans had long lost either ability or desire to throw off the rule of the Vatican; the danger to Pope Leo came from much nearer home. The Sacred College, the preeminent instrument of papal power, had committed an unprecedented act. It was no longer possible to assess the conspiracy as the impulsive action of a disgruntled youth. The college itself had made an attempt to destroy the person it had created. Why?

Why? demanded Leo in consistory. Had he not shown every kindness to the college, every favor possible? Why should he be met with such a return? The college was sullen, frightened, yet resigned. One by one, each member was called upon to affirm on oath whether or not he was guilty. Gradually, those implicated by Petrucci were isolated. Francesco Soderini first denied his guilt, and then after a tirade of abuse from Leo, threw himself prostrate and begged for mercy. There was a silence; then Leo remarked that there was another conspirator and Adrian of Corneto, under pressure from his colleagues, admitted that he had taken part in the treasonable discussions. With that, Leo professed himself satisfied. In a long and pathetic speech he declared that though the guilty deserved degradation and death, he would content himself with fining and pardoning them. The college, startled, applauded his generosity.

A few days later Petrucci, Riario, and de Saulis were stripped of all their dignities and handed over to the secular arm for that bloody punishment with which the spiritual hierarchy could not stain its hands. Soderini and Adrian, assessing Medici clemency for what it was worth, had made sensible use of the breathing space by leaving Rome, intending never to return until Leo's death. In the event, Petrucci and his personal servants alone suffered the torture of red-hot irons and the ignominious death at the end of a rope, for the powerful friends of Riario and de Saulis were able to force Leo to make practical application of his pretense of clemency.

It had been altogether a curious affair. Each of the accused men had had a grievance against Leo: Soderini's brother had been expelled from Florence by the Medici; Riario had been cheated of the tiara by Leo's election; Adrian and de Saulis had been relatives of the despoiled duke of Urbino. But probably every other member of the college could lay some such complaint against the pope. Taken singly or in their sum, the ostensible motives of the conspirators were not strong enough to impel a group of wealthy, powerful men to hazard their lives and liberty in such an inept attempt on Leo's life. And yet each had confessed—abjectly. The minutes of the "trial" had been kept secret, and swiftly rumor outside the college supplied its own motives—it was a Medicean trick to eliminate, finally, Medicean enemies and fill the coffers of a pope ever desperately in want of money.

Rumor appeared to receive startling confirmation a few weeks afterward when, on June 26, Leo made a massive creation of thirty-one cardinals. Each paid liberally for his hat, and the sum that passed into Leo's hand for the prosecution of his nephew's struggle for Urbino was probably more than half a million ducats from this single transaction alone. But, more important than the money was the fact that the college was now swamped with Medicean supporters. Those cardinals who had watched the continual aggrandizement of the Medici family in dislike and suspicion were now heavily outnumbered by those who owed everything to the Medici. From then until the close of his pontificate Leo had no more trouble with the Sacred College; it was, once again, an obedient instrument of papal power.

The gold that Leo had obtained in fines and investiture fees enabled him to bring the Urbino war to its inconclusive end in the autumn of 1517. There was nothing now too good for the young Medici duke of Urbino. Leo turned to the despised French to make another royal marriage for a relative and in March, 1518, young Lorenzo de Medici journeyed in regal state to Amboise for his marriage to Madeleine of Auvergne. On his return to Italy Lorenzo thought it prudent to take up residence not in Urbino, still chafing under a tyrant imposed from without, but in Florence. But he still enjoyed the title of duke and the Florentines, forgetting rapidly the republicanism that had been their driving force for centuries, cravenly accorded him the title in their official dealings with him.

Machiavelli, seeking some way to ingratiate himself with the family that had exiled him from Florence for his republican sympathies, dedicated *The Prince* to the young man. Lorenzo made good use of the handbook of practical politics but not, as Machiavelli hoped, in order to lead Italy against the barbarians that were despoiling her. Florence instead enjoyed the first application of Machiavellian politics in a reign that bade fair to resemble that of Cesare Borgia's. But Lorenzo died before he could develop his talents to the full, and with him died all Leo's hopes for the elder, legitimate branch of the Medici—not quite two years after della Rovere had been robbed of Urbino.

Luther

After the first months of his reign, money was Leo's dominant, consistent problem: money to pay those mercenaries who upheld the power of the Papacy; money to spend on the splendid trinkets flowing from innumerable workshops; money to pay the artists who were transforming the Vatican into one vast work of art; above all, money to spend on that titanic conception of his predecessor, the new basilica of St. Peter's. By any assessment, Leo was immensely wealthy, both as man and pope. He had inherited nearly three-quarters of a million ducats which the frugal Julius had laid up in Sant' Angelo; and the revenues of the Papal States, after trickling for so long through illegal conduits, gushed again directly into the apostolic palace. The Venetians, ever capable of assessing a potential client's income down to the last ducat, estimated that Leo could count upon something in the region of 400,000 ducats annually, drawn partly from the Papal States and partly from such monopolies as vinegar, salt, and that fortunate discovery, alum, which all Europe needed to dye its wool. In addition to such semifeudal revenues was the almost unassessable income drawn from all over Christendom in the forms of benefices, fees, and the like, which the Avignonese curia had so well established nearly two centuries earlier.

But Leo's expenses remained steadily in excess of his income. His court alone was four times the size of that of Julius, numbering now nearly seven hundred persons. His financial advisers calculated that he regularly spent eight thousand a month on casual gifts to favorites and at gaming. Nearly half the revenue of the Papal States went to pay for his endless banquets and all these vast sums were for purely domestic expenditures. More, much more, was needed to finance his dynastic ambition. The total cost of the Urbino war was something between 800,000 and a million ducats, and young Lorenzo had spent another 200,000 on his journey to France for his marriage. Seeking money where he could find it, Leo raised the number of salable offices in the curia to over two thousand. He founded a new order, that of St. Peter, and the fees paid by the new knights made their way rapidly through the Medici coffers. The bankers were approached again and again for ever more loans. Even a Florentine banker might hesitate at the sums demanded but Leo was young, his credit still high, and the bankers continued their golden flow.

But even had Leo balanced his own accounts and subjected himself to an unnatural restraint, the curia would still have continued in debt. The basilica of St. Peter's was an enormous conduit that relentlessly channeled away legitimate and illegitimate income alike. Work had been in progress for over ten years, bedeviled by bitter controversies, and would in fact continue for another century before the basilica's consecration as a completed temple. Leo had wholeheartedly adopted his predecessor's grandiose plan, and throughout his reign honorably gave it precedence over his own projects. But enthusiasm was no substitute for money and it was unthinkable that this crowning glory of the Papacy should be crippled for want of gold. Leo therefore exercised his spiritual authority and decreed that the basilica of St. Peter's was a fitting object for the care of the faithful. The income obtained from the dispensation of certain indulgences could legitimately be used for building the mother church of Christendom.

It was an epochal decision, but in making it, Leo had ample precedents. Over four hundred years earlier Urban II had granted indulgences and full remission of sin to all who went on crusade to liberate Christ's sepulcher from the infidel. Gradually the custom evolved that those pious Christians who desired to go on crusade but were prevented could obtain the same act of grace by providing a locum—in effect by making a cash contribution to the crusade. Thereafter, the custom hardened and spread, becoming yet another method of contributing to the upkeep of the curia, no more and no less defensible than the Avignonese system whereby a new incumbent paid his first year's income for the privilege of office.

Leo therefore found an existing machinery for his purpose: It needed only to be applied to this specific need. It so happened that in Germany the twenty-three-year-old Albert of Brandenburg found himself in grave financial difficulties. He had just received the expensive honor of being consecrated archbishop of Magdeburg and now owed something like 24,000 ducats to the curia. He had borrowed the money from the great banking house of the Fuggers, but it had to be repaid. Leo therefore proposed that an eight-year indulgence for St. Peter's and a new holy war against the Turk should be promulgated in Germany: Albert—or, rather, the Fuggers—should keep one half of the proceeds and the rest should go to Rome. Albert gratefully accepted the proposal and a Dominican monk named Johann Tetzel was given the task of promulgation.

The Church's doctrine on indulgences was highly complex, central to its thesis that the power to open or close the gates of heaven had been transmitted to the bishop of Rome from the founder of Christianity through the apostolic succession. In its essence, the doctrine declared that though a sinner might be absolved from the guilt of his sin by the sacrament of penance, there still remained the pains of temporal punishment attached to it, a punishment which would be administered in purgatory. Certain acts and certain objects, however, had the power to bring about the remission of all or part of the punishment due. Each indulgence obtained was the equivalent of a specified number of earthly days' penance which could be offered as payment for the outstanding punishment, and could be either reserved as future credit, or immediately used to deliver a soul from purgatory.

Tetzel reduced the complex theology to a simple formula, summed up by a satirical couplet that swiftly made its rounds:

> As soon as the coin in the coffer rings,
> The soul from out the fire springs.

The necessity for individual contrition was glossed over.

I have here the passports . . . to lead the human soul into Paradise. Inasmuch as for a single one of the mortal sins, several of which are committed every day after confession, seven years of expiation either on earth or in Purgatory are imposed—who, for the sake of a quarter of a florin would hesitate to secure one of these letters which will admit your divine, immortal soul to the celestial joys of Paradise? [19]

Tetzel too had his precedents even as did Leo, for in Wittenberg itself there was a rare collection of relics whose mere showing to a Christian could earn him a total of 1,443 years' indulgence on payment of the necessary fees. But Tetzel's indulgence slips, churned out by the marvelous new printing press, had all the charm of novelty and accessibility. It was no longer necessary for a Christian to make a long and costly journey to some sacred shrine: Indulgences were brought to his very door. Tetzel's entry into each town on his itinerary took the form of a triumph.

> He was preceded by the Bull of the Sovereign Pontiff, carried on a piece of scarlet and gold velvet. The peoples, priests, and monks, the scholars—all men and women went out in procession to meet him with lighted candles, standards unfurled while all the bells in the town rang out in gay carillons. In the middle of the nave of the principal church a huge red cross was raised upon which the pontifical banner was fixed. God himself could not have been given a more magnificent welcome.[20]

Discreetly on one side sat the Fugger agent, ensuring that 50 percent of all that came in was passed on to his master in repayment for the debt that had precipitated all this splendor. He was kept busy, for the money poured in without break. But not all who pressed around the booth were anxious to purchase passports to paradise. Some carping spirits made their payments, but passed the little slips of paper to the thirty-four-year-old doctor of theology at Wittenberg University. Would Dr. Martin Luther care to comment on the validity of this curious means of salvation?

On October 31, 1517, Luther nailed his ninety-five theses on the door of the palace church at Wittenberg. To later generations the clatter of the hammer on oak took on an immensely dramatic significance—the gesture of a free man defying a vast and corrupt authority with an undying symbol. Luther was merely following a common practice, the church door being a convenient place to display public notices. All he intended, and all he was understood to intend, was to offer to defend in debate ninety-five points which purported to establish the illegitimacy of the present use of indulgences. Some of the points were hard enough, however, particularly the glancing blow at the Medici wealth. If Leo was truly empowered to release souls from purgatory, why did he not himself pay for the building of St. Peter's from his own pocket, and thus empty purgatory of all its suffering souls at one instant? Tetzel later replied with his own antitheses and the war of words was on.

Leo heard of this "monkish squabble," as he termed it, with something between a smile and a sigh. He had just survived the most dangerous conspiracy a pope ever had to face, and summed up the difference between Luther's and Petrucci's actions with one of his neat epigrams. "The ax has been taken from the root and laid to the branches." [21]

There was no particular reason why he should be worried about Luther. Over the past two centuries there had been an endless procession of misanthropes who objected to this or that aspect of papal power and the corruption that inescapably went with it. Dante, Huss, Petrarch, St. Catherine of Siena, Arnold of Brescia, Jerome of Prague, St. Bridget of Sweden—each generation brought its vociferous critics. Some had been burned, some canonized; none, it seemed, had had the slightest effect in diverting or slowing the momentum of the Papacy. Leo had himself witnessed the rise and fall of the most recent in his own city. During the exile of the Medici, Girolamo Savonarola had reigned as a kind of priest-king and, thinking himself secure in the affection of the Florentines, had hurled at the Borgia pope missiles far more deadly than Luther's gentlemanly theses aimed at the Medici. Savonarola had gone the way of all such violent reformers. Alexander VI may have signed his death warrant, but it was his erstwhile adorers, the citizens of Florence, who lighted the fire in that same piazza which had witnessed his triumphs.

But Leo had forgotten that Savonarola's supporters had been drawn from the most volatile citizens of a volatile race; while Luther's supporters were those same earnest, dedicated Germans who again and again through the centuries had taken upon themselves the task of cleansing the stables of Rome. Otto the Great, who had descended from Germany six hundred years earlier to establish the Holy Roman Empire of the German nation, shared more than a common Saxon ancestry with Martin Luther: The

supporters of both saw them as divine instruments and were prepared to back their belief with gold or steel. Italians rarely saw
themselves obliged to go on holy wars; their energies were more
commonly employed in the suppressing of their fellow Italians.
But even had Leo immediately decided to take autocratic action
against Luther, he would have been checked by the political tangle which hedged and protected the as yet unwitting founder of
the Reformation. The temporal lords of Germany were faithful
sons of Holy Church, but they were also Germans eager to make
capital out of any situation that would protect or increase their
hegemony in an embattled Europe. The emperor, Maximilian of
Austria, wanted to ensure that the imperial crown continued in
the house of Hapsburg: Francis I of France saw no good reason
why the crown should not come to him instead of Maximilian's
grandson, Charles. Sooner or later the Papacy, fatally embroiled
in European politics, would have to ally itself with one side or the
other.

But Leo, in any case, ever preferred to use persuasion in intellectual matters, and when at length he was forced to take notice
of the squabble in Germany he reacted mildly. He agreed that the
doctrine of indulgences had been grossly oversimplified, issued an
edict condemning its abuse, and his nuncio Karl von Miltitz so
savagely castigated the wretched Tetzel that the monk was thereafter a spent force. Luther himself moved so reluctantly along
his path that again and again rapprochement seemed possible. But
both pope and monk gradually found themselves occupying a position where maneuvering was impossible.

It was Erasmus of Rotterdam who first noted that during the
vital early period Luther alone commanded the support of scholars.
"I know not how it has happened, but it is certain that those who
first opposed Luther were also the enemies of learning and therefore the friends of scholarship were less averse to him, lest by as-
sisting his enemies they should injure their own cause." [22] Repelled
by Luther's coarseness and intransigence, lacking perhaps the courage or the desire to launch himself into a new world, Erasmus
stayed on the side of the old. But his enemies in the Church charged
that his coolly cynical view of the Papacy contributed in no

small part to the success of the breakaway group. "He laid the egg which Luther hatched," was the accusation and there was truth in it.

But from the beginning, the brilliant group of scholars whom Leo had fostered, who depended for their very livelihood upon his goodwill, remained silent—so far as defense of the Papacy was concerned. Writing in his private diary, Francesco Guicciardini, the Florentine statesman and historian, summed up the reason in a candid if unheroic confession.

> No man is more disgusted than I am with the ambition, the avarice, and the profligacy of the priests. . . . Nevertheless, my position at the court of several Popes forced me to desire their greatness for the sake of my own interest. But, had it not been for this, I should have loved Martin Luther as myself—not in order to free myself from the laws which Christianity lays upon us but in order to see this swarm of scoundrels put back into their proper place, so that they may be forced to live without vices or without power.[23]

Luther could not better have summed up his own reasons for protest.

The defense of Pope Leo was therefore largely undertaken by the semiliterate and the bigoted, men who genuinely saw Luther as some Germanic monster, and who, incapable of employing the keen but delicate weapon of humanist scholarship, fell back on the ancient weapons of the gutter. Luther, capable of using both weapons with immense gusto and skill, completely outmatched them. He knew Rome—not as well as he thought he did, but enough to give a personal bite to his attacks. He was in the city for some months in 1511 and acted then like any other pious pilgrim, to his later disgust. "I dashed like a madman between one church and another, believing all their filthy nonsense. I even read a dozen masses and was very sorry that my mother and father were still alive, for I would gladly have redeemed them from Purgatory with these masses." [24]

He picked up the current lurid gossip about affairs in the Vatican. "If there is a hell, then Rome is built upon it—and this I have heard at Rome itself. Tiberius, the heathen Emperor, even if he were a monster such as Suetonius writes of, is nevertheless an angel in comparison with the present court of Rome. The same hath to serve the supper table twelve naked girls." [25] The last accusation went down well in Germany: Leo, the fastidious, would have deplored the grotesque juxtaposition of living and cooked flesh at the table.

It was a matter of open debate whether Italy had been corrupted by the Papacy, as Machiavelli contended, or whether the Papacy had been corrupted by Italy. To most northerners, the entire peninsula was an iridescent pool of corruption, attractive or repulsive according to the traveler's bent. Roger Ascham wrote:

> I was once in Italy myself, but I thank God my abode there was but nine days: and yet I saw in that little time, in one city, more liberty to sin than ever I heard tell of in our noble city of London in nine years. I saw it was there as free to sin, not only without punishment, but also without any man's marking, as it is free in the city of London to choose without all blame whether a man lust to wear shoes or pantofle.[26]

Italians might scoff at the delicate stomachs of English pedants, but all joined in heaping obloquy upon Rome. The Papacy was not the wealthiest of Italian powers, and neither was Rome particularly outstanding in the matter of moral corruption. Naples, Venice, and Milan each enjoyed a revenue greater than Leo's, and for sheer viciousness of habits Naples and Venice were preeminent in all Europe.

But Rome remained the target of satirists and moralists alike. Two centuries earlier, the same Giovanni Boccaccio who had joyously plumbed the depths of Neapolitan life coined the phrase that was to be repeated again and again. "If you want to convert a Jew, send him to Rome. The depravity of the Papal Court will not fail to convert him to a faith that can withstand such shame." And since Boccaccio's day the ferment of the Renaissance, working upon a highly intelligent, fiercely individualistic people, had exaggerated the lurid qualities of Roman life even while it gave a patina of culture.

"These vices, odious in themselves, are rendered infamous in men who make a profession of living in especial dependence upon the Deity," [27] Guicciardini observed. And it was this contrast which offended Italians as well as Germans—particularly Italians who lived on the perimeter and not in the center of the pool. The contrast was inescapable, for though Rome was the seat of the high priest of Christendom and his spiritual hierarchy, it was also the seat of the papal monarch, limited now in his pretensions to universal power but still one of the major monarchs of Europe. To Rome therefore came the ambassadors of all other powers, each well furnished with gold to buy favors and keep state: each accompanied by a train of servitors eager to taste the pleasures of the city. And the Romans, scenting the gold, were ready to oblige whether it involved the sale of a relic or a girl, an indulgence or an antique statue.

In the upper levels of society, pleasures were more polished but to the scandalized gaze of pilgrims infinitely more despicable, for they involved the members of the spiritual hierarchy in their capacity of temporal princes. Even some of those who took part in the endless round of festivities proclaimed their astonishment and disgust. The Venetian ambassador, no stranger to luxury in his own city, recorded how at the end of one of the marathon suppers "we rose from table gorged with the multiplicity of viands and deafened by the continual concert" to stagger on to yet more amusements. The beautiful Isabella d'Este, on a state visit to Leo, was entertained for four fantastic months, in which Rome appeared to her dazzled gaze as some kind of terrestrial paradise where one had only to ask, for a wish to be granted.

> Yesterday, His Magnificence Lorenzo de' Medici invited us to dine at his house where we saw a splendid bullfight in which four bulls were killed. When dusk fell, we fell to dancing for about three hours. At the festival appeared the most reverend the Cardinals of Aragon, Este, Petrucci and Cibo, all masked: but the Cardinals Bibbiena and Cornaro, who were likewise supping there, went unmasked. The sisters and nephew of the pope were present. The banquet was very fine and choice and lasted about two hours, after which we again set to dancing and enjoyed ourselves thus until eight of the clock.[28]

And through it all Leo made his happy way: At bullfights and hunting parties, at balls, banquets, comedies, music parties appeared the corpulent pontiff with his beaming smile, enjoying the sight of enjoyment. "God has given us the Papacy—let us enjoy it."

Luther took up the tale of Roman depravity in a curious letter to Leo that was presumably meant to be conciliatory—unless it was couched in profound irony. The pope was to be assured of his love and filial piety. Leo, after all, was not to be blamed.

> You sit like a lamb amidst wolves and live like Daniel amidst the lions or Ezekiel among the scorpions. The Roman court, which neither you nor any man can deny is more corrupt than either Babylon or Sodom and—according to the best of my information—is sunk in the most deplorable and notorious impiety. The fate of the court of Rome is decreed: The wrath of God is upon it, advice it detests, reformation it dreads. "We have medicined Babylon and she is not healed: Let us therefore leave her." I have always lamented, O most excellent Leo, that you, who are worthy of better times, should have been elected in such days as these.[29]

On June 28, 1519, the grandson of Maximilian was elected emperor as Charles V and the greater part of Europe fell under the control of a pale, silent young man of twenty-two. Two years later Charles convened a Diet at Worms to consider, in addition to various imperial matters, the case of the excommunicated monk Martin Luther, a subject of the empire. The imperial ban was added to the papal excommunication and Leo could feel that the troublesome interlude was passed. True, Luther was burned only in effigy, but he had fled from civilization and in his mountain asylum in the Wartburg could have little effect one way or the other on either Germany or Italy. Pope and emperor were in complete concord, and a month later, imperial armies were fighting alongside papal troops in Italy. Leo's nephew Lorenzo was dead but there were two illegitimate young Medici upon whom a dynasty could still be built. By the end of the year Florence was secured for them, and the French throughout Italy were on the retreat. On December 1, 1521, Leo heard that Parma had been recaptured for him: By the evening of the same day he was dead. Some said that his transports of joy at the news of Parma were too much for a weakened constitution—he had been ailing for some days past. Others swore that the cause was poison. The Romans, who had greatly benefited from his open-handed generosity, seized his cup-bearer, who was leaving Rome with suspicious haste, but the man was innocent. There were many accusations, but no direct evidence and no convictions.

Leo was fortunate in the time of his death. He had achieved that which had been denied Julius and seen the French on the run. The emperor was as yet respectful to the Papacy, Luther a fugitive monk, the Medici family established, the glow of the High Renaissance still upon Rome. Even in this matter of credit for the Roman Renaissance he was fortunate. It had been Julius who brought the great artists to Rome, urging them onward with his titanic energies. But it was Leo's rule that men were afterward to designate as the Golden Age. Many bitterly bewailed his death—none more bitterly than the bankers and wealthy cardinals, who, encouraged by his youth, had not called in their loans but increased them. None were repaid, for the treasury was quite empty.

VII

The Last Day of Italy

Giulio de' Medici
Pope Clement VII (1523–1534)

Giulio de' Medici

In the conclave that opened in the Sistine Chapel on October 1, 1523, the wooden cell of Cardinal Giulio de' Medici was, by chance, placed beneath Perugino's picture of St. Peter receiving the keys. This omen impressed many, for the cubicle of the cardinal who had emerged as Juluis II had stood in the same place.

It was the kind of lucky chance that had attended Giulio de' Medici all his life. Strictly speaking, he had no right to be here at all mixing on equal terms with the princes of the church on a portentous occasion, for his birth had been illegitimate; and though illegitimacy carried no social stigma it did create a legal bar—particularly to a career in the Church. If Giulio's life had followed a normal pattern he would probably now have been, at the age of forty-seven, a minor Florentine official boasting of the Medici blood in his veins and grateful for his useful connection with the ruling family of Florence. Instead, he was not merely cardinal and vice-chancellor but also *papabile*, one of the tiny handful of cardinals on whom Romans were placing bets that he would succeed to the vacant throne.

Good fortune, in the shape of an assassin's knife, had changed Giulio's life drastically when he was still a baby in arms, transferring him from a Florentine slum to the Medici palace. No one knew, or much cared, who his mother had been, except that she presumably had been pretty enough to attract the passing attention of his father, young Giuliano de' Medici, the handsome and popular brother of Lorenzo the Magnificent. Giuliano never bothered to justify her existence, for it was expected that a young nobleman would take his pleasure where he found it; as long as he did the sensible thing and married for solid political advantages when the time came, his private affairs were his own business. Giuliano, if he thought of the matter at all, would probably have intended to follow the compassionate custom of the day and bring his illegitimate son up in his own household once he acquired one. But he never had the chance to make any plans for Giulio: On an April Sunday in 1478 he was hewn down in the Cathedral of

Florence, victim of a conspiracy designed to topple the Medici rule in the city.

Lorenzo too was attacked on the same occasion but received only superficial wounds. The plot failed completely for the plotters had completely misjudged the temper of the Florentines. Giuliano had been immensely popular, and in a burst of corporate rage the Florentines rallied to the Medici and hunted down Giuliano's killers throughout the city. But though they exacted immediate vengeance for his murder, the spilled blood could not bring him back, and Lorenzo had loved his brother with all the deep family love of which a Medici was capable. In his passionate grief he learned that an obscure girl of the people had recently had a child by Giuliano, and ordered that she be found. It was not a difficult task in a city of a hundred thousand people; nor had the girl been at pains to conceal the illustrious parentage of her child. She made no difficulties about passing her son over to the lord of Florence and Lorenzo brought the child up as his own.

Giulio was only fourteen years old when Lorenzo the Magnificent died. In other families, perhaps, he would have been edged to one side or quietly put out of the way, now that his patron was gone. But again the strong Medici loyalty worked in his favor. Lorenzo's brilliant second son Giovanni became the boy's guardian, though Giovanni himself was scarcely three years older.

There developed a strong bond between the two half-brothers. Despite the narrow difference in their ages, it was Giovanni who took the lead in all their activities: He, the positive, articulate Giovanni, naturally earned and enjoyed the hero worship of the withdrawn, rather shy Giulio. And when in the course of time Giovanni achieved the heights of that career on which his father had started him and was crowned as Pope Leo X, nothing was more natural than that Giulio should have a large share of that cornucopia so lavishly poured out.

Leo legitimized him, created him cardinal, bestowed on him the powerful and lucrative office of vice-chancellor, and made him lord of Florence. On his part, Giulio served his half-brother honorably and competently in both his secular and sacred offices. He was not called upon to initiate policy: Always behind him he had

Leo's support and was therefore able to employ his considerable talents as an adminstrator without undue worry about their effects. People respected him even if they did not particularly like him. He was a conscientious worker and seemed to be free from the all-pervading crime of nepotism. He was proud of his name, but when he commissioned Niccolò Machiavelli to write the first true history of Florence, he insisted that he wanted realistic accounts of the Medici and not the conventional flatteries which passed for biography.

That name "Medici" stood him in very good stead when in company with thirty-five other cardinals he entered the conclave. Rome had had very poor pickings in the twenty months that had elapsed since the death of that other, more splendid Medici, Leo. Leo's successor Adrian had been an unmitigated disaster in the cardinals' opinion, forcing them to the assumption that he must indeed have been the candidate of the Holy Ghost for he certainly had not been theirs. Adrian, the earnest Dutchman who had never before been to Rome, was so ignorant of affairs that he had written asking that some suitable lodgings be obtained for him in Rome whence he could discharge his duties as pope. He was a barbarian who had been horrified at the pagan splendors of the Vatican when he at length arrived there. Barely able to speak Latin, Adrian seemed to believe that the prime duty of the supreme pontiff was to give spiritual guidance and set a Christian example to Christians. He lasted not quite two years and died, it was said, of a broken heart. The Romans rejoiced at his death, declared that a statue ought to be erected to his doctor, and on learning that a Medici was again in high favor in a conclave, impatiently looked forward to another golden age.

But the conclave dragged on, the days extending into weeks. Faithfully, the business of electing a pope continued to reflect the tensions in the outside world, but now all Europe was involved, not merely a handful of powerful Roman families. Whoever was elected pope would be forced to join one of the two camps into which the Continent was divided. He could choose either to throw in his lot with young King Francis of France, or he could follow the star of the equally young King Charles of Spain—who also happened to be emperor. What he could not do was to refuse to choose, to remain neutral.

The rivalry between king and emperor, soon to flare again into open war, found expression in the rough groupings of the cardinals in conclave. Giulio de' Medici had been a firm supporter of Spain during Leo's pontificate and was now openly regarded as the emperor's candidate—and the Spanish faction, though small, was united. The French party appeared powerful—so powerful that despite bitter protests from the Frenchmen present in the conclave, their opponents blandly began the proceedings before all the French had arrived in Rome. Shortly before the first scrutiny of votes on October 8, three indignant Frenchmen arrived at the wicket gate, brushed the attendants aside, and dressed as they were in boots, spurs, and plumes burst into the conclave and demanded to be included.

Giulio managed to reduce the opposition by a neat and typically Medicean trick. Not all those opposed to him were necessarily anti-Spanish. Pompeo Colonna, for one, simply disliked all Medici, and although he was a good imperialist he had forced his supporters to swear an oath that under no circumstances would they elect Giulio. The Colonna faction put up their own candidate, who, Pompeo had been assured, would be supported by the French. Secure in this knowledge, Pompeo Colonna approached Medici. With the combined French and Italian votes against him he stood no chance. Colonna urged his enemy: Would he continue to waste the votes of his faction? Medici agreed to vote for the Colonna candidate, provided that the Colonna voted for him if their candidate failed. He received Pompeo's promise in writing and then waited, untroubled, for the next scrutiny. What he knew, and Pompeo did not, was that the French had not the slightest intention of voting for the Colonna man.

When the results of the scrutiny became known, Colonna had to be physically restrained from attacking the French. Beside himself with rage, he accused them of double-dealing and then turned, babbling with fury, on Medici. Calmly waiting until the man had stammered into silence, Giulio pointed out that he now expected the votes of the Colonna faction to come to him—as

Colonna had sworn. Every member of the conclave knew that the Colonna had already sworn they would not vote for Giulio: Which oath would the unhappy Pompeo break?

But the constant groupings and regroupings all occasioned delay and by October 13 the omnipresent Roman mob was milling outside, bellowing for a pope. An irritated message was sent out from the conclave: "Seeing that you have already tolerated a foreign pope, we'll give you another one—he lives in England." This contemptuous reference was to Cardinal Wolsey, who had virtually considered himself pope at the beginning of the conclave. The Romans retorted in kind: "We don't care if he is a log of wood—just give us one." [1]

By now the city fathers were growing seriously perturbed by the dangers inherent in a protracted conclave. The administration of a conclave was, by law, in the hands of the civic authorities, so the magistrates, thus far remarkably lax, put into operation those powers which were designed to bring a conclave to a speedy conclusion. The constitution which governed a conclave laid down that the cardinals were to occupy a common room whose doors and windows were to be bricked up. One small wicket was to be left open, and this was to be just large enough to allow trays of food to be passed through. The fact that the three French cardinals were able to enter the conclave after it had begun argues that the walling up had not been very thorough. And certainly, throughout the six weeks of the conclave, all the cardinals were in open communication with the outside world, receiving and giving information and instructions.

But the city magistrates were able to put an additional, and very powerful, pressure on the conclavists: If a pope were not elected within three days then the cardinals' food could be reduced in quantity and quality. Faithfully the magistrates observed the regulation. From October 4, each cardinal was restricted to a single dish for the midday and evening meals, with the threat that five days later the menu would be reduced to bread, wine, and water.

Privation and threat had no effect except to increase the tensions within. After nearly a month without fresh air or natural light even the younger members of the conclave were suffering from the claustrophobic conditions—and most of the Sacred College were old men. The French revolted against the conditions, protested against the filth in which they were supposed to live, and demanded that they be allowed to take exercise in the Belvedere gardens for even a short time every day. The conclave was suspended briefly while the custodians inspected the cells and cleansed them of the grosser refuse, but when it met again the most rigorous of the conditions were imposed.

A diet of bread and water may finally have goaded the cardinals to a decision. A more likely spur was the news that war had again broken out between France and Spain, and that the emperor's forces had achieved a dramatic victory. Pompeo Colonna now knew which of his oaths he must break. Hurriedly, the members of his faction absolved each other from their oath that they would not elect Giulio de' Medici, and on November 17, Medici received the necessary majority and took the style of Clement VII. The Spanish ambassador jubilantly passed on the news to his master. "This pope is entirely your majesty's creature—so great is your majesty's power that even stones become obedient children." [2] It might perhaps have been better for the peace of Italy if indeed the new pope had been the submissive creature of the emperor.

Pope Leo, the legitimate Medici, had more closely resembled a butcher than an aristocrat; Pope Clement, the illegitimate Medici, truly resembled the ideal nobleman. He had inherited from his unknown mother a curious grace of form: In figure he was tall and slender, and despite a slight cast in his left eye he was handsome enough in a saturnine manner. But even as Leo's engaging character had compensated for his unprepossessing appearance, so a basic flaw in Clement's personality robbed him of majesty. The expression on his face was permanently sour, permanently suspicious, substantiating Guicciardini's opinion that "he was rather morose and disagreeable, reputed to be avaricious, by no means trustworthy and naturally disinclined to do a kindness" [3]—an unkind if accurate assessment by a man who genuinely liked him.

But despite his lack of personal popularity, Clement entered upon his reign with an immense fund of goodwill. During the short but dismal pontificate of Adrian, the artists and writers he had banished from the Vatican made their way to Medici's palace, there to keep alive the flame of the Golden Age until it could blaze again in a more congenial atmosphere. Clement, both as cardinal and pope, gave every indication that he too intended to be a Maecenas. It was doubtless a coincidence that on the very day of his election work began anew on Raphael's uncompleted Hall of Constantine in the Vatican, but it was a happy augury for the future.

Again Clement followed Leo's lead, allowing his court painters to portray his features under the guise of some heroic figure from the past: In the *Baptism of Constantine* he appeared as the near-legendary St. Sylvester, supposed inheritor of Constantine's empire of the West, a portrayal which Clement's own reign was to prove ironic. He lacked Leo's flair for picking new talent over a wide field. He loved jewelry above all other arts and the friendship he struck up with the bragging, murderous genius Benvenuto Cellini was one of the odder aspects of his career. In his tumultuous *Autobiography*, Cellini—who ever preferred to destroy a reputation rather than give one—had nothing but good to say of the pope whom almost all other writers united in execrating. In Cellini's company Clement seemed almost happy: fingering a brooch, discussing with eagerness the design for a vase, Clement was perhaps in his true element.

Clement's very virtues as a subordinate now proved his defects as a ruler. Men had admired his statecraft as a cardinal, but that statecraft had been employed merely as the instrument of Leo's policy. Now he was called upon to initiate policy, to make decisions—and he failed. Marco Foscari, the Venetian ambassador at the curia, observed Clement at close quarters for over four years and created one of his incisive pen portraits of the pope for his government in Venice.

The Pope is forty-eight years old and is a sensible man but slow in decision, which explains his irresolution in action. He talks well, he sees everything, but is very timid. He suffers no control in state affairs—he listens to everyone and then does just as he pleases. He is just and God-fearing. If he signs a petition he never revokes it—as did Pope Leo who signed so many. He withdraws no benefices and does not give them in simony. He gives away nothing, nor does he bestow the property of others. But he is considered avaricious. Pope Leo, however, was very liberal—he presented and gave away a great deal but this Pope is the opposite and therefore people grumble in Rome. He gives largely in alms, but is nevertheless not liked. He is very abstemious, and is a stranger to all luxury. He will not listen to jesters or musicians and never indulges in the chase or any other amusement. Since he has been Pope he has only twice left Rome—to go to Magliana, and has very rarely visited his vineyard, which is only two miles away. His entire pleasure consists in talking to engineers about waterworks.[4]

Clement lacked that easy Medici charm which had enabled Leo to persuade the unwilling even against their better judgment. His very virtues of sobriety and frugality were stigmatized, as Foscari noticed, as coldness and avarice. He was forced to be frugal, for he had inherited a bankrupt treasury. Leo would merely have borrowed more, for some banker, somewhere, would have accepted his large promises. Clement struggled on as best he could, for even had he tried to borrow, no banker would have trusted him, despite the fact that his financial probity was undoubtedly greater than his half-brother's had been. Foscari, with his ready ear for public opinion, remarked upon the effect of his parsimony: "The people grumble in Rome." The Romans who had looked forward to a continuation of the Medicean saturnalia felt themselves cheated. They did not turn upon him; they merely disassociated themselves from him, so that when the day of testing came Clement found himself alone.

But Clement's inability to inspire loyalty was as nothing compared with his main defect: his inability to make up his mind. It sprang perhaps from a too great sensitivity, a too vivid imagination: Even as he arrived at a solution to a problem, so immediately he could see only too clearly the problems to which that solution must inevitably give birth; attempting always to anticipate, he succeeded only in vacillating. "I will and I won't," the Venetians christened him derisively. Francesco Guicciardini, who had known and respected the cardinal, came to despise the pope. At Clement's urgent request Guicciardini came to Rome in the late spring of 1525, when trouble with Spain was imminent, to give the pope the benefit of his vast political experience.

Guicciardini did his work well, and in a series of vigorous briefs he addressed the pontiff in remarkably frank terms. Clement at least could not afterward complain that flattery had kept him in ignorance of the true state of affairs. Guicciardini, having outlined the current problem in the most lucid terms, again and again returned to the theme that "it is bad to make a bad decision—but worse to make none at all." Clement must make up his mind: if he offended one man by favoring another—well, that was unavoidable, but he would at least secure the support of the party favored. But if he attempted to please all men at the same time, disaster must inevitably result.

Nothing better illustrated Clement's painful vacillation than the messy business of the divorce of Henry VIII of England. Henry wanted to put aside his current wife Catherine on the grounds that her previous marriage with his brother had been consummated; therefore her marriage with Henry was technically incestuous. True, it was well known that Henry wanted to marry again, but Clement, the English argued, was not being asked to establish any shattering precedent. All that Henry wanted was what Rodrigo Borgia had granted to his own daughter Lucrezia.

Clement desperately wanted to please Henry, for had not the English king come forward with his earnest, if prosy, defense of the Papacy against Luther, and gained from a grateful Leo the resounding title "Defender of the Faith"? But if he pleased Henry, infallibly he would displease Charles V, the formidable nephew of Catherine. And Catherine herself strongly denied that her first marriage had ever been consummated. How could anyone possibly know? Was Catherine to be condemned for lying, on the strength of a coarse remark by her dead first husband? The despised Adrian VI would have made short work of Henry's claim but Adrian had only the limited vision of a spiritual pastor, whereas Clement was tormented by the vista of endless political repercussions. He first sent a secret brief to Henry and Wolsey, agreeing in principle to Henry's wish—if consummation could be proved. Then in turn he revoked it abruptly, temporized, sought more advice, and at length lost not only the dubious fidelity of Henry but the respect of the vast body of Englishmen who otherwise did not doubt that the head of the English Church resided in Rome, not London.

All this Guicciardini observed, and, observing, despaired and finally condemned, as others condemned. In the larger matter of the struggle between France and Spain, he believed that much of Clement's difficulties arose from the fact that his two favorite counselors, Giammatteo Giberti and Nicholas von Schomberg, were respectively French and imperial in their sympathies. According to Guicciardini, Giberti was the "heart of the Pope," for there was a strong personal bond between them. Giberti too was illegitimate, the child of a Genoese sea captain; he too had been brought up in a Medici household and enjoyed the favors of Leo. Clement made him secretary of state, an honorable choice, for Giberti was an honorable man—as, too, was Schomberg.

But even here, Clement became the victim of his own virtues, for his two honorable counselors, honorably appointed, pulled him in exactly opposite directions. Nothing that France could do was wrong for Giberti: Schomberg believed that the salvation of both Italy and his native Germany lay in a powerful emperor. As each gained a temporary ascendancy over Clement, so temporarily would Clement swing from the opposite side.

The Gathering Storm

In 1523 the two men who were to decide the fate of Pope Clement VII had not yet reached the age of thirty. The emperor Charles was just twenty-three while Francis was six years older. Their youth was about the only thing they had in common and even that was deceptive: Charles had never been young while Francis had never grown up.

Francis was typical of that class of monarch which his country had so often thrown up to its cultural profit and political loss. Highly intelligent, sufficiently learned to pass as scholar in a flattering court, he yet was blinded by that doctrine which ultimately brought the French monarchy to bloody ruin: The king, in his judgment, was a being outside and above human laws. His vast opinion of himself was fed and maintained by his mother, Louise of Savoy, as foolish in everything that pertained to her son as she was astute in everything else. It was Louise who acted as regent in a sullen France while her son sought "honor" in brilliant but useless military campaigns. It was Louise who organized the fantastic Field of the Cloth of Gold so her son could posture in showy splendor before the English king. And it was Louise who, against her better judgment but in order to gratify his vanity, scraped up the money that allowed Francis to enter the ruinous auction sale of the imperial crown. Henry VIII of England also entered the bidding but wisely backed out when he saw the colossal price the electors were demanding for the bauble. Francis, with his mother behind him, grimly bid higher and higher, and yet higher, pledging the royal credit to its utmost, forcing taxation to dangerously high levels in order to keep up the pace.

Charles of Spain eventually outbid him, for Charles was backed by the bottomless coffers of Europe's greatest banking house, the Fuggers. The coldly assessed generosity of the Fuggers was the best possible indication of the relative standing of the two young men. The crown cost Charles over half-a-million pieces of gold—and the enmity of Francis. A clash between the two major monarchs in Europe was always probable: It was raised to certainty when one of them was a vain young man who felt he had been cheated of his rights.

The emperor Charles V had been born to greatness, for he came at the converging point of royal lines whose ramifications covered all Europe. In 1506 at the age of six, he inherited the Netherlands through his father; at the age of sixteen he fell heir to Naples and a united Spain through his mother; at the age of nineteen he became archduke of Austria on the death of his grandfather, the emperor Maximilian. And now that he himself was emperor, the vast but shadowy claims of the empire were reinforced for the first time in centuries with the real powers of a territorial monarchy.

But Charles had not only been born to greatness: He would have achieved it even without the accidental advantages of inheritance. He was a man who in thirty years' time, at the height of his powers, would voluntarily abdicate, turning his back deliberately on the splendors he had created to spend his declining years as a private person. He had immense moral and physical courage, and was capable of pursuing to their logical end the most complex, most hazardous, affairs of state; but he was capable too of staking his life and crown on an offer of single combat.

War was for him a means, not an end, as it was for Francis. After the battle of Pavia when he had eventually crushed his great rival, he declined to make the usual ostentatious celebrations. Instead he prayed—as he prayed every day of his life—a devout and humble Christian who bore the great weight of power as a duty even though he found little joy in it. He could be inflexible and harsh in judgment when politics so demanded, but he gained the love of those who served him. Less ostentatiously cultured than Francis, he nevertheless knew greatness when he saw it: Titian received his patronage and repaid it with compound interest in those great portraits in which the soul of the man stood clear— the irony, the humor, the essential tolerance giving the ugly, lantern-jawed face an unforgettable attraction.

Clement VII, caught up between these two men, was in an impossible position from the very first days of his pontificate. Conflict between the two monarchs was inevitable; equally inevitable was the fact that they would fight out their differences in Italy, for each was too strong to be attacked on his home ground and each laid claim to the wealthy duchy of Milan. Common sense urged Clement to throw in his lot with the emperor. He owed his election very largely to Charles's support, and only a few years earlier his half-brother Leo had made common cause with the Spaniards to drive the French out of Italy.

But Charles as king of Spain was quite a different proposition to Charles as emperor. The king of Spain was an ally—the emperor could very easily become a master. Legally Charles could claim not only Milan but Naples, and if he established himself in both the north and south of Italy the States of the Church which lay between would be at his mercy. It was in defense of this territory, the Patrimony of Peter, that Clement began playing the same game that the more fortunate Leo had played with such success: threatening Charles with Francis, and when necessary, Francis with Charles. The chain of events that followed would end in the destruction of Rome.

In the early months of his pontificate Clement professed to be neutral, but even while he was still negotiating with Charles, he concluded an alliance with Francis. When Charles learned of the deception, his courtiers witnessed a most rare event—the emperor in a rage. "I shall go into Italy," he stormed, "and revenge myself on those who have injured me—particularly on that fool of a pope. Martin Luther, perhaps, was not so far wrong." [5]

In the autumn of 1524, eighteen months after Clement's election, two great armies were converging upon Milan. From the north came Francis, dragging great pieces of artillery across the Alps in an epic march that earned the admiration of Europe; Francis excelled at such dramatic gestures. From the southwest came the imperialists—slow, lumbering, dejected, for they had been soundly beaten outside Marseilles. At the head was the Constable of Bourbon, who had betrayed his king after a bitter quarrel and now served the emperor Charles. Francis swooped upon Milan, the imperial garrison fled, and the French were once again masters of the duchy. Impressed, Clement made his disastrous secret treaty with the temporarily ascendant power of France. Francis promised to keep his hands off the States of the Church and protect Medici rule in Florence. In return, Clement would recognize him as duke of Milan and allow the passage of a French army through the States in order that it could attack the Spaniards in Naples.

Dazed by the tempestuous French entry into Lombardy, the imperial army halted, but by the beginning of February it was once again on the move. Now it was the turn of the French army, camped before Pavia, to go on the defensive. Urgently, Francis' generals advised him to retreat northward to Milan, leaving hunger to destroy the already ill-provisioned imperialists. Clement joined his entreaties to those of the generals. Already he was regretting his now open alliance with this headstrong young man who unlike Charles thought of war in terms of glory and honor. The threatened battle would be no mere engagement between detached units but a head-on clash between the powers of France and Spain. He who lost the battle, lost all. And if Francis went down, Clement would be dragged with him. In Rome, the faithful Giberti took the papal nuncio to Francis on one side, begging him to use all his influence to prevent the clash. Let Francis not put too much reliance on treaties, was the veiled burden of his advice. "As no sailor ever risks the storm of the open sea with one anchor only so the Pope, confident though he is in the strength of King Francis, will not stake all on the single throw of a battle before Pavia." [6] The elaborate fancy was merely a restatement of the Medici policy of making simultaneous promises to both sides: If Francis failed, Clement would abandon him—rapidly.

Francis made the throw, and failed. In a tremendous battle outside Pavia on February 25, the French army was destroyed, the king taken captive, and the balance of power in Italy—in all Europe—tilted toward the emperor. Clement received the terrible news on the following evening. He was as one dead, an observer rcorded: Not only was Rome at the mercy of the imperialists if they chose to march south, but long dormant faction warfare broke out again in the city as the pro-imperial Colonna, savagely elated, fell upon their ancient enemies, the Orsini, who had linked their fortunes with the French. Those who feared Charles blamed the wretched Clement. Even Alessandro Farnese, the Petticoat Cardinal, paused in his round of pleasures to contribute to the obloquy heaped upon the pope. "This willing and not willing has brought the inevitable result. All Rome is dismayed, and dreads the ruin that may easily follow." [7]

But ruin did not follow immediately, for Charles, though still far distant in Spain, was in control of events in Italy. He wanted an ally, not a sullen, smoldering victim, and he therefore proposed an alliance with Clement, believing the pope must have learned his lesson. Swift as ever to secure a transient advantage, Clement accepted; on April 1, 1525, just three months after he had signed his pact with Francis, he signed another treaty, which in effect merely replaced the name of the French king with that of the emperor. Charles now was to be recognized as lord of Milan with the right to bestow it upon whom he pleased. In return, he too would take the States of the Church under his protection and ensure the continuance of Medicean rule in Florence—for which privilege the Florentines had to pay 100,000 florins.

The bridle of the emperor was cast over Italy but he rode still with a gentle hand. Satisfied that he had established his right to Milan, he reinstated the Sforza in their rule: Even his subtle brain apparently could not conceive the possibility that Clement would deliberately walk again to the edge of chaos. But indeed little that Clement did was deliberate. During the endless summer of 1525 the sign of imperial power was visible everywhere. Feverishly Clement sought advice as to its removal, but to his anguished inspection, each plan brought added dangers. Machiavelli, lucid as ever, precisely summed up the situation in which Clement had found himself from the beginning of his reign. "The Church, being possessed of a temporal sovereignty in Italy, was not sufficiently powerful to unite the rest of Italy under her scepter—yet feared to forfeit that temporal dominium by invoking a potentate who would defend her against the mighty ones of the land." [8] Any overt move that Clement might make threatened the safety of the Patrimony of St. Peter. In desperation he allowed himself to be involved in that prime expression of Italian politics—the plot.

The secretary of Francesco Sforza, the duke of Milan, who now ruled only by favor of the emperor, was Girolamo Morone, a highly skilled, much experienced, and thoroughly unscrupulous politician. It had been due largely to his exertions that Sforza possessed even the limited power that he did. Viewing the complex political pattern in Italy, Morone came to the conclusion that the easiest way out of the situation was to seduce the commander-in-chief of the imperial forces, the marquis of Pescara, an Italian by birth though now a loyal servant of the emperor. If Pescara could be offered a big enough bribe—say, the crown of the kingdom of Naples—the whole military strength of the emperor in Italy would be lost to him. Morone took the project to Clement: It precisely suited the Medicean talent for double-dealing and Clement made the plot his own. He would crown Pescara king of Naples if Pescara would betray his master and join an Italian alliance against him.

Pescara listened to the proposals made to him—listened and agreed in principle and asked for more details—and kept the emperor minutely informed of what was happening. It speaks much for Charles's confidence in his ability to choose lieutenants that he left the handling of the affair entirely in Pescara's hands. At the exact moment, Pescara struck. Morone, convinced that everything was going according to plan, accepted an invitation to confer with Pescara, and was arrested. Every detail of the inept plot then went awry. Instead of the imperialists being driven from Milan, Sforza lost even his small foothold, for as a felon vassal, he now forfeited the duchy, and Spanish troops occupied Milan and its subject cities permanently and in full strength. Bitterly, Clement cursed the name of Pescara—a "double traitor," he called him, conveniently ignoring his own elastic code. He waited in trepidation for the emperor's reaction, but none came. Charles had tightened his grip upon Italy and was content for the moment to leave it at that. Italy was only one of his many problems. Encouraged by the silence, Clement blundered on to his last deception.

King Francis had reacted characteristically to the disaster of his imprisonment. As a king in France his wishes had passed for laws. As a prisoner he was reduced to the status of an ordinary human being. And that Francis could not tolerate. "All is lost save honor," was the message he sent to his mother after his capture. But Francis' concept of honor was highly personal: It was that which allowed him to express his personality untrammeled by the actions of others. He had been prisoner for just a year when Charles offered him his freedom on harsh conditions. By law of conquest, Charles pointed out, he could lay claim to all France: He would, however, content himself merely with reclaiming what was his own. Charles knew perfectly well that he would not have been able to maintain the great kingdom of France as a vassal state, but so anxious was Francis to be free that he accepted the conditions. Burgundy was to be given to Charles and Francis was to renounce all claims to any part of Italy. Genoa, Asti, Naples, Milan—generations of Frenchmen had shed their blood to maintain the royal claims to these Italian territories. Smoothly, Francis agreed to obliterate that proud and bloody memory from French consciousness. He swore an oath, and was released. "Once again I am king!" he cried in triumph as he set foot on French soil. He left behind two small sons as hostages, but he had already made a secret reservation when making the oath: He had not the slightest intention of keeping it.

Francis was still on the way home when a papal nuncio was sped from Rome to meet him. Clement wanted to know, most urgently, whether the young king would undertake to perjure himself. The oath had been wrung from him under duress and papal absolution would be forthcoming if he would take up arms again against the emperor. Francis needed no Italian entreaties to urge him to the game of empire; it was pleasant to know that the supreme pontiff would absolve him from the crime of perjury, but it was not vital. All Europe agreed that Charles must have been nodding momentarily to have accepted Francis' word under the circumstances.

On May 22, 1526, a holy alliance was formed at Cognac, an alliance consisting of the Papacy, Venice, Milan, and France, directed against the emperor Charles V. Clement had committed himself to a war that would have taxed the abilities of even the terrible Julius II.

"This war is not for a point of honor, or for a vendetta, or for the occupation of a city: this war concerns the well-being, or the eternal servitude of all Italy." [9] So Giberti confided to a friend, exulting that at last a direct challenge had been hurled at the emperor, that Italy now was aligned with his beloved France. But it was not the egregious Giberti alone who rejoiced. Guicciardini considered that all Italy desired it as a painful surgery necessary to remove the hand of the barbarian, though later he bitterly regretted his judgment. Machiavelli too looked upon it as the long-awaited war of liberation. "For the love of God, do not allow this chance to slip by," [10] he wrote to his friend Guicciardini. The pope, on this occasion at least, must be kept firmly to the true path. Ever hopeful, Machiavelli brought to Clement his optimistic scheme of reviving Italian arms and Italian virtue by establishing an Italian militia, instead of relying upon treacherous mercenaries. Clement first grasped at the idea, then shrank from it: War was not yet declared, negotiations were still possible, they should not unnecessarily irritate Charles. Wearily, Machiavelli went back to Florence to superintend the strengthening of the city's fortifications, bedeviled by Clement's long-distance nagging and worrying. Even in this supreme crisis, Clement thought first of Florence, the seat of his family's power, and Machiavelli at length begged Guicciardini to use his influence with the pope and tell him that "he does not know what he is talking about" in the matter of civic defenses at least.

By a supreme irony, Clement the vacillator found himself cast in the role of patriotic leader, the head of a national movement. The emperor might be in overall political control of his varied forces in Italy, but even he could not place day-to-day restraint upon them. And the imperialists treated Italy as the occupied country that it was. The Spaniards in Milan particularly earned for themselves a ferocious but impotent hatred, for the common soldiers were quartered in private houses and treated their involuntary hosts as slaves. Every locality in which the imperialists were in strength had its tale to tell of casual murder and rape, of ceaseless pillage. For over a generation the Italians had been writhing under foreign overlords; rebellion was inevitable, but it was tragic that it came in the pontificate of Clement VII.

Charles made an effort to come to terms with Clement, but spurred on by his nationalist advisers, the pope rejected every proposal outright. The Spanish ambassador left the Vatican in a violent rage on June 20—whether by accident or design he had mounted his court fool behind him on his horse, and as they rode away the man mouthed and gestured obscenely at the sullen Italians. Three days later, still on the crest of his new wave of determination, Clement wrote a bitter letter to Charles detailing his grievances, denouncing the emperor's every action, justifying his own.

The letter was dispatched to Baldassare Castiglione, the papal nuncio at the imperial court. Castiglione, the gentle Italian whose virtues reflected the high standard he himself demanded of a Christian gentleman, was horrified. Throughout the previous feverish months he had been attempting to cool the atmosphere in Rome and present the emperor's case in a rational manner. If Castiglione had been near at hand, Clement would indubitably have added the nuncio's advice to the sum already collected; in distant Spain he was merely the recipient of disastrous instructions. Castiglione would have been even more horrified had he known that Clement had regretted writing the letter two days afterward, and had hastily dispatched a more conciliatory missive. By then it was too late. Obedient to his instructions, though deploring them, Castiglione had already conveyed the tenor of the first letter.

The great war for the liberation of Italy began, continued, and ended, disastrously. The first, and continuing, error which Clement countenanced was the appointment of the duke of Urbino as commander-in-chief of the papal armies. Doubtless it was at the insistence of Venice, the last truly independent power in Italy, and Clement was forced to travel far along the road of Venetian demands. But he would have been better advised had he employed the famed long memory of the Medici and remembered that it had been a Medici who despoiled the duke of Urbino. The duke stood by with a large army while a rebellion in Milan was bloodily put down, the first fruit of that deep mutual suspicion which fatally weakened the holy alliance against Charles.

But while the agony of Milan was distant, almost immediately afterward Clement was subjected to immediate and personal humiliation and danger. The Colonna launched a vicious attack upon Rome itself. The ancient Ghibelline seed had been dormant, not dead; even the great Boniface VIII had been unable to destroy it. Now, in the weakness of the Papacy in the person of Clement, it put out vigorous shoots.

The leader of the raiders was Cardinal Pompeo Colonna, Clement's rival in conclave and as loyal a supporter of Charles as it was possible for a Colonna to be. The raiders galloped into Rome on the morning of September 20 and the Romans welcomed them as though they were a circus. Five thousand men gathered outside the Colonna palace to refresh themselves after their furious ride across country and to plan the attack upon the Vatican. Clement called upon the people to defend him. They were deaf, as Marco Foscari, at least, knew that they would be to such a call. Clement, with a last flickering of self-respect, announced that he would meet his enemies as Boniface had met these same Colonna at Anagni—robed, crowned, and throned. At the last moment he thought better of it and retreated to Sant' Angelo where, trembling, he remained while the forces under the command of a cardinal of the Christian Church plundered the Christian churches of Rome, not even sparing St. Peter's itself. For the remainder of that day and all through the next, the Colonna troops gorged themselves with spoil and cruelty. Belatedly, the Romans had cause to regret their passiveness, for citizens as well as ecclesiastics were held to ransom, private houses as well as churches plundered.

Late on the afternoon of September 21, Clement signed a hasty treaty with the Spanish ambassador, who returned now without his buffoon but in triumph. The pope agreed to abandon his allies for four months—and to pardon the Colonna. Reluctantly the raiders withdrew and it seemed the danger was past. But the Colonna raid was only the overture to a tragedy.

The Sack of Rome

On December 7, 1526, less than six months after he had written his triumphant call to arms, Giberti was despondently confiding to the papal nuncio in England that "we are on the brink of ruin. Fate has let loose upon us every kind of evil so that it is impossible to add to our misery. It seems to me that sentence of death has been passed upon us and that we are only waiting its execution which cannot be long delayed." [11]

The armistice extracted from Clement had not run even its brief course of four months. Reproached by his allies, urged by the protestations and fiery promises of Francis, Clement swung back to the role of Italian patriot. There were initial successes in the bloody fighting in Lombardy but his allies, in their turn, betrayed him. The duke of Ferrara went over to the emperor, the duke of Urbino continued his disturbingly equivocal tactics—and no help came from France. Clement took the succession of blows very badly. "Unless something turns up he will make a separate peace or run away," the Milanese ambassador wrote. "He looks to me like a sick man whom the doctors have given up. From France nothing is heard and this drives everyone to despair."

The ambassador was wrong in his opinion that Clement contemplated flight from Rome, for there was no refuge for him elsewhere. Charles had at last replied to that fatally hasty letter of the pontiff's in language as intemperate as Clement's own. The pope was accused of having plunged Italy into war, causing the blood of Christians to be shed in defense of worthless worldly possessions. He was threatened with talk of that council which hung over the heads of all popes since the fifteenth century, when councils had at last resolved the scandal of the schism. Clement knew only too well to whom the tiara might be transferred—to the rebellious cardinal Pompeo Colonna, who would not hesitate to seize him should he leave the shelter of Rome and the last refuge of the Papacy, the great Castel Sant' Angelo.

The military situation was as bad as the political. The emperor had thrown his whole weight into the struggle and a fleet was already approaching Italy from Spain, bearing more armed men to be thrown into the caldron. But these were for the most part Spaniards—cruel enemies but Catholic. In the north, in Germany, a new menace was stirring—mercenaries known as landsknechts, who exaggerated the existing nationalist divisions with the new one of religious difference.

Lutheranism was already a recognizable force in Germany but it still was not strong enough to sever the mystic German bond between a man and his tribal leader. Charles V was a devout Catholic, and later a fierce persecutor of heretics, but he was also emperor and archduke of Austria; when news came to Germany of how the German emperor had been deceived and threatened by the Italian priest, the landsknechts flocked to the banner of his general in Germany, George Frundsberg. The great imperial victory at Pavia had largely been the work of this stolid, elderly man whose loyalty could not be undermined even by the meagerness of the rewards he had received for his service.

There had been sufficient ambiguity about Pescara to tempt Morone to his plot; no man would have deemed it worthwhile even to consider seducing Frundsberg. He mortgaged his own property to provision the company of some 12,000 landsknechts whom he gathered together in October, 1526. It was a small enough army with which to launch an attack upon Lombardy, and Frundsberg's friends attempted to dissuade him. For though the feudal tie was strong enough to get the force moving, the landsknechts were, after all, mercenaries, and if funds were not forthcoming in Italy certainly there would be trouble. Frundsberg replied with the kind of remark that coming from any other man would have been dismissed as rhetoric: "Many enemies—much honor: with God's help we will succeed in saving the Emperor and his people."

Frundsberg's crossing of the Alps was even more hazardous than Francis' had been, for the passage was made at the beginning of winter when snow and ice made the precipitous paths doubly dangerous. The general himself, grown fat with age, was bodily pushed and heaved up many a slope while his bodyguard made a fence of pikes along the dangerous outer edges. His 12,000 men were for the most part swashbuckling youngsters, clad in incongruous finery of plumes and fantastically slashed baggy trousers, supremely confident in themselves and their commander. But their resilience was tried to the utmost. Starving, exhausted, they stumbled down into the plain of Lombardy to find themselves faced with the only competent military force in Italy—the mercenary company known as the Black Bands under the command of Giovanni de' Medici.

Giovanni delle Bande Nere was the resounding nickname by which most men knew him. But he too was a Medici, though belonging to a junior branch of the family, and he had been consistently slighted by Clement who was both jealous and fearful of his growing fame. But in the supreme crisis of affairs Machiavelli had been able to persuade the pope that the salvation of Italy probably lay in the hands of this last of the condottieri, and to Giovanni had been given the defense of the approaches to the river Po.

The Black Bands fell upon the advancing Germans and might perhaps have halted them had not a lucky shot killed Giovanni. The company collapsed and the route south was open. Frundsberg sent an urgent request for money to Bourbon, then commanding a large Spanish force in Milan. Bourbon blackmailed the Milanese, threatening them with a return to the terror his arrival had ended, raised an emergency fund, and marched to join Frundsberg. On February 7, 1527, the Spanish and German forces in the north united to form an army of some 25,000 men and began the march on Rome.

Clement did not immediately appreciate the significance of the advancing horde, for a month earlier the imperial fleet had landed midway between Rome and Naples and an army was even now crossing the southern frontiers of the Papal States. In Rome he was subjected to almost exactly equal pressures from both sides, symbolized by the arrival, on the same day, of French and imperial envoys, the one bearing more promises, the other immediate threats. His Italian allies, fearful of having their entire southern front torn open, urged him on, but there were almost as many Italians in the ranks of the enemy as there were following the papal standard. He had no money, for Francis had again let him down. He considered creating some cardinals to raise funds but eventually declined to go against his own principles—making more fuss about the selling of a handful of hats, Guicciardini contemptuously remarked, than other popes had made about disposing of entire territories.

Yet again Clement's virtues proved more disastrous than other men's vices. Francophile still, Clement feared the emperor more: A lucky victory stiffened his resolve; a sudden threat sent him veering back again. But at last even he could understand the menace from the north, and two weeks before Frundsberg and Bourbon joined forces, he signed yet another treaty with the Spanish ambassador. He agreed an armistice of eight months, thereby abandoning his allies once more. He agreed to pardon even the Colonna, to withdraw his troops from Naples, and to pay 60,000 ducats to the starving landsknechts—on condition that they immediately withdraw from Italy.

Such a treaty might have saved Rome had it been signed a few weeks earlier. As it was, it merely eroded the last barrier that stood between the mercenaries and the city. Frundsberg had been able to keep them under control only because they believed that the plunder of Florence or a vast ransom from Rome would repay them for their sufferings. On the news that a beggarly 60,000 ducats for an army of 25,000 was to be their sole reward, they mutinied. In vain, Frundsberg harangued them, appealing to their loyalty; they howled him down and even threatened him. He collapsed onto a drum and shortly afterward died—of a broken heart, it was said, for he had loved his men.

Bourbon inherited the command, but if a German tribal leader could not restrain his men, a French renegade had no hope. The Spanish viceroy came in person to the camp in an attempt to ensure that the treaty would be recognized. Bourbon declared that he needed at least 250,000 ducats to satisfy the men. Resolute on this matter, Clement refused to pay such a fantastic sum and the southern march was resumed. The original plan had been to attack Florence, but that city's defenses were in good order after generations of intercity warfare. Rome was less prepared, trusting as it did in its sacred character to act as its defense. And in a burst of optimism Clement had disbanded his expensive troops and the capital of Christendom lay almost undefended before the advancing Spanish Catholics and German Lutherans.

They broke through at six A.M. on May 6, 1527—a cold morning with a thick mist that hampered the sparse defenders. Bourbon fell early in the assault. Benvenuto Cellini, goldsmith and master gunner to Clement VII, claimed the distinction of killing the only man who might have been able to prevent the worst excesses of the sack of the city. Cellini was with a party of gunners on the walls, and defeated by the fog was about to leave, when he caught sight of a group of men apparently trying to raise ladders against the wall. He drew his companions' attention to them

> . . . and then directing my arquebus where I saw the thickest mass of men, I aimed exactly at one who seemed to be higher than the rest—the fog prevented me from seeing whether he was on horseback or on foot. . . . When we had fired two rounds apiece I crept cautiously up to the rampart and, observing an extraordinary confusion among the enemy, I discovered afterwards that one of our shots had killed the Constable of Bourbon.[12]

By midmorning the defense had collapsed and the enemy was already beginning to plunder the Leonine City. Cellini was conscripted as a member of the papal household by the captain of the papal guard and ordered, much against his will, to man guns in Sant' Angelo. "I ascended to the keep and at the same instant Pope Clement came in through the corridors of the castle. He had refused to leave the Palace of St. Peter earlier, being unable to believe that his enemies would effect their entrance into Rome." [13] Paolo Giovio, the historian, had accompanied the pontiff in the hazardous dash from the Vatican Palace to the castle and had thrown his violet cape over Clement's too distinctive white vestments to give him some protection from sharpshooters.

Clement was at his prayers in the chapel when the horde broke in and he escaped only minutes ahead of time. He was not the only person who could not believe that Rome might fall. A few weeks earlier he had attempted to raise the Roman militia: The people remained indifferent while the nobles offered to lend small sums—at interest. Belatedly the militia rallied, but it was little more than a gesture, for the handful of softened citizens was no match for thousands of veterans spurred on by hunger, and national and religious rage. By the following morning, May 7, the city was at their mercy and remained so for five hideous months.

"Hell has nothing to compare with the present state of Rome," a Venetian wrote on the tenth. Two days later another Venetian appealed to his brother to raise ransom money.

> For God's sake do not abandon me. I am a prisoner of the Spaniards who have fixed my ransom at one thousand ducats. They have already tortured me twice and finished by lighting a fire under the soles of my feet. Dear brother, do not let me perish thus miserably. If I do not pay the ransom in twenty-six days they will hack me to pieces. For love of God and the blessed Virgin help me. All the Romans are prisoners, and if a man does not pay his ransom he is killed. Help me, dear Antonio, help me for God's sake.[14]

The Italian who fell into the hands of the Germans was marginally more fortunate than those who fell into the hands of Spaniards or fellow Italians. The German taste inclined toward drunkenness rather than cruelty, and ignorant of Italian ways, they could be fobbed off with lower ransoms. The Spaniards and Italians, able to assess wealth, exacted the last ducat and if the robbed man then fell into the hands of more Latins he could count only upon a cruel death. The Germans excelled in religious desecration. Their old general Frundsberg, it was rumored, had carried a golden halter to hang the pope and his troops did their best to carry out his intentions. Clement was safe in Sant' Angelo, giving absolution to his gunner Cellini—"for all murders I should perpetrate on behalf of the Apostolic Church"—but there were thousands of undefended priests and nuns to serve as hecatomb to Frundsberg. A mob of soldiers dressed an ass in bishop's vestments and demanded that a priest should offer it the Host. The man, in last defense of his office, swallowed the wafer himself and was murdered—slowly. Those nuns who were killed after being raped were fortunate, for their sisters were dragged around like animals, to be auctioned off to man after man before finding the relief of death. Luther was proclaimed pope in a mock ceremony. The venerable relics of Rome, the very tombs of the popes, were despoiled.

Every soldier became a wealthy man. Some of the more astute set up asylums in which the wealthier Romans could find temporary safety. Camp followers had their hats stuffed with coins. Men swaggered around with garments of costly silk and brocade thrown over their stinking rags, bearing sacks clinking with precious vessels looted from palaces and churches. Rome had not been sacked since the eleventh century and the city had become a treasure-house, a fraction of whose value would have furnished sufficient defense had it been offered in time.

Over two thousand murdered citizens had been thrown into the Tiber by the end of May and nearly ten thousand more were inefficiently buried, so that with the advent of summer plague arose in the city. There was gold in undreamed-of quantities—but no bread. Hunger and plague struck victors and vanquished alike and gradually the more sensible invaders left the city. By the middle of June Rome was a dead city: "No bells ring, no churches are open, no masses are said. The stench of dead bodies is terrible— men and beasts have a common grave and in the churches I have seen corpses that dogs have gnawn." [15] Some soldiers remained to garner the last ducats at risk of their lives, others would be forced to return as events in the outside world set the tide moving toward Rome again. But those who remained and those who later returned were alike: They were rummaging over a corpse.

> We expect that your majesty will give us accurate instructions as to whether some form of Apostolic Chair is to remain or not. I will not conceal from your majesty the view of some of your servants that the Sacred Chair in Rome should not be utterly and finally abolished. If this happened the King of France could immediately install a Patriarch in his dominion, and England and every other monarch would do likewise, refusing obedience to the Holy See.[16]

So, on June 8, a Spanish bureaucrat could discuss the future of the Papacy, coming to the conclusion that the spiritual should again be divorced from the temporal power. Three days earlier Clement had signed his last effective treaty of the war, putting himself utterly at Charles's mercy. Throughout that appalling summer Clement remained a prisoner in Sant' Angelo while his fate, and that of his office, was debated in Spain. Charles himself had been deeply shocked by the events of May and June, and Europe as a whole reacted violently in favor of the pope. "If he came here he would be worshipped," Castiglione reported from Spain. Even had he wished, Charles could not have adopted the extreme measures urged upon him: To destroy the Papacy would be to create a vacuum—and no man could tell how it would be filled. By the end of October the emperor had made his decision. His troops would be removed from Rome and the States of the Church returned to Clement, on condition that he would give hostages, agree to a council for the reformation of the Church, and remain politically neutral.

There was no fear that Clement would break this last agreement. The papal treasury was totally empty, for he had been forced to pay the vast fine of 400,000 ducats to gain his freedom—one of Cellini's last tasks in Sant' Angelo had been to remove the jewels from the regalia and melt down the gold to be used as ransom. Clement had no troops: His Italian allies were already fighting between themselves for his territories, and Florence—his own city —had risen in revolt and chased out the two young Medici bastards who had been given the city as though it were the pope's private property.

With the aid of the more responsible imperial officers Clement made his escape from Rome disguised as a merchant, on December 8, and found refuge of a sort in Orvieto, a city set high on a rocky hill some eighty miles to the north of Rome. To him came almost immediately the envoys of the English king, Henry VIII, still bent on securing their master's release from an irksome marriage. Clement was as evasive as ever, they reported, and his condition was truly pitiable.

> The pope lieth in an old palace of the bishops of the city, ruinous and decayed, where or we came to his privy chamber we pass three chambers, all naked and unhanged, the roofs fallen down, and as one can guess, thirty persons—riffraff and others—standing in the chambers for a garnishment. And as for the Pope's bedchamber all the apparel in it was not worth twenty nobles.[17]

In June famine drove him out of Orvieto and he wandered on to his next temporary lodging through a land that seemed to be in the convulsions of death. Spaniards, French, Germans, Italians continued to fight each other and prey upon the demoralized people. A brief French victory raised his hopes, but the death of the French general dashed them even lower than before. The only power in Italy was that of the emperor, and perforce Clement accepted the position.

Charles desired a coronation and Clement agreed, crowning him in Bologna in December, 1529—the last pope to crown an emperor. In return Charles lent him troops to destroy the resurrected republic of Florence and to place upon a throne its first duke—the evil young Alessandro de' Medici, whom men believed to be Clement's own son, so overweening was the love he bore him. Out of the wreck of papal power this at least was gained, the glory of the Medici purchased cheaply enough by the agony of all Italy.

Clement had survived, but there was still one great danger that lay ahead of him: the emperor's insistent desire that a council of the Church should be called to discuss the whole question of reform. Reluctantly Clement again took the road to Bologna where Charles was impatiently waiting. Again an English envoy accompanied the pope, for the Bologna meeting was designed not only to discuss the question of a council but also to pronounce, finally, on the business of Henry's divorce.

It was a miserable journey in the depth of winter through a starving land. Clement, the envoy wrote,

> . . . did not dare take the high road which, as you know, is by Florence and foul enough, but by Perugia and the lands of the Church. The said journey to the pope, by reason of the continual rain and foul way, with other unfortunable accidents, as the loss of certain of his mules and the breaking of the leg of one Turkish horse that he had, and above all for the evil lodging that he had with his company was wondrous painful. The pope divers time compelled, by reason of the foulness and dangers of the way, to go on foot the space of a mile or two: besides that pleasure and past-time, for lack of a feather bed, compelled to lie in the straw.

He entered Bologna on the evening of December 7, "riding in his long white kirtle, having his rochet upon the same and a stole upon his neck and so coming to his palace. Of any miracles done upon any halt or lame, I heard not of." [18]

The malicious jest was not wholly correct, for Clement did manage to bring off a miracle of sorts—the avoidance of a council. Obediently he censured Henry of England for his adultery, tardily if uselessly defending the honor of the emperor's aunt. He agreed to another league which would strengthen Charles's hand against France. But with considerable skill he sabotaged the movement toward the establishment of a council, which even at this late stage might have healed the rift in Christendom. The emperor's desire to end the schism was as much political as religious, for it gravely weakened his power. But any effective council, in examining the morality and structure of the existing system, could not have failed to take into account Clement's own career and pronounce him unfitted to hold the supreme office.

The Venetian government, at least, was unsurprised when the meeting dissolved with the vital question still unanswered, for their ambassador at Bologna, with the pessimism of an experienced diplomat, had warned them to expect nothing else. "As far as the Council is concerned, Your Serenity can be assured that Clement will avoid it by any means. Indeed, the fear of it, more than any other thing, vexes the soul of His Holiness—so much so that he is prepared to forfeit the friendship of the Emperor and the others, and even his own life." [19] Charles was not so strong in Italy that he could afford to risk the desperation of a weak man who would rather that Rome be destroyed for the second time than that the tiara should be taken from his head.

In addition to the negative triumph, Clement achieved a positive one at Bologna: the emperor's consent to the marriage of Catherine de' Medici to the son of the king of France. Catherine, then an unattractive girl of fifteen, was the great-granddaughter of Lorenzo the Magnificent and the sole surviving legitimate Medici of the elder branch. At the same time, the emperor agreed to affiance his own daughter to Clement's alleged nephew Alessandro.

It was no little matter to place—simultaneously—relatives in the families of two mortal enemies, but where Medici interests were at stake, Clement proved himself a statesman of the first rank.

Seven months after the Bologna meeting Clement went in state with his ward Catherine to Marseilles, where he himself celebrated her marriage to Henry of Orléans, the son of King Francis. The prolonged festivities that followed were decorous and mild enough, but unsettling for one of his abstemious habits and undermined constitution. He returned to Rome in December, 1533, and almost immediately afterward fell ill, lingering on until the following autumn. One of his last official acts was to write a long, pathetic letter to Charles, confiding his nephew Alessandro to the imperial protection, "since I fear that the position which your magnanimity has bestowed on him may be destroyed by those enemies who are encouraged by the fact that his marriage to your daughter has not yet taken place." [20] At the end, as at the beginning of his career, the Medici were his major care. There was a pious hope that Charles would respect the dignity of the holy chair, but the letter was concerned throughout only with the fate of the house of Medici after his death.

Cellini visited him three days before the end, bringing some medals that Clement had commissioned.

> He ordered his spectacles and a candle to be brought in, but nevertheless he could discern nothing of my workmanship. So he set to examine the medals by the touch of his fingers, but after feeling thus for some length of time he fetched a deep sigh, and told one of the courtiers he was sorry for me, but if it pleased God to restore his health he would make me a satisfactory payment. Three days later he died and I had only my labor for my pains.[21]

Clement died on September 25, 1534, in the fifty-sixth year of his age. His ward Catherine did in time ascend the throne of France, but his two nephews survived him only briefly. One was poisoned by the other and then was himself murdered, and the hard-won ducal crown passed to the despised younger branch of the family.

In all but his personal attributes, Clement VII was the protagonist in a Greek tragedy, the victim called upon to endure the results of actions committed long before. Each temporal claim of his predecessors had entangled the Papacy just a little more in the lethal game of politics; even while each moral debasement divorced it just a little more from the vast body of Christians from whom ultimately it drew its strength. Its supernatural role for centuries had buttressed its temporal claims. So Dante could excoriate the men who had attacked Pope Boniface VIII, even though Boniface as a man had been his most hated enemy. So Cesare Borgia's victim could plead for absolution from his murderer's father—and neither victim, murderer, nor father was aware of the inherent irony.

But the buttress was being eroded at its base as the faith of Christians was weakened by the more bizarre activities of those who claimed to hold the sword as well as the keys. The first crack had appeared during the reign of Clement's splendid and fortunate relative Leo. It had been papered over. Leo's successor Adrian had had the desire—and perhaps the ability too—to repair the crack. He had been mocked into his grave by those who could have supported him. Clement had inherited an impossible situation for a man of his caliber. In addition to the formidable problems of state that every pope had to face, he had to cope with the fact that Luther, far from being suppressed, was flourishing; that a precedent had been established for religious purposes that could be used only too easily for political purposes; and that the two major Catholic powers in Europe were engaged in combating each other while demanding that he declare for one or the other.

A greater man than Clement might have turned his back upon the political problems and concentrated the vast energy of the Roman Church upon destroying the cancer in its heart, reforming itself before it again sought to lead others. But Clement was no more than the product of the forces which for centuries had been directed to one end: the maintenance of papal power. In moments of clarity he saw that himself. After the sack of Rome, when the fires of arson had at last died down, when the last gold-gorged mercenary had departed, and the populace was wearily stirring, still dazed, still fearful, the Venetian ambassador Gaspar Contarini tried to rally the stricken man.

> Your Holiness must not imagine that the welfare of the Church of Christ rests in this little State of the Church: on the contrary, the Church existed before she possessed the State, and was the better for it. The Church is the community of all Christians; the temporal state is like any other province in Italy and therefore your Holiness must seek above all to promote the welfare of the True Church which consists in the peace of Christendom.

Clement agreed heavily with everything the Venetian said, and admitted that "as a conscientious man I know that I ought to act as you tell me."

But what else could Clement do but attempt to defend those temporal rights he had inherited, at no matter what cost to his spiritual role? Had he done otherwise, "I would have been plundered to the last farthing, unable to recover anything of my own. I repeat—I see clearly that the way you point out is the right way, but in this world the ideal does not correspond to reality, and he who acts from amiable motives is nothing but a fool." [22]

Three weeks after Clement's death, Alessandro Farnese ascended the throne as Paul III. He did at least countenance the summoning of a council—but the Council of Trent did too little and met too late and its failure strengthened the Inquisition that was to drive a wedge into the crack in Christianity. Clement had bartered the last opportunity to restore the prestige of the Papacy for the sake of an uneasy power under the shadow of the emperor. And for that Italians cursed him. "He died loathed by the Curia, distrusted by monarchs, leaving behind him a hated and oppressive memory," [23] wrote Guicciardini, his quondam admirer. Francesco Vettori, fellow citizen of both Guicciardini and Clement, made perhaps a better judgment. Clement had been a good man, he thought, particularly if compared with his immediate predecessors. "If one considers the lives of previous popes one may truly say that, for more than a hundred years, no better man than Clement VII sat upon the Throne. Nevertheless, it was in his day that the disaster took place while these others, who were filled with all vices, lived and died in felicity—as the world sees it. Neither should we seek to question the lord our God, who will punish—or not punish— in what manner and in what time it pleases him." [24]

Appendix

The Sources

Each of the seven popes linked together in the present book precipitated a crisis in the affairs of the Roman Church through the interaction of a defective personality and theoretically unlimited power. In the vast context of papal history they were neither unique nor typical in their crimes. But each, in pursuing the lure of temporal power and pleasures, caused a profound modification in the structure he had inherited, his actions reaching forward to chain his successor to the path that led at last to the European crisis of the Reformation and the Italian tragedy of the Sack of Rome in 1527.

According to his Church's teaching, the spiritual capacity of each remained unaffected by his temporal activities, the waters of divine grace continuing to pass through him unaffected by the possible foulness of the conduit. This, a mystery of religious faith, is outside argument but reflects the abiding dilemma of the historian: the assessment of personal motives. No man can say what was in the innermost hearts of these seven men. There is no possible way of knowing whether Borgia committed sacrilege each time he broke the Bread, or whether at those moments he was utterly and humbly absorbed. We cannot tell whether Boniface really believed that he could not commit simony because the pope and the church were one, or whether the belief was a subtle sophistry. They can be judged only as other historical figures are judged, on their actions as observed and recorded by their contemporaries.

But any exploration of the papal past encounters at the outset an additional hazard beyond the normal historical lacunae and accidental distortions: the religious fanaticism which undermines the value of those contemporary chronicles and diaries, histories and private letters, without which official documents are inert substance. An extreme example of this effect occurred in the sixteenth century when Cardinal Cesare Baronius was charged to write the first of the papal histories, as corrective to that produced by the Protestant reaction. Encountering the darkness of the tenth century, Baronius found that the only sure guide was Liudprand of Cremona; and Liudprand, though a bishop, was filled with a bitter hatred for the Roman Papacy which colored all his work. As it was impossible to ignore him, Baronius accepted him, though reluctantly, and so enshrined Liudprand's version of the "pornocracy" as official history.

It seems impossible for even the greatest writers to maintain, on the subject of the Papacy, their habitual honesty and balance. Polemics alone survived the trauma of the Reformation unchanged, seventeenth-century Puritans joining hands with fifteenth-century anti-papalists even while papal apologia achieved its extreme forms. The fierce partisanship of historians maintained the tradition on both sides of self-illusion and mendacity, weakening the objective value of their compendia upon which a general historian, faced with the immense scope of papal history, is forced to rely. So, in the sixteenth century, Francesco Guicciardini could equably record anti-papal stories on flimsy bases he would have scorned to use for other purposes. So, in the mid-nineteenth century, the entire French edition of the work of the Protestant historian von Ranke could be so doctored that he declined to recognize it as his own.

In the late nineteenth century the violent swings of the pendulum began to abate, the moment of rest best marked, perhaps, when Pope Leo XIII opened the Vatican archives to the great Catholic historian, Ludwig Pastor, with the single injunction: Tell the truth. There were still limitations—even Pastor found that certain classes of documents were not accessible—but from then onward the historical treatment of the Papacy as a temporal institution has been marked by a degree of objectivity lacking in earlier centuries.

The present book has been written between two guidelines, as it were, erected to left and right—the work of the Protestant historian Ferdinand Gregorovius, whose history of medieval Rome is, in effect, a continuation of Gibbon and the papal histories of two Catholics, Horace K. Mann for the earlier period and Ludwig Pastor for the later. The bibliography on pp. 291–296 lists those books, by both contemporary and later writers of all degrees of partisanship, which have enabled the writer to work in depth between the lines.

Bibliography

Alberi, E. *Documenti sull' assedio di Firenze* 1529–1530. Florence, 1840.

————, *Le relazioni degli Ambasciatori Veneti al Senato durante il secolo decimosesto*. Florence, 1839–1855.

Alfieri, Vittorio, *Del Principe e delle Lettere*. Milan, 1919.

Alvisi, E., *Cesare Borgia, duca di Romagna: Notizie e documenti*. Imola, 1878.

Analecta Bollandiana, T. IX, pp. 147–200: *Vita et miracula Sancti Petri Caelestini Auctore coaevo*. Brussels, 1890.

Antonelli, G., *Lucrezia Borgia in Ferrara*. Ferrara, 1897.

Atti e memorie delle RR deputazione di storia patria per le provincie Modenensis e Parmensis. Modena, 1863–1876.

Bale, John, *The Pageant of the Popes . . . Englished with sundry additions by I.S.* London, 1574.

Baluze, S., *Miscellanea*, Vol. IV. Paris, 1761.

————, *Vitae Paparum Avenonensium*. Paris, 1693.

Balzani, Ugo, *Le cronache italiane nel Medio Evo*. Milan, 1900.

Baronius, Caesar, *Annales ecclesiastici*: continued by Raynaldus. Lucca, 1738–1756.

Benedict of Soracte (Benedictus, S. Andreae Monachus), *Chronicon*, in Migne, *Patrologia Latina*, T. 139.

Bergenroth, G. A., *Calendar of Letters, Despatches and State Papers Relating to the Negotiations Between England and Spain*, etc., Vols. I and II. London, 1862–1866.

Bisticci, Vespasiano da, *Lives of Illustrious Men of the 15th Century*, trans. by William George and Emily Waters. London, 1926.

Boase, T. S. R., *Boniface VIII*. London, 1933.

Bouquet, Martin, *Recueil des historiens des Gaules*. Paris, 1738.

Breisach, Ernst, *Caterina Sforza: a Renaissance Virago*. Chicago and London, 1967.

Brown, Rawdon, *Calendar of State Papers*, etc. Vol. I. London, 1864.

Bryce, James, *The Holy Roman Empire*. London, 1887.

Burchard, John, *Diarium,* 1483–1506, Vols. I–III, L. Thuasne, ed. Paris, 1883–1885.

———, *The Diary of John Burchard,* Vol. I, 1483–1492, trans. from Thuasne's text by A. H. Matthew. London, 1910.

———, *At the Court of the Borgia: Being an Account of the Reign of Alexander VI Written by His Master of Ceremonies,* ed. and trans. by Geoffrey Parker. London, 1963.

Burckhardt, Jacob, *The Civilisation of the Renaissance in Italy,* trans. by S. G. C. Middlemore. London, 1878.

Capecelatro, Alfonso, *Storia di S. Caterina da Siena e dal Papato del suo tempo.* Siena, 1878.

Cappelli, Antonio, *Lettere di Lorenzo de' Medici, dette il Magnifico, conservate nell' Archivio Palatino di Modena.* Modena, 1863.

Capuana, Raimundo, *S. Catharinae Senensis Vita* (*Acta Sanctorum Aprilis,* Tom. III). Venice, 1738.

Cellini, Benvenuto, *Autobiography,* trans. by J. A. Symonds. London, 1896.

Cipolla, C., *Le signorie dal 1300 al 1500.* Milan, 1881.

Compagni, Dino, *La cronica delle cose occorenti ne' tempi suoi,* ed. by Isidoro del Lungo. Città di Castello, 1913–1916.

Creighton, M., *A History of the Papacy During the Period of the Reformation,* Vols. I–II. London, 1882.

Dante Alighieri, *The Divine Comedy,* trans. by Henry Wadsworth Longfellow. London and New York, 1895.

Dell' Arco, Mario, *Pasquino e le Pasquinate.* Milan, 1957.

Dietrich von Niem, *De Scismate,* ed. by G. Erler. Leipzig, 1890.

Döllinger, J. J., *Beiträge zur Politischen, Kirchlichen und Kultur-Geschichte der Sechs Letzen Jahrhundert,* Vol. III. Vienna, 1882.

———, *Fables Respecting the Popes in the Middle Ages,* trans. by Alfred Pummer. London, 1871.

Dupuy, P. (ed.), *Histoire du Differend d'entre le Pape Boniface VIII et Philippe le Bel.* Paris, 1655.

Eugenius Vulgarius, *Invectiva in Romam,* in Migne, T. 129.

Fabronius, A., *Laurentii Medicei Magnifici vita.* Pisa, 1784.

Finke, Heinrich, *Acta Aragonensia. Quellen zur deutschen, italienischen, franzosischen, spanischen zur Kirchen und Kulturgeschichte aus der diplomatischen korrespondence Jaymes II (1291–1327)*, Vols. I–III. Berlin and Leipzig, 1908.

———, *Aus den Tagen Bonifaz VIII*. Berlin, 1902.

Flodoard, *Histoire de l'église de Rheims: Chronique sacrée*, in Guizot. Paris, 1824.

Florence of Worcester, *Chronicle*, trans. by Joseph Stevenson. London, 1853.

Froissart, Jean, *Chronicles*, trans. by Thomas Johnes. London, 1849.

Gardner, Edmund, *St. Catherine of Siena*. London, 1907.

Garinci, G. B., *Documenti scelti del archivio dei Gaetani*. Rome, 1846.

Gayet, Louis, *Le Grand Schisme d'Occident d'après les documents contemporains*. Florence, 1889.

Gibbon, Edward, *The Decline and Fall of the Roman Empire*. London, 1830.

Giovio, Paolo, *La vita di dicenove huomini illustri*, trans. by L. Domenichi. Venice, 1561.

Giustinian, A., *Dispacci, 1502–1505*, ed. by Pasquale Villari. Florence, 1876.

Glaber, Raoul, *Chronique*, see Guizot. Paris, 1824.

Glasfurd, Alec, *The Antipope: Peter de Luna 1342–1423*. London, 1965.

Graphia aureae urbis Romae, in Ozanam. Paris, 1850.

Grassis, Paris de, *Diarium*, in Döllinger, *Beiträge*. Vienna, 1882.

Gregorovius, Ferdinand, *History of the City of Rome in the Middle Ages*, trans. from the 4th German ed. by Annie Hamilton. London, 1894–1902.

———, *Lucretia Borgia: According to Original Documents and Correspondence of Her Day*, trans. by John Leslie Garnet. London, 1903.

Grottanelli, F., *Leggenda minore di S. Caterina da Siena e lettere dei suoi discepoli*. Bologna, 1868.

Guicciardini, Francesco, *Counsels and Reflections*, trans. by N. H. Thomson. London, 1890.

———, *Storia d'Italia*, ed. by Constantino Panigada. Bari, 1929.

Guicciardini, Luigi, *Il sacco di Roma*. Cologne, 1758.

Guizot, M., *Collection des mémoires relatifs à l'histoire de France*, Vol. VI. Paris, 1824.

Hodgkin, Thomas, *Italy and Her Invaders*, Vol. VII. London, 1899.

Infessura, Stefano, *Diario della Città di Roma*, ed. by Oreste Tommasini, in *R.I.S.*, III, 2. 1890.

Jacopo da Volterra, *Diario Romano 1479–1484*, ed. by E. Carusi, in *R.I.S.*, N.S. XXIII, Pt. iii.

Jacopone da Todi, *Le Satire*, ed. by B. Brugnoli. Florence, 1914.

Kervyn de Lettenhove, *Etudes sur l'histoire du XIIIᵉ siècle* (*De controversia Bonifac.*), in Migne, T. 185.

Köhler, Walther, *Dokumente zum Ablasstreit von 1517*. Tübingen, 1934.

Labbe, P., *Sacrosancta Concilia*, Vol. VI. Venice, 1728–1733.

Landucci, L., *Diario Fiorentino*, ed. by I. Del Badia. Florence, 1883.

Leva, G. de, *Storia documentata di Carlo V in correlazione all' Italia*. Venice, 1863.

Liber Pontificalis, Text, introduction and commentary by L. Duchesne. Paris, 1884.

Liudprand of Cremona, *Works* (*Antapodosis; Liber de Rebus Gestis Ottonis; Relatio de Legationes Constantinopolitana*), trans. by F. A. Wright. London, 1930.

Luther, Martin, *Tischreden*, Vols. I–VI. Weimar, 1912–1921.

Luzio, Alessandro, *Isabella d'Este ne' primordi del Papato di Leone X*. Milan, 1907.

Machiavelli, Niccolò, *Discorsi sopra T. Livio*, Vol. III of *Opere*. Milan, 1804.

———, *The History of Florence and the Affairs of Italy; The Prince; Jerome Savonarola; Murder of Vitellozzo*. London, Bohn Library, 1847.

———, *Le lettere familiari*, ed. by E. Alvisi. Florence, 1883.

Magnan, J. B., *Histoire d'Urbain V*. Paris, 1862.

Malmesbury, see William of Malmesbury.

Mann, Horace K., *The Lives of the Popes in the Early Middle Ages*. London, 1902–1932.

Marullus, M. T., *Hymni et epigrammata*. Florence, 1497.

Migne, J-P., *Patrologia Latina*, Vols. 139, 145, 185. Paris, 1853–1855.

Mollat, G., *The Popes at Avignon*. Edinburgh, 1963.

Muratori, Ludovico, *Annali d'Italia dal principio dell' era volgare sino al 1750*. Rome, 1752–1754.

Muratori, Ludovico, *Rerum Italicarum Scriptores*, etc. Milan, 1723–1751; *New Series*. Città di Castello, 1900–1913.

Okey, T., *Avignon*. London, 1926.

Ozanam, A. F., *Documents inédits pour servir à l'histoire littéraire de l'Italie depuis le VIIe siècle jusqu'au XIIIe*. Paris, 1850.

Pastor, Ludwig, *The History of the Popes from the Close of the Middle Ages*, ed. by F. I. Antrobus, Vols. I–VI. London, 1891–1898.

Penni, Gian-Giacomo, *Chronicha delle magnifiche et honorate pompe fatte in Roma per la creatione et incoronatione di Papa Leone X*. Rome, 1513.

Pertz, G. H., *Monumenta germaniae historica*. Hanover, 1873.

Petrarch, Francesco, *Lettres sans Titre*, trans. by V. Develay. Paris, 1885.

———, *Lettere delle cose familiari*, trans. by G. Fracasseti. Florence, 1892.

Platina, B., *The Lives of the Popes*, trans. by W. Benham. London, n.d.

Ptolemy of Lucca, *Historia ecclesiastica*, in R.I.S., XI, 1727.

Pulver, Geoffrey, *Machiavelli: The Man, His Work and His Times*. London, 1937.

Ranke, Leopold von, *The Ecclesiastical and Political History of the Popes During the 16th and 17th Centuries*, trans. by Sarah Austin. London, 1866.

Raynaldus, see Baronius.

Richer, *Histoire*, trans. by A. M. Poinsignon. Paris, 1855.

Ridolfi, Roberto, *The Life of Francesco Guicciardini*, trans. by Cecil Grayson. London, 1967.

R.I.S., *Rerum Italicarum Scriptores*, see Muratori.

Roscoe, William, *The Life and Pontificate of Leo the Tenth*, ed. by Thomas Roscoe. London, 1864.

———, *Illustrations, Historical and Critical, of the Life of Lorenzo de' Medici . . . , with an Appendix of Original and Other Documents*. London, 1822.

Ruscelli, G., *Lettere di Principi*. Venice, 1562–1581.

Salembier, L., *The Great Schism of the West*. London, 1907.

Sanuto, Marino, *La spedizione di Carlo VIII in Italia*, ed. by R. Fulin. Venice, 1873–1882.

———, *I Diarii*, Vols. I–LVIII. Venice, 1879–1902.

Schertlin, Sebastian, *Lebensbeschreibung . . .* , ed. by C. S. von Holzschuber. Nuremberg. 1777.

Sigismondo de' Conti, *Le storie de suoi tempi dal 1475 al 1510.* Rome, 1883.

Sismondi, J. C. L., *Histoire des Républiques Italiennes du Moyen Age.* Paris, 1809–1818.

Spiapasto, Guidotto, *Cronica,* in *Archivio Veneto,* XVII. 1887.

Stefaneschi, Jacopo, *Vita Coelestini V,* in *R.I.S.,* N.S. III, 1900.

Symonds, John Addington, *Renaissance in Italy: Age of the Despots.* London, 1897.

Tangmar, *Vita Bernwardi,* in Migne, T. 140.

Thietmar, *Chronik.* Berlin, 1935.

Tommaseo, Niccolò, *Le lettere di S. Caterina da Siena,* Vols. I–IV. Florence, 1860.

Tyler, R., *The Emperor Charles V.* London, 1956.

Ullmann, Walter, *The Growth of Papal Government in the Middle Ages.* London, 1955.

Valla, Lorenzo, *Treatise on the Donation of Constantine,* trans. by C. B. Coleman. New Haven, 1922.

Valois, Noel, *La France et le Grand Schisme d'Occident,* Vols. I–IV. Paris, 1896–1902.

Vasari, G., *Le Vite de' più eccellenti pittori, scultori ed architettori.* Florence, 1878.

Vaughan, Herbert M., *The Medici Popes.* London, 1908.

Ventura, G., *Chronica Astensis,* in *R.I.S.,* XI.

Vettori, Francesco, *Sommario della storia d'Italia dal 1511 al 1527,* in *Archivio storico Italiano,* App. VI. 1848.

Villani, Giovanni and Matteo, *Cronica.* Florence, 1825.

Villari, Pasquale, *La storia di Girolamo Savonarola e dei suoi tempi.* Milan, 1895.

———, *Medieval Italy from Charlemagne to Henry VII,* trans. by Costanza Hulton. London, 1910.

———, *The Two First Centuries of Florentine History,* trans. by Linda Villari. London, 1905.

Visconti, P. E., ed., *Lettera sulle antichità di Roma scritta da Raffaello d'Urbino a P. Leone X.* Rome, 1834.

William of Malmesbury, *The History of the Kings of England,* trans. by John Sharpe. London, 1854.

Notes

PART I The Golden City
1. *Graphia*, Chap. 1
2. Malmesbury, Chap. 5
3. Epistle 52, quoted in Gregorovius, *Rome*, I, 188
4. Liudprand, *Antapodosis*, Chap. xlv
5. Quoted in Labbe, VII, 7
6. Quoted in Hodgkin, VII, 135–37
7. Eugenius, 828

PART II The House of Theophylact
1. Gibbon, Chap. xlix
2. Liudprand, *Antapodosis*, Chap. xlviii
3. *Ibid.*
4. Benedict, Chap. 5
5. Liudprand, *op. cit.*, Chaps. iv, xlv
6. Liudprand, *Ottonis*, Chap. x

7. Thietmar, IV, 22
8. In Pertz, IV, 29
9. Liudprand, *op. cit.*, Chap. x
10. *Ibid.*, Chap. v
11. *Ibid.*, Chap. x
12. Quoted in *ibid.*, Chap. xiii
13. Quoted in Gregorovius, *Rome*, III, 405
14. Tangmar, Chap. 25
15. *Liber Pontificalis*, II, 269
16. Glaber, Chap. xlvi
17. *Ibid.*
18. Florence of Worcester, An. 1031
19. Epistle 1, in Migne, 145
20. Malmesbury, Chap. 13

PART III The Lord of Europe
1. Stefaneschi, II, Chap. i
2. *Analecta*
3. Dupuy, 259
4. Jacopone, 25

5. Spiapasto, 428
6. Dante, *Inferno*, III, 59
7. Finke, *Tagen*, iii
8. Quoted in Gregorovius, *Rome*, V, 9
9. *Analecta*
10. *Ibid.*
11. Dupuy, 46
12. *Ibid.*, 80
13. G. Villani, VIII, Chap. 64
14. Dante, *op. cit.*, XXVII, 67
15. G. Villani, X, Chap. 50
16. *Ibid.*, VIII, Chap. 64
17. Compagni, I, Chap. 21
18. Quoted in Villari, *Florentine History*, 505
19. Dante, *Paradiso*, XXVII, 22
20. Finke, *Acta*, I, 104
21. *Ibid.*, 100–106
22. Ventura, Chap. 26
23. G. Villani, IX, Chap. 65
24. Geoffrey of Paris, quoted in Bouquet
25. Dupuy, 44
26. *Ibid.*, 65
27. *Ibid.*, 70
28. *Ibid.*, 54
29. Ptolemy, XXIV, Chap. 36
30. Dante, *Purgatorio*, XX, 87
31. Quoted in Gregorovius, *Rome*, V, 591

PART IV The Wandering Pope
1. Baluze, *Vitae*, I, 481

2. *De planctu ecclesia*, quoted in Pastor, I, 72
3. Petrarch, *Lettres sans Titre*, XIX
4. Baluze, *op. cit.*, I, 241
5. *Ibid.*, 239 ff.
6. M. Villani, III, Chap. 43
7. Petrarch, *op. cit.*, XVI
8. Capuana, 152
9. Froissart, II, Chap. 12
10. Valois, I, 52
11. Dietrich, 122–23
12. Petrarch, *Lettere familiari*, XIV
13. Raynaldus, An. 1379, 16
14. Grottanelli, Letter 3
15. BM Harleian 3480, 312, quoted in Gardner, 282

PART V The Spanish Bull
1. Raynaldus, An. 1460, 31
2. Sigismondo, I, 49
3. Dante, *Inferno*, XIX, 115
4. Valla, 28
5. Jacopo, 130
6. Infessura, Chap. 14
7. Quoted in Pastor, V, 237
8. Marullus, 16
9. Volterran, *Innocent VIII*
10. Burchard, *Diarium*, An. 1484
11. Infessura, Chap. 10
12. Sigismondo, II, 53
13. Guicciardini, *Storia*, I, 20
14. Carte Strozziane, quoted in Gregorovius, *Lucretia*, 65

15. *Ibid.*, 69
16. Antonelli, 34
17. Burchard, *op. cit.*, An. 1487
18. *Ibid.*, An. 1493
19. Dispatch quoted in Gregorovius, *op. cit.*, 59
20. Guicciardini, *op. cit.*, III
21. Dispatch quoted in Gregorovius, *op. cit.*, 89
22. Burchard, *op. cit.*, An. 1497
23. *Ibid.*
24. Brown, I, 74
25. *Atti . . . Modenensis*, I, 433
26. Dispatch quoted in Gregorovius, *op. cit.*, 57
27. Machiavelli, *The Prince*, VII, 426
28. Sanuto, *Diarii*, III, 500
29. Baluze, *Miscellanea*
30. Quoted in Gregorovius, *Rome*, VII, 486
31. Sanuto, *op. cit.*, III, 625
32. Machiavelli, *op. cit.*, VII, 428
33. Giustinian, I, 64
34. Sigismondo, II, 67
35. Sanuto, *op. cit.*, V, 74
36. Guicciardini, *op. cit.*, Chap. 27

PART VI The Golden Age
1. Alberi, *Documenti*, Ser. iii, III, 51
2. *Ricordi*, quoted in Roscoe, *Lorenzo*, App. iii
3. Alberi, *Relazioni*, 52
4. Burchard, *Diarium*, An. 1489
5. Fabronius, II, 308–12
6. Penni, 231
7. Giovio, *Leo X*, IV
8. Quoted in Groli, *Le caccie di Leone X*
9. Grassis, An. 1515
10. Fourth Satire
11. Bale, *Pageant of the Popes*
12. Vettori, 322
13. Visconti, 14
14. *Ibid.*, 20
15. Alberi, *Documenti*, Ser. ii, III, 290
16. Bergenroth, II, 240
17. Quoted in Roscoe, *Leo*, II, 72
18. *Ibid.*, 73
19. Köhler, 128
20. Myconius, *Historia reformationis*
21. Quoted in Roscoe, *op. cit.*, II, 95
22. *Ibid.*, 104
23. Guicciardini, *Counsels*, n. 1, 123
24. Luther, II, 1612
25. *Ibid.*, III, 3478
26. *The Scholemaster*
27. Guicciardini, *op. cit.*, n. 1, 125
28. *Luzio*, 45
29. *On Liberty*, quoted in Roscoe, *op. cit.*, II, 213

PART VII The Last Day
of Italy
1. State Papers, Henry VIII, VI, n. 4
2. Bergenroth, II, n. 610
3. Guicciardini, *Storia,* XX, 417
4. Alberi, *Relazioni,* 126
5. Leva, II, 233
6. Ruscelli, II, 67
7. *Ibid.,* I, 155
8. Machiavelli, *Discorsi,* I, Chap. 12
9. Ruscelli, I, 160
10. Machiavelli, *Le lettere familiari*
11. Ruscelli, II, 20
12. Cellini, 66
13. *Ibid.,* 67
14. Sanuto, *Diarii,* XLV, 237
15. Quoted in Pastor, IX, 427
16. Quoted in Gregorovius, *Rome,* VIII, 621
17. State Papers, Henry VIII, VII, 63
18. *Ibid.,* 394
19. Alberi, *Documenti,* Ser. ii, V, 3
20. Quoted in Raynaldus, An. 1534, n. 67
21. Cellini, 141
22. Leva, 658
23. Guicciardini, *op. cit.,* XX, 417
24. Vettori, 381

Index

Aachen, capital of, 18-19, 46
Abbeys, 83, 166, 211
Abdication, legality of, 85-86, 88, 100, 158, 264
Abruzzi, 79
Absolution, rite of, 103, 129, 269, 278
Acre, 78
Adalbert, influence of, 50-51, 55, 58, 60
Adrian VI, Pope (1522-1523), 259, 261, 284
Adrian of Corneto, 222, 235-37, 255
Adriana, Madonna, 175-76, 184
Adriatic coast, 17, 92, 154
Adriatic Sea, 62, 147, 180, 196
Adultery, papal, 56
Albalato, 111-12
Alban Hills, 69, 71
Alberic, marquis of Camerino, 29-31
Alberic, son of Marozia, 29, 30, 33, 34, 36-43, 53, 61, 63, 67
Albert of Brandenburg, 240
Aldus, printing house of, 222
Alexander V, Pope (1409-1410), 158
Alexander VI, Pope (1492-1503) 171-205, 214-15, 231, 243; character of, 186-89; death of, 200, 204-5; and France, 195-98; reforms of, 190-91, 193; sickness of, 201-4. *See also* Borgia, Rodrigo
Alfonso, king of Naples, 181
Alighieri, Dante, poetic works of, 85-86, 102, 108, 110, 114, 122, 127, 165, 243, 285
Almsgiving, 260
Alps, 32, 120; crossing of, 16, 182, 265, 274
Amalfi, 149
Amboise, 237
Anagni, 120, 123, 144, 272
Anarchism 19, 31, 71
Anchorites, sect of, 79
Ancient republics of Italy, 210
Ancona, 17; cardinal of, 233
Andrew, husband of Joanna, Queen of Naples, 148-49

Angevin dynasty, 147, 149, 181
Anjou, house of, 85, 147, 149-50
Ansfried, swordbearer, 48
Anti-Christ, the, 112
Anti-popes, 157-58. *See also* Avignon period
Appian Way, 164
Aquila, 82; bishop of, 154
Aragon, cardinal of, '247; Catherine of, 261; house of, 181; Isabella of, 180; king of, 111
Archangel Michael, 9
Architecture, treatise on, 6, 164
Aretino, Pietro, 222
Ariosto, Lodovico, 222-23
Ark of the Covenant, 9
Arnold of Brescia, 243
Arnolfo, statue of, 107
Arson, premeditated, 42, 284
Art and artists, 4, 106-7, 133, 259
Ascham, Roger, 246
Assassins and assassinations, 68, 150, 198-99
Asti, 269
Attila, scourges of, 223
Augsburg, battle of, 47
Augustan Rome, 5
Augustinian monks, 190
Augustus, Caesar, 5, 40
Aurelian, Emperor, 4
Aurelian walls, 5, 8, 48
Austria, 244, 264, 274
Autobiography (Cellini), 259
Autonomy, 180
Auvergne, 237
Aventine Hill, 29, 64
Aversa, 151
Avignon period, 127-36, 140-52, 155, 157-58, 214, 239

Baglioni, prince of Perugia, 180
Bajazet, Sultan, 168, 182-83
Bandits, Italian, 44, 48
Bankers and banking houses, 216, 220, 231, 240-41, 249
Baptism, 134; of Constantine, 14, 259; of Jews, 11
Barbarians, invasions by, 10, 16, 48, 78, 145

Index

Bari, archbishop of, 128
Baronius, Cardinal, 21, 27
Basilica, St. Peter's, 6-8, 14, 43, 67, 165, 213, 239-40
Battistina, Donna, 178
Belvedere Gardens, 258
Bembo, Pietro, 222-23
Benedict, Cardinal, 56
Benedict, the chronicler, 32
Benedict IX, Pope (1032-1048), 66-74. *See also* Theophylact
Benedict XI, Pope (1303-1304), 123
Benedict XII, Pope (1304-1332), 131-32
Benedict XIII, Pope (1394-1423), 158
Benedictines, Order of, 83
Benefices, grants of, 87, 141, 239, 260
Benincasa, Catherine, 127, 134
Berengar, influence of, 44, 48-54, 59-60
Bibbiena, Cardinal, 247
Bisceglie, duke of, 192, 199, 201
Black Bands, 275
Blasphemies, 19, 173
Boccaccio, Andrea, 193
Boccaccio, Giovanni, 147, 246
Bologna, 17; meeting at, 281-83
Bolsena, Lake, 219
Boniface VII, Pope (974-985), 157
Boniface VIII, Pope (1294-1303), 86-90, 93, 96-97, 104, 106-8, 111-15, 118, 157, 163, 165, 182, 272, 284; character of, 100; capture of, 121-22; coronation of, 91-92; domestic policies of, 94, 98; election of, 100; fall of, 129. *See also* Gaetani, Benedict
Book of the Popes, The, 21, 28
Borgia: Cesare, 162, 174, 178-79, 185, 187-89, 191-203, 205, 209, 230, 238, 284; Giovanni, brother of Cesare, 174, 178-79, 183, 186-89, 192; Giovanni, cousin of Rodrigo, 193, 201-2; Giovanni, son of Giulia Farnese, 197; house of, 166, 168, 170, 173, 179, 181, 186, 192, 194, 199, 205, 232; Joffré, 174, 178-79, 181, 190; Lucrezia, 174, 176-79, 190, 191-94, 197-99, 201, 205, 261; Pedro Luis, brother of Rodrigo, 162; Pedro Luis, son of Rodrigo, 174; Rodrigo, 158, 161-62, 166-68, 170-71, 213, 223, 261. *See also* Alexander VI, Pope (1492-1503)
Bourbon, Constable of, 265, 275-77
Bramante, 224
Brandenburg, Albert of, 240
Breton, 136

Bridget of Sweden, St., 243
Bulls, papal, 106, 114, 117-20, 130, 137, 173, 189-90, 209
Burchard, John, papal master of ceremonies, 167, 169, 171, 177, 183-85, 188, 198-99, 201, 203-4, 211, 224, 233
Bureaucracy and bureaucrats, 84, 129, 140, 146, 157, 224, 280
Butillo, *see* Prignano, Francesco
Byzantine Empire, 10, 13, 16-17, 30, 51, 54, 64, 146, 180, 221

Calixtus III, Pope (1455-1458), 161-62, 172
Camerino, fall of, 200
Camp followers, 279
Campani, Dino, 108, 110
Campo di Fiore, 166
Canon lawyers, 129, 157
Canute, King, 69
Capua, 149
Cardinals of the Roman Church, 77-78, 82, 85, 93, 95, 98, 111, 135, 138, 140; French, 256-57; non-French, 141; rebellious, 144; in Rome, 88, 157; torture of, 154
Carlotta, 192, 195
Carnivals, Christian, 164
Carolingian Empire, 8, 19, 46
Cartagena, bishopric of, 166
Caserta, 95, 149
Castiglione, Baldassare, 271, 280
Castile in Spain, 180
"Catalans," 161
Catherine of Siena, St., 130, 134-36, 143, 145, 148, 150, 243, 283
Celestine V (1294), 82-85, 89, 92, 95-97; abdication of, 86, 88; death of, 93, 100
Cellini, Benvenuto, 259, 277-78, 280, 283
Censorship of books, 198
Cesena, butcher of, 137; fall of, 136, 200
Charlemagne, Emperor, 18, 20, 34, 46-47, 223
Charles, king of Naples, 77-78, 81-82, 84-85, 88, 92
Charles V, Emperor, 244, 248, 255, 261, 263, 280-83; character of, 273-74; and France, 265-66, 268-69, 282; and Holy Alliance, 271; and Pope Clement, 265, 267, 270
Charles VIII, king of France, 181-85, 193, 211, 227

Charles of Durazzo, 149-54
Charles of Valois, 182
Chigi, Agostino, 215, 221
Chinon, 195
Christianity, ethics of, 7, 12, 100;
  Euopean, 182; persecution of, 8, 14;
  primitive, 11; theological centers of,
  11-12; traditional, 3, 6; Western,
  38-39
Christophorous, papal official, 14-15, 18
Chronicles and chroniclers, 32, 106,
  108, 137
Church, doctrines of, 3, 14, 169, 241,
  281; English, 262; fiscal machinery of,
  129; lands of, 281; plunder of, 149,
  272; reform of, 181, 185, 189, 280;
  states of, 265-67, 280
Church of St. John, 71
Cibo, Cardinal, 167-68; *see also* Innocent
  VIII, Pope (1179-1180); Cardinal of,
  247; Franceschetto, son of Pope
  Innocent VIII, 168, 173, 211
Cicero, 62, 163, 222
Cistercian monastery, 97, 117
Civil authority, 4, 32, 120, 190, 257
Civil war, 11, 133-34, 136, 147, 196,
  236, 271, 278-81
Civitavecchia, papal villa near, 219
Classicism and culture, 48, 163-64, 213,
  215, 221
Clement V, Pope (1305-1314), 106, 123,
  131
Clement VI, Pope (1342-1352), 133,
  145-146, 148, 151
Clement VII, Pope (1523-1534), 158,
  258-86; character and evaluation of,
  258, 260-61, 267, 270, 272, 276-77,
  284, 285; death of, 283, 285; election
  of, 144, 265; fate and imprisonment
  of, 263-64, 267, 271, 273, 278, 280-85;
  foreign affairs of, 259, 261, 265, 267,
  270, 283. *See also* de' Medici, Giulio
Clergy, 134, 217, 242; European, 71;
  French, 144, 151; morality of, 189;
  taxation of, 118
Cognac, Holy Alliance formed at, 269
College of Cardinals, Sacred, 74, 77, 78,
  84, 86, 88, 96, 100, 129, 138, 140-41,
  144 157, 166, 172, 186, 200, 209,
  211-12, 217, 231, 235-37, 258
Colonna, house of, 78, 80, 85, 97, 100-
  101, 109, 111-14, 158, 183, 196-97,
  216, 266, 271, 276; James, 96, 98,
  103; John, 102; Peter, 81, 96, 98, 103;

Pompeo, 256, 258, 272-73; Sciarra,
  103-5, 120-21; Stephen, 98, 103
Colosseum, 84
Commoner Peter, the, 56
Condottieri, 275
Conrad, 68, 70
Consistory, 85, 100, 172, 178, 189, 233,
  235
Conspiracies, 140, 243
Constantine, Emperor, 6, 9-10, 14-16,
  90, 165, 224, 259
Constantinople, 10, 18, 40, 52, 53; fall
  of, 180; patriarch of, 11
Contarini, Gaspar, 285
Cornaro, Cardinal, 247
Corneto, Cardinal Adrian, 202-3, 235-
  237
Coronation, papal, 49, 89, 91-92, 143,
  213-14, 281
Corruption and depravity, 33, 38, 59,
  74, 162-63, 245-46, 248
Cossa, Baldassare, 158
Council of Trent, 285
Councils, ecclesiastical, 56, 59-60,
  157-58, 163, 181, 197, 273, 280-82
Court, Avignon, 130, 135; Byzantine,
  64; Ferrarese, 201; Frankish, 16;
  Greek, 40; of imperial Rome, 63-64;
  Pope John XII's, 50; Pope Leo X's,
  221; painter, 259; Roman, 248; Saxon,
  54
Cremona, bishop of. *See* Liudprand
Cruelty, 13; Greek, 47; papal, 154, 235;
  Saracen, 47; Spanish, 154, 278
Crusades, 101, 113, 149, 181, 183
Curia, 111, 140-41, 144, 189, 221, 259,
  285; Avignonese, 127-29, 146, 239;
  French, 117; Roman, 133-34, 150-154;
  upkeep of, 239-40

d'Albret, Charlotte, 195
da Todi, Jacopone, 84, 97, 100, 103
Damascus, 130
Damian, Peter, 71, 74
Dante. *See* Alighieri, Dante
Dauphine, 193
de Barbiano, Alberico, 145, 154
de Bari, Jean, 138
de Beaufort, Pierre Roger, 133
de' Catanei, Vannozza, 174, 176, 178,
  187-88
Deeds of Otto, 53
de Grassis, Paris, master of ceremonies,
  213-14, 219, 233, 235

Index

de Luna, Cardinal Pedro, 137, 139-40
de' Medici: Alessandro, 281, 283;
Catherine, 282-83; Giovanni, 172,
209-13, 223, 234, 253-54, 275;
Giovanni (delle Bande Nere), 275;
Giuliano, brother of Lorenzo the
Magnificent, 253-54; Giuliano, son of
Lorenzo the Magnificent, 210-11, 216,
228-30, 233; Giulio, 158, 176, 216,
228, 253-58; house of, 220, 226, 249,
266-67; Lorenzo the Magnificent, 168,
210-13, 253-54, 282; Lorenzo,
grandson of Lorenzo the Magnificent,
229-31, 237-239, 247-48; Piero, 211,
229. See also Clement VII, Pope
(1523-1534); Leo X, Pope
(1513-1521)
de Montfort, Simon, 87
de San Marco, Antonio, 215
de Saulis, Genoese, 235-37
della Rovere, Franceso Maria, 230
della Rovere, Cardinal Giuliano, 168,
170, 181, 205, 238; excommunicated,
230-32
delle Bande Nere, Giovanni, 275
Demonic visitations, 11-12, 43, 68, 203
Denmark and the Danes, 47
Description of the Golden City, 4
Despotism, 180
d'Este, Cardinal Alfonso, 180, 201, 247
d'Este, Isabella, 247
di Cambio, Arnolfo, 107
di Cordoba, General Gonsalvo, 186
Diet at Worms, 248
Divine Comedy, 106, 110
Divorce, 281
Djem, Sultan, 182-85
Dominicans, Order of, 241
Donation of Constantine, 15-18, 25,
165, 223
Durazzo, 147, 149-54
Dynastic struggles, 95, 147

Easton, Adam, 152, 155
Edicts, iconoclastic, 11; imperial, 13
Edward, king of England, 87, 94, 133
Elections, papal, 66-68, 73-74, 77-78, 80,
83, 88, 96, 100, 123, 136, 138, 140,
144-48, 157, 167, 171, 181, 189, 209,
228, 255, 259, 265
Emperor versus Pope controversy, 11-15,
33, 61, 67, 70, 73, 114
England, 47, 69, 94, 106, 116-17, 145,
147, 152, 280; benefices in, 87;

Church of, 262; kings of, 78, 94, 133,
155, 261, 263, 281-82; papal envoys
to, 273, 281
Erasmus of Rotterdam, 222, 244
Estes, cardinal of, 247; prince of
Farrara, 180
Eternal City. See Rome
Etruscan power, 26, 40, 62
Europe, new nations of, 227; northern,
10; peoples of, 3; politics in, 18, 47,
63, 71, 94, 101, 141; religion in,
12, 59-60, 69, 113, 182; unity of, 46;
western, 47
Excommunication, ban of, 13, 60, 70,
100, 105, 109, 117, 120, 143, 153,
230-31, 248

Faenza, fall of, 200
Fanaticism, religious, 8, 79, 83-84, 97,
183
Farnese, Alessandro, 175, 219, 233, 266,
285; see also Paul III, Pope (1534-
1549); the Petticoat Cardinal;
Girolama, 175-76; Giulia, 175, 178,
184, 197
Ferdinand of Castile, 180
Ferrante, king of Naples, 181
Ferrara, 17, 170, 180, 201; duke of,
273; envoy from, 167, 178, 193
Feudalism, 101, 116, 274
Field of the Cloth of Gold, 263
Flanders, 94
Fleet, imperial, 275; Saracen, 8;
Spanish, 273
Florence, 102, 104, 106-9, 112, 134,
138, 163, 175, 183, 210, 212, 215,
222, 237-38, 243, 248; archbishop of,
216; bankers in, 220, 231; cardinal of,
138-39; Cathedral of, 253-54;
defenses of, 270, 276, 281; history of,
170, 255; nobility in, 109, 180,
229-230, 253-54; plunder of, 276
Flores, Bartolomeo, 190
Fondi, 149
Forgeries, 15
Formosus, Pope (891-896), 19;
character of, 22; trial of, 20, 28, 48
Fornuovo, battle of, 185
Fort Douce, Abbot of, 211
Foscari, Marco, 259-60, 272
Fournier, Jacques, 131
France, 19, 105-6, 123, 140, 147-48,
181, 196-97, 199, 231, 237, 273, 281;
army of, 116, 137, 145, 266; influence
of, 94, 120, 200, 275; and Italy, 183-

184, 186, 211, 227-28, 248, 265-66, 270; monarchy of, 78, 106, 116, 118, 123, 141, 144-45, 149, 170, 182, 200, 228, 263, 268, 279, 282-83; and Papacy, 195, 227-28, 269; religion in, 59, 87, 117-18, 131, 138, 256-58; and Spain, 228, 258, 262-65, 268-69, 282

Francis I, King of France, 228, 244, 255, 264, 266, 273-75, 283

Franciscans, Order of, 97

Frankish nation, 16-17

Fratricide, 101

Friars, 102, 131

Froissart, Jean, 137, 140

Frundsberg, Goerge, 274-78

Fugger banking house, 241-42, 263

Fumone, fortress of, 93

Furioso, Orlando, fictional character, 223

Gaetani, Benedict, 77-82, 85-88, 94-98, 114, 120, 122, 157, 197, 216. *See also* Boniface VIII, Pope (1294-1303)

Gandia, duke of. *See* Borgia, Giovanni, brother of Cesare

Geneva, Robert of, Cardinal, 136-37, 142-44

Genoa, republic of, 154-55, 157, 170, 269

Gerald of Albalato, 111-12

Germany, 46-49, 61, 64-65, 73, 106, 184, 197, 218, 227, 240, 243-46, 262, 274-278, 281

Gibbon, Edward, 26-27

Giberti, Giammatteo, 262, 266, 269, 273

Giotto, Florentine painter, 107

Giovio, Paolo, 218, 222, 277

Giustiniani, Antonio, Venetian ambassador, 200, 202

Glaber, Raoul, 67

Golden Age, the, 46, 166, 218, 249, 255, 259

Golden Basilica, 9

Gonfalons of the Holy See, 216

Gratiano, Giovanni, 71-73

Greece and the Greeks, 9-10, 47, 64, 92, 221

Gregory II, Pope (715-731), 12-13

Gregory VI, Pope (1045-1046), 71

Gregory VII, Pope (1073-1085), 72-74, 127-28, 134, 136, 140

Gregory XII, Pope (1406-1415), 158

Gregory of Tusculum, 63-65

Gubbio, 17

Guglielmina, 97

Guicciardini, Francesco, 173, 182, 204, 222, 245, 247, 258, 261-62, 270,

275, 285

Guy, Lord of Tuscany, 34, 36

Hadrian's mausoleum, 8-9. *See also* Sant' Angelo, Castle of

Hall of Constantine, 259

Hapsburg, house of, 244

Hedonism, 151, 165, 194, 213

Henry III of Germany, Emperor, 74

Henry VIII, king of England, 261-63, 281-82

Henry of Orleans, 283

Heresy and heretics, persecution of, 57, 100, 112, 118, 120, 123, 131, 135, 152, 164, 274

Hildebrand, Chaplain, 71, 73-74

History, papal, 21, 27, 106

Holy Alliance, organization of, 269, 271

Holy Ghost, incarnation of the, 96-97; supplication to the, 79-80, 82, 86

Holy Lance, 168

Holy Lands, the, 101

Holy Roman Empire, 49, 60, 63, 74, 115, 243

Holy See, 95, 117, 141, 162, 216. *See also* Vatican, the

Holy wars, 120, 149, 241, 244

Hugh of Provence, reign of, 34-40, 43-44, 46, 54

Humanism and scholarship, 164-65, 223, 226, 245, 260

Hundred Years' War, 94

Hungary, 147-48; king of, 90

Huns, devastations of, 14, 30, 47 51-52

Hunting parties, papal, 219, 248

Huss, John, 243

Iconoclasts, 11

Idols and idolatry, 11-12, 106

Iesi, 17

Images, worship of, 11-13

Immorality, 40, 142. *See also* Corruption

Imperiola, the commoner Peter, 56

Incarnation, 97

Incest, charges of, 205

Index, papal, 198

Indulgences, doctrine of, 240, 242, 244, 247

Infidels, disputes with, 11, 101, 113

Innocent VIII, Pope (1179-1180), 167-168, 170, 172-73, 177-78, 182, 211

Inquisition, 285

Interdict, papal, 109, 118, 134, 153

Intrigues, political, 11, 109, 232

Investiture, cost of, 237. *See also*

Index

Coronation
Ireland, 106
Isabella of Aragon, 180
Islam, 180
Italy, central, 182, 219; government of,
18, 30, 72, 101, 163, 180, 196, 200,
210, 227, 262, 271; kings of, 19,
34-36, 40, 44, 49; north, 30, 44, 136,
177, 265, 275; peace in, 226, 258;
peoples of, 11-12, 64, 243; religion in,
12, 68, 87, 166, 275; revolution in,
54, 133-34, 278-81; south, 146-50,
265; warfare in, 8, 129, 131, 144-46,
162, 181, 185, 195-96, 227, 268-275,
278, 281

James, the brother of Jesus, 12
Jerome, 7, 243
Jerusalem, 113, 181
Jesters, court, 260
Joan, "Pope," 25-26, 91
Joanna, Queen of Naples, 129, 143,
146-51
John, bishop of Narni, 56
John, bishop of Ravenna, 29
John, cardinal deacon, 56
John X, Pope (914-928), 28, 29, 34, 35
John XI, Pope (931-936) 25, 28, 33-36,
38
John XII, Pope (955-964), 42-43, 45,
48-57, 60, 67, 70. See also Octavian
John XXII, Pope (1316-1334), 131
John XXIII, Pope (1958-1963), 158
Jubilee year of the Roman Church,
113-114, 119, 197-98
Judaism, 11, 90
Julius II, Pope (1503-1513), 205, 209,
214-15, 217, 220, 223-24, 227-28,
230, 239, 249, 269
Julius Caesar, 104, 163

King and emperor, rivalry between, 256
Kingdom of the Two Sicilies, 146. See
also Sicily
Knight of Rhodes, 216
Knights Templar, Order of the, 101

Landsknechts, military unit of, 274, 276
Landulf, Cardinal, 111
Lateran Palace, center of Roman
government, 9, 14, 20, 43, 67, 89, 91,
98, 122, 137, 214-15
Laterani, house of, 9
Latin language, 10, 40, 50, 57, 64, 71,
83, 97, 163, 222, 225, 255

Legends of Peter, 79
Lent, postponement of, 201
Leo I, Pope (440-461), 223
Leo III, Pope (795-816), 11, 18, 46, 223
Leo IV, Pope (847-855), 8, 223
Leo VIII, Pope (963-965), 58-60
Leo X, Pope (1513-1521), 210, 214-49,
254-56, 258-62, 265, 284; ambitions
of, 227, 229-30; character of, 210, 219,
259-60; coronation of, 213; court of,
221; dangers to, 234, 236-37; election
of, 228; expenditures of, 220, 225,
239, 245; illnesses of, 218, 234;
policies of, 212, 215-18, 224, 230,
232-33, 254-56, 258; scholarship of,
215, 222, 260; treaties of, 228. See
also de' Medici, Giovanni
Leonine Age, 214
Leonine City, 8, 55, 164, 223, 277
Library, Vatican, 164
Limoges, cardinal of, 138, 143
Limousin group, 137-38
Liudprand, bishop of Cremona, 27-28,
33, 35, 46, 53-58, 61, 67
Lombardy and the Lombards, 16-19, 30,
44, 69, 177, 227, 229, 273-75
London, 246
Lorraine, 19
Louis, son of Charlemagne, 19
Louis XII, king of France, 193-96, 200
Louis of Anjou, 149-50
Louise of Savoy, 263
Lucanius, Roman citizen, 3
Lucca, 155
Lucullus, 62
Lupercalia, 164
Luther, Martin, challenge of Papacy by,
163, 166, 190, 242, 244-45, 248-49,
261, 265, 274, 278, 284
Lyons, 121

Machiavelli, Niccolò, 195, 197, 200, 202,
205, 222, 238, 246, 255, 267, 270, 275
Madeleine d'Auvergne, 237
Magdeburg, archbishop of, 240
Magliana, 260
Maifreda, 97
Malabranca, Latino, 78-80, 85
Malatesta, prince of Rimini, 180
Malliana, villa of, 220
Malmesbury, William of, 3
Marignano, battle of, 228
Marozia, senatrix of Rome (926-932),
ambitions of, 26-27, 31, 35, 46, 53;
descendants of, 22, 61-62; imprison-

ment of, 38; marriage of, 28-29, 33, 36; myth of, 96; personality of, 32-33

Marseille, battle of, 265

Marseille, Catherine of, 283

Martin V, Pope (1417-1431), 158

Martyrdom, 12, 84

Maximilian, emperor of Austria, 244, 248, 264

Mediterranean Sea, 146, 180

Mercenary troops, employment of, 72, 136, 149-50, 154-56, 205, 227, 239, 274, 276, 285

Merchant class, 43, 141, 216

Michelangelo, 165, 209, 223-24

Milan, 97, 140, 191, 227; invasion of, 196, 246, 265, 267-70, 273, 275; Sforza, prince of, 180; rebellion in, 196, 271

Milan, archbishop of, 69-70

Milan, cardinal of, 138-39

Milvian Bridge, 211

Mistresses, 28, 34, 174-75, 190

Mob rule, 37, 42, 67, 137, 257. *See also* Anarchism

Modena, revenues from, 228

Monasteries, 21, 97

Monks, 11, 67, 71, 74, 83, 85, 88-89, 97, 117, 185, 190, 241-42, 244, 248

Monte Cassino, 83, 211

Monte Morone, 79, 83, 89

Montefeltro, Count Guido of, 102

Montfort, defeat of, 87

Monuments and statues, 5, 107

Morality, 33, 52, 88, 246. *See also* Corruption

Morone, Girolamo, 267-68, 274

Morone, Peter of, 79-82

Mount Soracte, 21, 32

Murder and rape, 42, 44, 198, 269

Music and musicians, 97, 190, 260

Muslims, 11, 30

Mysticism, 135

Naples, kingdom of, 145, 181, 199, 246; monarchs of, 77-78, 81-85, 88, 90, 92, 129, 140, 143, 146-49, 153, 179, 181, 191-92, 200, 229, 264, 268; rebellion in, 150; Pope Urban VI in, 151; war in, 149-50, 154-56, 185, 201, 265-66, 269, 275-76

Narni, bishop of, 56

Nationalism, 117-18, 270, 274

Neapolitan war, 150

Nepotism, crime of, 94, 97, 118, 131, 149, 166, 182, 189, 197, 230, 255

Nero, Emperor, persecutions under, 5-6

Netherlands, the, 264

Nicholas V, Pope (1447-1455), 164, 166

Ninety-five theses, the, 242

Nobility, hereditary, 189; Roman, 17, 96, 174, 197, 247; Spanish, 176

Nocera, siege of, 151, 153

Nogaret, William, 119, 121

Normans, 146

Nuovo Castello, 83

Octavian, 39-42. *See also* John XII, Pope (955-963)

Office for the Dead, ritual of, 203-4

On Pleasure, 165

Oriental civilization, 10

Orleans, 283

Orsini, Cardinal, 138; house of, 78, 80, 96, 98, 101, 144, 183, 186, 188, 196, 216, 266; Napoleon, 79

Orvieto, 281

Otto, husband of Queen Joanna, 143

Otto I (Otto of Saxony, Otto the Great), 33, 46-60, 63, 243

Otto II, 61, 63

Otto III, 61, 63-65

Paganism, 3, 11, 165, 255

Palestrina, 96, 102-4, 120

Pallas, body of, 4

Papacy, the, army of, 101, 109; government of, 9, 16, 18-19, 22, 26, 28, 33, 38-39, 71, 245; historians of, 21, 27, 106; monarchical office of, 4, 17, 41, 106, 119, 127, 136, 148; and the Renaissance, 95, 205; sins of, 14, 94, 105, 144, 149, 154, 235; temporal power of, 18, 25, 42, 61, 72, 91, 122, 129, 182, 284

Papal States, the, 17, 42-43, 55, 71, 90, 109-10, 146, 196, 209, 230-31, 236, 239, 248, 275

Paris, 88, 121

Paris, University of, 87, 100

Parma, recapture of, 248-49; revenues from, 228

Parricide, 100, 118

Passigano, abbey of, 211

Patrimony of St. Peter, 15-16, 62, 69, 162, 182, 186, 265, 267

Paul, the Apostle, 9, 14

Paul II, Pope (1464-1471), 172

Paul III, Pope (1534-1549), 175, 190, 285. *See also* Farnese, Alessandro; the Petticoat Cardinal

Index

Pavia, 54; battle of, 264, 266, 274
Peasants and the peasantry, 101, 141, 220
Penance, sacrament of, 241
Penni, Gian-Giacomo, 215, 217
Pepin, king of the Franks, 16-18
Perjury, 102
Perugia, 77, 79, 81-82, 87, 155, 180, 186, 281
Perugino, Umbrian painter, 253
Pescara, marquis of, 268, 274
Peter. *See* St. Peter the Apostle
Peter of Morone, 79-82
Peter's pence, 141
Petrarch, 127, 131, 133, 142, 147, 243
Petrucci, Cardinal Alfonso, 217, 234-36, 243, 247
Petticoat Cardinal, the, 175, 190, 219, 266. *See also* Farnese, Alessandro; Paul III, Pope (1534-1549)
Philip IV, king of France, 105, 116, 118-20, 123
Philip the Fair, 94, 100
Piacenza, revenues from, 228
Piccolomini, Aeneas, 161-62
Pilgrims and pilgrimages, 4, 43, 52, 72, 79, 82, 113, 116, 119, 150, 197-98, 220, 245, 247
Pinturicchio, 183
Pisa, 139
Pius II, Pope (1458-1464), 161, 172, 190
Plague, ravages of, 77
Plunder, 42, 44, 62, 72, 100; of Florence, 276; of Rome, 149, 277; of St. Peter's Cathedral, 55, 70, 270, 272
Po River, 13, 275
Poetry and poems, 97, 106, 164-65, 221-22
Poison, use of, 202, 234
Politics and politicians, ecclesiastical, 41, 87, 97; female, 32, 135; Neapolitan, 33, 54, 63, 147.
Pompeii, 151
Porcari, Stefano, 166
Portugal, 197
Portus, bishopric of, 166
Power, exercise of, 62, 64, 147, 205; military, 33; Spanish, 266; spiritual, 18, 38; temporal, 18, 25, 38, 42, 61, 72, 91, 122, 129, 182, 284
Prague, 243
Prelayo, Alvaro, 131
Pretenders, 47, 49, 55
Prignano, Bartolomeo, 128-30, 134-35, 138, 140. *See also* Urban VI, Pope

(1378-1389)
Prignano, Francesco, 149-53
Prince, The, 238
Printing press, 242
Prisons and prisoners, 268, 278
Provence, 19, 34-35, 38, 40, 43-44, 51, 54
Pucci, Lorenzo, 175-76
Purgatory, 241

Racism, 227
Ransom, pressure of, 272, 276
Raphael, 223-25, 259
Ravenna, battle of, 13, 17, 34
Rebellion, 51, 59, 133-34, 150, 196, 271, 278-81
Reform of the church, 25, 71, 74, 181, 185, 189-90, 244, 280-81, 284
Renaissance, ferment of, 6, 25, 32, 95, 106, 108, 133, 162-65, 173-74, 194, 205, 210, 221, 246, 249
Republicanism, 16, 109, 180, 237
Revenues, papal, 34, 43, 94-95, 118, 141, 199, 216, 220, 225, 228, 239
Riario, Cardinal, 233, 235-36
Richard II, king of England, 155
Rieti, 103
Rimini, 180
Riots, 35, 44, 59
Roger, Cardinal Hugh, 141
Romagna, campaign in, 196, 200-201, 231
Rome, bishop of, 9-10, 12, 14, 17, 20, 28, 39, 46, 51, 58, 69; curia in, 133-134, 150-52, 154; glories of, 3-5, 8, 15, 40, 63, 91, 104; invasion of, 5, 7-8, 30, 41, 67, 87, 149-50, 273, 275, 277, 281-82, 284; life in, 4-5, 7, 41, 64, 67, 94, 107, 203, 246; nobility in, 17, 33, 58, 63-64, 94, 96, 109, 170, 174, 197, 200, 247-48, 255; politics in, 33, 54, 63, 69, 71, 113, 147, 162, 217; synod in, 13, 55, 88, 90, 157
Roncalli, Angelo, 158. *See also* John XXIII, Pope (1958-1963)
Rosiers, lord of, 132
Rotterdam, 222, 244

Sabine Hills, 70
Sacred College, 77, 84, 96, 100, 129, 138, 140-41, 144, 172, 209, 212, 217, 235-37, 258
Sacred Lance, 46
Sacrileges, 16, 56
Sacro Possesso, ceremony of the, 214-215, 218

308

St. Catherine Disputing, 183
St. Francis of Assisi, 84
St. Lucy's Day, 86
St. Mark, Palace of, 173
St. Peter the Apostle, 6, 14, 18, 48, 100;
    chair of, 12, 17, 21, 26, 66, 71, 78, 91,
    177, 279; legends of, 79; Order of,
    239; Patrimony of, 15-16, 62, 69, 162,
    182, 186, 265, 267; shrine of, 7, 49;
    statue of, 9, 12; tomb of, 4, 8, 17, 41,
    114, 224
St. Peter's Cathedral, altar of, 89, 114;
    basilica of, 6-8, 14, 43, 67, 165, 213,
    239-40; cardinal of, 138, 144;
    construction of, 6-7, 9, 165, 224, 243;
    majesty of, 17, 20, 69, 89, 107, 110,
    113, 138, 224, 277; plunder of, 55,
    70, 270, 272; treasures in, 8, 34, 43,
    71, 133
St. Peter's Square, 137
Sala di Constantini, 223
Sala Reale, 177
Salerno, 149
Salt monopoly, 239
San Pietro, Piazza, 199
Sancia, daughter of ruling house in
    Naples, 179
Sangro, Cardinal, 151-53
Sant' Angelo, Bridge of, 166
Sant' Angelo, Castle of, 9, 34, 36-38,
    113, 137, 140, 145, 184, 197, 209,
    234-39, 272-73, 277-78, 280-81
Santa Croce, house of, 216
Saracens, 8, 30, 47, 51, 78, 146
Savelli, house of, 197, 216
Savonarola, Girolamo, 183, 185, 243
Savoy, Louise of, 263
Saxonicus, 64
Saxony, 45, 54
Schism, scandal of, 144, 146, 148, 152,
    163, 273, 282. *See also* Avignon period
Scholarship. *See* Classicism and culture
Sciarra-Quarreler. *See* Colonna, John
Scotland, 145
Senigaglia, fall of, 200
Sergius III, Pope (904-911), 21, 26,
    28-29, 34-35
Sforza, Cardinal Ascanio, 170, 177, 184,
    188-89; Caterina, 196-97; Francesco,
    267-68 Giovanni, 191-92, 199;
    Ludovico, 180-84, 191, 196
"Sicilian Vespers," the, 147
Sicily, 8, 78, 105, 146-47
Siena, 25, 134, 161, 217, 234
Simony, scandal of, 94, 97, 118, 140,

142-43, 149, 172, 181-82, 184, 189,
    209, 260
Sistine Chapel, 170, 209, 253
Sixtus IV, Pope (1471-1484), 172, 178
Slaves and slavery, 8, 37, 101
Society, strata of, 27, 32, 100, 164
Soderini, Francesco, 235-36
Sodomy, 118
Sorrento, 149
Spain, belligerency of, 47, 106, 158, 180,
    186, 193, 197, 199, 227, 231, 235,
    256, 261-64, 281; Catholics in, 140,
    166, 276; cruelty of, 278; envoys of,
    270-72, 276; kings of, 200, 228, 232,
    244, 248, 255, 261, 265-71, 273-74;
    Navy of, 273; nobility in, 176
Spirituals, the, 79, 83-84, 97
Stefaneschi, James, 81, 83, 92
Stephana, 56
Stephen II, Pope (752-757), 16-17
Stephen VII, Pope (896), 19-21
Stephen the martyr, 12
Strolling players, Italian, 190
Strozzi, Lorenzo, 220
Suetonius, 246
Sweden, 243
Swiss Guards, 217, 227
Sycophants, 50
Sylvester, St., legendary life of, 14-16,
    90, 259
Sylvester II, Pope (999-1003), 61, 63,
    65, 68, 70
Sylvester III, Pope (1045), 73
Synod horrenda, 19-21, 28

Tables of the Law, 9
Taranto, 147
Tartars, 114
Taxes and taxation, 116, 131, 141, 231,
    263
Temple of Solomon, 7
Tetzel, Johann, 241, 243-44
Teutons, 146
Theodora, 26-30, 34, 40, 61
Theophylact, house of, 26, 28-30, 33-34,
    40-41, 52, 62, 66, 68, 74. *See also*
    Benedict IX, Pope (1032-1048)
Three Estates, meeting of, 119
Tiber River, 5, 8, 20, 30, 64, 187, 198,
    221, 279
Tiberius, Emperor, 245
Tithes and tithing, 14
Titian, 264
Tivoli, 55, 57-58
Tower of London, 87

Index

Traditions, pagan, 3
Treachery, 44, 63, 102, 144, 146, 180, 185
Treaties and alliances, 16, 28, 265, 267, 280
Tripoli, 78
Troy, fall of, 3
Turenne, countess of, 133
Turkey and the Turks, 181, 241
Tuscany, 34, 36, 109, 121, 130, 185, 200, 219
Tusculum, 26, 40, 61-67, 70, 73-74, 90, 96, 120
Tyranny, 37, 40, 147

Umbria, 156, 200
Umbrian hills, 55
Unam Sanctam, 119
Urban V, Pope (1362-1370), 133
Urban VI, Pope (1378-1389), 136, 140, 142-57, 163, 224. See also Prignano, Bartolomeo
Urbino, bishop of, 231; duke of, 271, 273; fall of, 200, 237, 239

Valencia, bishopric of, 166, 171, 179
Valla, Lorenzo, 165-66, 223
Valois, 116, Charles of 182
Vasari, 107

Vatican gardens, 199
Vatican Hill, 5, 7-8, 14, 177
Vatican Palace, 8-9, 91, 137-40, 164, 173, 177, 194-98, 202-3, 211, 214-215, 236, 239, 245, 255, 272, 277
Venice and the Venetians, 114, 130, 171, 180, 183, 196-98, 202, 235, 239, 247-48, 259, 282, 285
Vetori, Francesco, 285
Villani, Giovanni, 102, 104, 108, 110, 114, 116, 133
Villanova, Arnold of, 112
Villeneuve, 142
Vinegar monopoly, 239
Virgil, 3
Viterbo, 184, 219
von Miltitz, Karl, 244
von Niem, Dietrich, 140, 152-53, 157
von Schomberg, Nicholas, 262

Wartburg Castle, 248
Wealth, amassing of, 18, 131
West, emperor of, 18, 33
William of Malmesbury, 3
Wittenberg University, 241-42
Wolsey, Cardinal, 257, 262
Women, political power of, 32, 135
Worldliness, 97
Writers, classical, 108, 163, 259